Advances in African Economic, Social and Political Development

Series editors

Africa is emerging as a rapidly growing region, still facing major challenges, but with a potential for significant progress—a transformation that necessitates vigorous efforts in research and policy thinking. This book series focuses on three intricately related key aspects of modern-day Africa: economic, social and political development. Making use of recent theoretical and empirical advances, the series aims to provide fresh answers to Africa's development challenges. All the socio-political dimensions of today's Africa are incorporated as they unfold and new policy options are presented. The series aims to provide a broad and interactive forum of science at work for policymaking and to bring together African and international researchers and experts. The series welcomes monographs and contributed volumes for an academic and professional audience, as well as tightly edited conference proceedings. Relevant topics include, but are not limited to, economic policy and trade, regional integration, labor market policies, demographic development, social issues, political economy and political systems, and environmental and energy issues.

More information about this series at http://www.springer.com/series/11885

Hanna Kociemska

Public-Private Partnership for Sub-Saharan Africa

Springer

Hanna Kociemska
Wroclaw University of Economics
Wrocław, Poland

ISSN 2198-7262 ISSN 2198-7270 (electronic)
Advances in African Economic, Social and Political Development
ISBN 978-3-030-14752-5 ISBN 978-3-030-14753-2 (eBook)
https://doi.org/10.1007/978-3-030-14753-2

Library of Congress Control Number: 2019933201

This Springer imprint is published by the registered company Springer Nature Switzerland AG
The registered company address is: Gewerbestrasse 11, 6330 Cham, Switzerland

Contents

Chapter 1
Introduction

> *The core of the theory is the study of how best to allocate and deploy resources across time in an uncertain environment and of the role of economic organizations in facilitating these allocations. Time and uncertainty are the central elements that influence financial economic behaviour. It is the complexity of their interaction that provides intellectual challenge and excitement to the study of finance. To analyze the effects of this interaction properly often requires sophisticated analytical tools..., of course, not all that is beautiful in science need also be practical. And surely, not all that is practical in science is beautiful. Here we have both* [1].
>
> R. C. Merton

Robert C. Merton presented a sound characteristic of the development of financial theory and, above all, the financial market theory. The interesting and innovative interactions referred to in the quote that preceded this introduction shape our economic reality. Uncertainty and risk accompany most business relationships. The variability and complexity of these phenomena over time, as well as the need to react to them faster and faster, but also in different ways, make it necessary to look for new methods of financial management. Convergence of the principles and philosophy of management of conventional and Islamic investors understood as convergence in selected areas are not always possible. The theoretical heterodox approach to such cooperation in the formula of public-private partnership (PPP) does not have to be useful everywhere, although, according to R. C. Merton, can be scientifically beautiful. Hence, the author made an attempt to describe the cooperation of public and private sector actors from different legal and religious orders, between which the selected canons of the economy, often perceived as separate, tend to permeate. In economics, heterodoxy is pertaining to an evolutionary approach to the economy. It analyses phenomena in many aspects, including social, historical and religious ones. It is not a part of the mainstream economics, as it often stands in opposition to it. Heterodox economists attempt to explain phenomena and data that mainstream science often

H. Kociemska, *Public-Private Partnership for Sub-Saharan Africa*,
Advances in African Economic, Social and Political Development,
https://doi.org/10.1007/978-3-030-14753-2_1

takes for granted.[1] Thus, the heterodox approach proposed in the monograph in the context of the implementation of PPP projects in the conditions of conventional and Islamic finance in emerging or developing countries will be a manifestation of the search of theoretical solutions in the sub-discipline of public finances and evolution of finances. For the purposes of these analyses, three orders have been distinguished, systematising the types of countries and economic systems, the interactions of which will be the subject of research. These are:

- a system of conventional financial rules, hereinafter referred to as the conventional finance system (Western finance), covering the area of Europe, America and East Asia;
- the Islamic financial system, which includes the Gulf countries, Malaysia and other regions of Asia;
- a system that is not clearly defined from the point of view of the dominant financial system, covering the area of dysfunctional, emerging and developing countries, in particular, the countries of sub-Saharan Africa.

The nature of the proposed terminology is purely conventional, as it only allows to outline features of particular types of partners, appearing in correlations in the PPP structures described. A private or public investor operating in the conventional financial system is one who uses generally accepted financial principles, in particular: cost and outturn account, profit maximisation, interest on borrowed capital, operating in the Western financial system. An Islamic investor is a public or private investor who bases his decisions on the *Islamic Moral Economy*, the *Quran* and the principles of *Shari'ah* law. Each of these types of investors has its own specific characteristics and faces different economic challenges. The difficulties for the conventional partners are increasing, and the existing financial instruments and public finance management rules are no longer sufficient. The repeating financial crises in the USA and Europe proved to be key moments in disrupting the stable development of many conventional economies. Although the very concept of crisis is often treated in a journalistic way, in economic reality it is still estimated that many economic indicators are in decline.[2] In connection with unfavourable demographic changes and growing needs of societies, deteriorating economic indicators may contribute to the crisis of public finances and to disturbance of the relationship between incurred expenditures and accumulated public revenues, as a consequence may lead to an uncontrolled increase of public debt.

At the same time, under conditions of uncertainty in the economic systems of conventional countries, Islamic countries have a specific position. They have become more resilient to the effects of financial crises through their application of the principles of the Islamic Moral Economy. Additionally, they have not suffered in terms of their ability to finance public infrastructure and provide their citizens with a

---

[1]Rogowska [2].

[2]http://www.kozminski.edu.pl/pl/aktualnosci/aktualnosc/eksperci-kozminskiego-ostrzegaja-polsce-grozi-kryzys-spoleczno-gospodarczy-w-2016-i-2017-roku-moze-nastapic-zachwianie-rownowagi-spoleczno-ekonomicznej-w-polsce-twierdza-badacze-z-alk-tworcy-indeksu-zrownowazonego-rozwoju-spoleczno-ekonomicznego/, accessed on 05.07.2016.

certain quality and quantity of public goods in their implementations of public policies, which are largely based on ongoing cooperation with private actors. Nevertheless, they face significant demographic problems, shortages of crucial raw materials, which are needed for development, such as water, and the need for intensive education or the acquisition of knowledge and technology from outside. The countries of the Gulf Cooperation Council (GULF) also need opportunities to further diversify their sources of income and to look for them beyond the market for their natural resources. The expansion of these countries can be hampered by the lack of acceptance and full understanding of Islamic finance principles in conventional countries and in new markets not defined in terms of systems.

In sub-Saharan Africa, it was not until the 1980s and 1990s that individual states began to regain independence and shape their territories, economies and societies. Power in newly formed states often fell into the hands of dictators and highly corrupt administrations, without any experience and knowledge regarding managing a country, which often led to fratricidal wars and the loss of valuable assets—such as raw mineral deposits—to "new colonisers".[3] At the end of the 1990s, the transformation process began slowly, with growing openness to investors, while the need for political and economic changes was noticed in most of the countries of the region, especially Nigeria, Botswana, Angola and South Africa. The lack of stable pillars of public policy is currently prompting the authorities of these countries to consider models of managing public funds adequate for their states. These economic systems still form a "plastic mass" that can be shaped in a way that is fair, benefiting both the society and investors and stable in the context of long-term development through knowledge and experience. Therefore, I propose the implementation of solutions in the PPP formula, using selected principles of conventional and Islamic finance in sub-Saharan Africa.

The functioning of these conventional financial systems is affected by the progressive globalisation, which for the purposes of this paper is broadly understood as a manifestation of both the internationalisation of individual economies and the increasingly free movement of knowledge, experience and human capital between countries. At the same time, the globalisation process has revealed deep disparities in the development of individual regions of the world. These can be seen particularly in sub-Saharan Africa, including some emerging countries such as Nigeria and Botswana. These countries need support and intervention so that their development becomes possible and beneficial. For investors from developed countries, both conventional and Islamic, it is an opportunity to expand in a new social and economic environment. This requires knowledge of local circumstances, particularly in view of the progress of Islamisation in sub-Saharan in Africa, and the increasing use of the Islamic financial rules.

Thanks to the broader use of PPPs, which involve the interpenetration of selected principles of conventional and Islamic finance, it may prove possible to ensure stable development of the region of sub-Saharan Africa. Moreover, the involvement of foreign investors will be fairer, adequate to local needs and supporting the process

---

[3]Tiffen [3].

of shaping the political, economic and social order. Under the proposed conditions, PPPs will significantly reduce the current processes of over-exploitation of natural resources, linked to the transfer of all profits outside the continent. What is more, the postulated heterodox approach towards formulating PPP projects will become a platform for fitting and coexistence of selected elements of conventional and Islamic finance in order to achieve synergy in the development of these countries, as well as to carry out joint investments in new economic areas. Territories such as emerging countries or countries characterised by atrophy of statehood in sub-Saharan Africa, where until recently there were no rigid frameworks of the financial systems, will gain access to knowledge and a basis for new socio-economic solutions that are appropriate to local circumstances, including religious ones. The new forms of management can be manifested with a heterodoxic approach to PPP, which inherently combines the goals and rules of management implemented by both the public and the private partners. Reaching a consensus always requires giving up some authorisations, as well as foregoing maximising revenue in order to work out common goals that will be satisfactory for both parties in the course of long-term formal collaboration.[4]

A strong desire for development and economic progress, as well as the search for ways to overcome the crisis and wake the economy from a slumber, is evident not only in the countries of Europe but also in many countries of the Middle East and in Africa. The willingness of many investors to grow and expand often means that new markets have to be found. For example, for a few years now, the Polish government has been operating a programme of investment promotion, entitled "Go Africa". According to the statistics of the Economic Department of the Polish Embassy in Pretoria, which deals with the region of sub-Saharan Africa, the number of Polish companies investing in this region is constantly increasing. This is confirmed by the data of the Central Statistical Office (GUS), which indicates that the exports by Polish entrepreneurs to Africa in 2015 increased by 13% compared to 2014 and in the third quarter of 2015 amounted to 8.11 million PLN.[5] Thus, the attention of scientists and finance experts is also increasingly focused on the new, emerging, developing economies of the Gulf countries, as well as some African countries. Our cognitive aspirations urge us to get interested in how the world's economic centres will change, how the importance of the so far insignificant emerging and developing countries will grow, especially in sub-Saharan Africa.

The functioning of other financial systems, such as Islamic finance, the more widespread use of which could be supported by the proposed heterodox approach to the implementation of public-private projects, is another interesting matter. The understanding of the emerging turning points in the development of international relations and the financial situation within many countries should contribute to the awakening of "sluggish" and troubled conventional economies. Paying greater attention to emerging countries and countries with Islamic financial systems can bring multilateral benefits to economies that undergo the process of globalisation.

---

[4] Kociemska [4].

[5] http://www.stosunki.pl/?q=content/polska-rusza-na-podbój-afryki.

Meanwhile, science is often ahead of the strongly globalising world economy. In 1930, during the economic crisis, J. M. Keynes predicted that in the next 100 years, living standards in progressive countries would be between five and eight times higher. At the time, it was treated as something absurd. However, despite the historical, political and economic turmoil, the forecasts turned out to be true.[6] At present, the argument of the crisis of paradigm in the contemporary economy, which is defined differently by many authors, is often raised.[7] The most frequently cited definition of paradigm is the one coined by T. Kuhn, who is considered to be the creator of the concept of paradigm, in which he describes it as an original and open work, which is sufficiently unprecedented to attract an enduring group of adherents and sufficiently open-ended to leave all sorts of problems for the redefined group of practitioners to resolve; it is consistent logically and conceptually, but not once and for all, it also evolves [...]. Therefore, we are looking for theoretical models explaining the ever-changing reality, calling into question the existing models and improving them. The aim is to find solutions to the emerging economic turbulences that are occurring in such rapidly changing economies. The demands of enriching science with the heterodox economy are becoming more and more visible. This is illustrated for example by an article titled: *On the outskirts of economics. The importance of modern heterodoxy*.[8] During the 9th Congress of the Polish Economic Society, Professor Jerzy Hausner stressed that the global economic crisis provoked a revision of many paradigms of the neoclassical economy.[9] During the meeting, Professor Grzegorz Kołodko asserted that economy itself will evolve towards an interdisciplinary approach to sciences and that heterodoxy will dominate in the future.[10] T. Kuhn believes that sweeping revolutionary changes will bring about new areas of scientific research, as well as specialisation of paradigms. This specialisation would imply the emergence of narrower research trends and new disciplines as a result of permeation of other, already existing fields.[11]

In the sub-discipline of public finance, a clear trend of the dominance of the science of *New Public Management* (NPM) is currently visible. In Islamic finance, religious and ethical norms stemming from the interpretation of the *Quran* and from the rules set forth by the *Shari'ah* law continue to form the main basis of economic relations. Heterodox scientific dissertations in financial sciences, especially in public finance, are rare. Hence, the study was motivated by the following challenges regarding forms and rules of carrying out investments in the public sector:

---

[6]Wąsowski [5].

[7]Cf. Guziejewska [6] and *Ekonomia dla przyszłości. Odkrywać naturę i przyczyny zjawisk gospodarczych,* Polish Economic Society Congress materials, http://kongres.pte.pl/kongres/upload/files/Kongres_streszczenia_internet.pdf, p. 57.

[8]Cf. Rogowska [7].

[9]www.kongres.pte.pl/kongres/upload/files/Kongres_streszczenia_internet.pdf, p. 58.

[10]Ibid., p. 68.

[11]Cf. Kuhn [8, 9].

- searching for opportunities of developing PPP investments in new territories, taking into consideration the effect of convergence between conventional public finance and Islamic finance;
- searching for practical financial solutions for shaping a stable, long-term development of economies in emerging and developing countries, which often function according to the Islamic finance system;
- searching for new investment methods in the field of the provision of public goods based on PPP in mixed, conventional and Islamic market conditions.

The aim of this monograph is to make an attempt at elaborating on issues pertaining to public-private partnership, based on the theory of conventional public finance and Islamic finance, to discuss the interdependence of both systems, leading to the evolution of existing assumptions of public finance science and risk management in infrastructure projects implemented in the PPP formula. The research case points to a gap in public finance theory, which, if supplemented, would fully reflect the possible correlations of conventional financial theory and Islamic Moral Economy to the implementation of PPP investments in related financial systems and emerging markets. The research conducted is motivated by the desire to draw a specialised paradigm in the theory of public finance, i.e. a heterodox approach to public finance, concerning public-private structures. It will be based on the convergence between selected private conventional investors "objectives, such as profit maximisation and Islamic investors" goals—maximising social well-being and profitability, as well as public service objectives, i.e. delivering public services characterised by quality and accessibility.

The objective defined in this way, extensive studies of the existing achievements of economic sciences, especially in the field of finance, the obtained research material and the author's own experience enabled the author to formulate key research hypotheses:

- There is a possibility of convergence, understood as the emergence of convergence in selected areas of conventional public finance and Islamic Moral Economy for the development of emerging and developing economies willing to implement investments in the PPP formula.
- The promotion of public-private partnerships in emerging countries can contribute to the stabilisation of the economic situation in those countries.
- Risk management in the implementation of public-private projects under the conditions of conventional finance and Islamic finance is possible.
- The application of the proposed heterodox approach to PPPs may help increase the involvement of investors from countries with conventional finance systems in Islamic finance countries, including new markets.
- The heterodox approach to PPP is a potential solution to the crisis of public finance in various economic conditions, especially those assuming convergence of principles and philosophy of management of conventional and Islamic investors.

This objective and the presented research hypotheses determined the structure of work in a fundamental way. The whole publication consists of five chapters, as well as an introduction and a conclusion, which have substantive links with each other. This enabled the author to formulate general conclusions. The introductory chapter defines the aim of the paper and research hypotheses and explains the general concepts used in the paper.

Chapter 2 provides an overview of the most important issues in the field of *project finance* and PPP. General legal conditions of PPP and standard organisational principles of this process are presented. The chapter also presents sub-Saharan Africa as a region where many countries with dysfunctional economic systems and numerous emerging countries seeking forms of stable economic development can be found. The potential of the PPP market in Europe, the Middle East and Africa was briefly summarised, signalling how the situation of conventional countries and Islamic investors may affect the implementation of PPP infrastructure investments. The presentation of the experience of conventional and Islamic countries in the implementation of PPP projects makes it possible to transfer knowledge and technology in this field to new markets.

In Chap. 3, in order to verify the proposed heterodox approach to PPP, risk areas specific for this type of investment projects in the theory of public finance and in Islamic finance were identified. Risks to the performance of public finance functions were also identified in the analysed systemic areas, for which the proposed approach to the implementation of investment projects constitutes a significant reduction of uncertainty and risk. The key financial, social, demographic and geopolitical turning points in the global economy, which contributed to the creation of a heterodox approach to PPPs, were also emphasised. Their understanding and correct interpretation will encourage the search for innovative theoretical and practical solutions in the field of shaping the rules of public finance, especially in the failed, emerging and developing countries of sub-Saharan Africa.

This outline of important concepts and general determinants of contemporary selected conventional and Islamic economies provides a substantive background for further theoretical considerations presented in Chap. 4. The chapter identifies the key features and the most important trends in the development of both conventional principles of the theory of public finance and Islamic finance. The features of the Islamic Moral Economy are presented in a synthetic way in order to show the possibility of permeating and converging the agency theory, public choice theory and the social choice theory with the norms of the principles of the *Quran* and the *Shari'ah* law in the further part of the chapter. Identification of the axioms of the role of the state and society in the discussed financial systems has also become an important field of research. The main proposal of the PPP in a heterodox perspective, which indicates the possibility of the interpenetration of selected areas of conventional finance and Islamic finance in public-private projects, is the culmination of the considerations presented in this work.

In Chap. 5, the theoretical presentation of the heterodox approach to PPP was expanded to include factors of its attractiveness for conventional, Islamic and public administration investors wishing to implement investments using the *project finance* method, with the involvement of conventional and Islamic partners.

The last part of the work, Chap. 6, offers a summary of the existing deliberations in the form of presentation of risk matrices in PPP projects based on a heterodox approach for a selected developing country in sub-Saharan Africa and the implementation of a PPP investment method together with exemplary financial forecasts for such an enterprise.

The work is mostly theoretical, only complemented by empirical experience, and the basic discourse is conducted from the macroeconomic perspective of public finances. It is in line with the nomenclature of basic research, which aims to formulate a new heterodox approach to cooperation in the PPP formula. It also pointed out the possibility of applying the results of work in economic practice, especially in the area of functioning of emerging and developing countries, seeking, on the one hand, stable forms of development, and on the other hand, access to knowledge and technology. The main aim of the research was to discover and justify the general pillars of the heterodox approach in PPPs, applied between conventional and Islamic partners in the area of emerging and developing countries. Thanks to carrying out a related research project at the Rhodes University in South Africa and numerous economic visits to sub-Saharan Africa, where the author represented European investors, it was possible to conduct qualitative research directly. The research was characterized by the fact that the collection of data and source information was carried out through direct observation of both public entities and foreign investors, operating in the socio-economic conditions of sub-Saharan Africa. Thanks to the understanding of the phenomena taking place, as well as the researcher's curiosity regarding the broader financial reality of conventional and Islamic investors, it was possible to develop a new heterodox approach to PPP. A method of scientific induction was used to formulate research hypotheses. The use of synthetic analysis enabled the development of a platform for consensus regarding the principles of conventional public finance and Islamic finance, particularly regarding the PPP formula for carrying out public tasks. The presentation of models for risk analysis in PPP in the proposed heterodox approach using causal link matrices, correlation indicators and financial simulations of the company significantly enriched the methods employed for the purpose of this research. The research methods used mainly included scientific observations, primary source and statistical data analyses and, in addition, an extensive analysis of foreign language sources. Ordinary descriptive and comparative, historical as well as predictive methods were also employed in this study.

The author intended to create a common ground for consensus among private and public investors who are particularly active in emerging and developing countries in the sub-Saharan region, where the political and socio-economic order is lacking, and the conditions of operation are constantly changing by combining the theoretical characteristics of public finance and Islamic finance systems. The heterodox approach in public finance does not only develop upon or supplement the existing financial theories but also proves to be a practical solution for meeting the objectives of various investors in the PPP cooperation model. It places particular emphasis on changing the principle of allocating public resources in the uncertain legal and economic environment of the region discussed. It also promotes departure from financing public needs primarily by debt towards cumulating assets and using them efficiently in order to carry out infrastructure investments through PPP. Even the partial introduction of the principles of Islamic finance to the economic and public life may seem to be a "revolutionary proposition" from the standpoint of conventional public entities. This means interrupting the stable development of sciences by intellectual and revolutionary thought, after which one conceptual scientific view is replaced by another.[12] Due to the inadequacy of the existing theoretical models, which do not fully explain the reality[13] and do not indicate the possibility for the selected principles of conventional and Islamic finance to permeate, new and more reliable solutions are sought. The heterodox approach to PPP presents a solution that is beneficial to many types of partners, including: public entities and multicultural societies, conventional and Islamic investors, as well as emerging nations, in particular of sub-Saharan Africa. Additionally, it contributes to the aforementioned continuous development of the field of finance and the search for new trends in the field of public finance.

Perhaps the presentation of the heterodox approach to PPP is a manifestation of transcendental idealism and a presentation of the elementary conditions that must be fulfilled in order to enable further research into the potential for the permeation of achievements in the fields of conventional finance and Islamic Moral Economy. Immanuel Kant was critical of both the a priori synthetic judgements of rationalists and those that denied a priori synthetic judgements of empiricists. He wrote: "It has hitherto been assumed that our cognition must conform to the objects; but all attempts to ascertain anything about these objects a priori, by means of conceptions, and thus to extend the range of our knowledge, have been rendered abortive by this assumption. Let us then make the experiment whether we may not be more successful in metaphysics if we assume that the objects must conform to our cognition".[14] This is the guiding principle of this monograph.

The current problems of conventional public finances are based on credit and financing of public tasks with debt. The achievements of financial theory so far have not been of any great help in describing market trends and public policies. Despite the achievements of the Nobel Prize winners, such as Robert Lucas, who believed in models based on an idealistic economic equilibrium theory, the problem of the recession has not been solved. Other, new solutions are still being sought. Paul Ormerod presented a valid analysis of the situation in *The Death of Economics*. In his opinion, a positive attitude to the emergence of new trends and innovative solutions in the field of economics is necessary. "(...) At the end of 2000, debt in the global economy exceeded the level of debt noted in 1929, at the beginning of the Great Depression. But economies have grown, despite the fact that according to current theories they should have collapsed, and it has turned out that they can function with debt." The same author gives another example of a quick rebound from the 1980 crisis and a very slow or insignificant rebound after 2008, where private investors, who were the driving force behind the economy, did not see the future of the economy in a positive light. They raised funds without investing, with a

[12]Cf. Kuhn, T. S. *The Structure of Scientific Revolutions...*, pp. 34–38.

[13]Cf. Ostaszewski [10].

[14]Karpinski [11].

negative outlook on the future.[15] Thus, the proposed heterodox approach to PPP is an unconventional attempt at finding other pillars of public funds management, full of optimism and interdisciplinary perception of economic principles. Perhaps the field of finance is similar to philosophy and the assumption that certain approaches do not always lead to pragmatism in describing, explaining, predicting and controlling economic phenomena is logical. Evolutionary rules are increasingly being sought, not yet included in the rigid schemes of objectively accepted market principles. This scientific paper does not suggest that we should all wear rose-tinted glasses and hope that the proposed heterodox approach to PPPs and their implementation will mean that all public finance problems will disappear and that Islamic finance could easily be implemented in the conventional public finance systems of the countries of the Old Continent; however, it aims at raising awareness and showing that the heterodox approach to public finance verifies the existing approach to shaping the financial policy and may become an adequate solution, especially for emerging or developing countries located in sub-Saharan Africa. The basis for this would be the principles of the heterodox approach to PPP, i.e. the departure from profit maximisation as the exclusive investment objective, stronger consideration of social welfare in financial plans of the investments, greater collaboration of public and private entities in long-term perspective, with greater use of assets belonging to the public sector and less debt. Perhaps such assumptions are not fully rational, yet both the economy and society are constantly evolving, and not only rational mathematical models, but also psychological abilities and intuition, cognitive passion, and perhaps even imagination based on broad mental horizons are required to describe these phenomena. Creating science always entails balancing between scientist's responsibility and adventure, even if sometimes it sounds naïve.

References

1. Merton RC (1992, July) Continuous—time finance, revised edn. Wiley-Blackwell, Preface, p III and V
2. Rogowska B (2015) Ekonomia społeczna a współczesna heterodoksja. Studia Ekonomiczne, Wydawnictwo UE, Katowice, pp 209–210
3. Tiffen A (2014, August) The new neo-colonialism in Africa. www.globalpolicyjournal.com. Accessed 10 Sept 2016
4. Kociemska H (2010, November) Public private partnership—projects success circumstances. J Mod Account Auditing 6(11):58, series no 66
5. Wąsowski M (2017, January) Polsce grozi poważny kryzys. 'Populizm może pacyfikować niezadowolenie' [WYWIAD]. Business Insider. http://businessinsider.com.pl/finanse/kryzys-w-polsce-i-na-swiecie-w-2017-roku-niepewnosc-i-populizm/k0fng82
6. Guziejewska B (2013, November) Meandry sanacyjnej roli finansów publicznych. In: 9th Congress of the Polish Economic Society. www.pte.pl
7. Rogowska B (2016) Na obrzeżach ekonomii.Znaczenie współczesnej heterodoksji. Studia Ekonomiczne, Zeszyty Naukowe UE, Katowicach, p 259

[15]Ormerod [12].

8. Kuhn TS (2000) The road since structure: philosophical essays, 1970–1993. University of Chicago Press, Chicago
9. Kuhn TS (1962) The structure of scientific revolutions. University of Chicago Press, Chicago
10. Ostaszewski J (2014) Zamiast wstępu. In: Ostaszewski J, Kosycarz E, Katedra Finansów SGH (eds) Rozwój nauki o finansach. Stan obecny i pożądane kierunki jej ewolucji. Kolegium Zarządzania i Finansów, Warszawie, p 10
11. Karpinski JA (2015) Wstęp do nauki o mądrości, vol 1. Gdańska Szkoła Wyższa, Gdańsk, pp 247–249
12. Ormerod P (1997) The death of economics. Wiley, pp 3–22

Chapter 2
Development of Public-Private Partnerships (PPPs) in Diversified Economic Areas

2.1 Genesis and Concepts: *Project Finance* and Public-Private Partnerships

Project finance, including PPP, is an economic concept strongly connected with the development of theories of conventional and Islamic finance. In the light of ongoing changes on the financial markets and scientific progress in the development of the field of finance, the need for cooperation between the areas of conventional finance of companies and public finance is becoming more and more apparent. So far, the rather orthodox assumptions of Islamic finance have been evolving towards stronger cooperation between public and private partners, aimed towards the benefit of the Islamic community and obtaining positive financial results. Thus, PPPs have proven to be a good example for presenting the heterodox approach proposed in this monograph as a scientific direction that leads to a consensus on the expectations of public and private investors, as well as local communities in different markets and based on different systemic canons in economics. In connection with the continuous development of social needs and economic expansion of many countries, the governments of these countries are constantly interested in the formula of *project finance* as a comprehensive way of implementing infrastructural investments. This concept is more broadly defined as the implementation of infrastructure investments with the use of long-term external financing in projects requiring high financial outlays. In view of the difficult situation of states in terms of both public finances and local government finances, their own possibilities of implementing investments, as well as management of the resulting infrastructure, are becoming increasingly limited. Moreover, the knowledge that using conventional methods of financing public investments is less effective is becoming more and more widespread, which leads to the search

H. Kociemska, *Public-Private Partnership for Sub-Saharan Africa*,
Advances in African Economic, Social and Political Development,
https://doi.org/10.1007/978-3-030-14753-2_2

for alternative organisational and financial solutions to the provision of public services and goods.[1] Thus, *project finance* has become a mechanism responding to the challenges related to the above-mentioned circumstances.

In the scientific literature, it is most often equated with the idea of the so-called 3E (economy, *efficiency*, *effectiveness*) within the *New Public Management* (NPM) theory.[2] The principles of economy, efficiency and effectiveness are promoted as key principles in this scientific field. The most important factors determining the increase in efficiency, in this case in the allocation of public funds and the performance of the redistributive function of public finance, include:

- principles of vertical division of public tasks between the state and local government;
- the sphere of tasks and the dual nature of local government;
- instruments for the collection of government revenue;
- instruments allowing to invest surplus financial resources and serving to cover liquidity shortages;
- tax and debt instruments aimed at minimising demotivating systemic solutions limiting the initiative and creativity of the local community;
- promoting the concept of equivalence of tax burden and moving away from the concept of financial capacity to pay;
- popularisation of economic balance, care in the implementation of public tasks, care for the financial results achieved;
- making the system of financing public tasks more flexible, e.g. by using PPP.[3]

The above arguments proving the need to increase the effectiveness in the performance of state operations, as well as other scientific contributions in this area,[4] constitute a manifestation of the search for a way to improve the financial standing of the entity in the public world. In addition, gains connected with increasing efficiency should be linked to improving the quality and availability of public services, including the uninterrupted delivery of all public finance functions. In the face of the subsequent financial crises, growing disproportions in the scope of development of individual countries, seeking new investment areas, interest in creating tools for effective public management in various economic, social and religious conditions are growing. The proposed heterodox approach in public finance, applied in the *project finance* structures, should be a potential solution to the problem of seeking optimal efficiency in the management of public administration in theory and practice. For several decades, *project finance* has been a solution to the public finance sector in terms of conducting public activities without the need to privatise the sector. The notion of the organisation of investments in the *project finance* formula was presented by, among others, P. K. Nevit and F. Fabozzi, describing the process as "the financing of a specific economic entity based on the principle that the principal

---

[1] Hua Jin et al. [1].

[2] Hausner [2].

[3] Filipak [3], after Sochacka-Krysiak [4].

[4] Cf. Kosikowski [5].

source of repayment acceptable to the lender is the financial surplus generated by the entity, and the collateral for the loan is provided in the form of the assets held by the entity".[5] A number of approaches to the understanding of the *project finance* phenomenon can be distinguished in this field, emphasising many of its diverse aspects. For some, such as D. J. de Nahlik, this process is a way to manage projects, including the risk areas, assuming a minimum impact of the process occurring in the established purpose vehicle on the sponsors—the entities organising it.[6] For others, such as H. Harries, the essence of this phenomenon lies in the structure of financing with repayable capital, where the repayment of the investment loan in the project takes place exclusively with the cash flow generated by the project.[7] The European Investment Bank (EIB) and the International Project Finance Association (IPFA) provide a definition, widely used in science as well as in economic practice, where *project finance* is used for long-term financing of infrastructural or industrial projects based on the lack of recourse to the sponsors of a special purpose vehicle. Debt capital and equity are used to conduct business and repay the liabilities arising from the financial flows generated by the project. The basic difference in such a financing structure compared to the traditional financing of entities is based on the inability of the investors to use financial resources, assets and the previous creditworthiness of the sponsor in the project as a basis for anything.[8] Thus, on the basis of the literature review and the studies, the following set of *project finance* characteristics can be distinguished in the case of infrastructure projects:

- used to finance investments on the basis of the *ring-fenced* principle, meaning economic, legal and organisational independence of the special purpose vehicle established to implement the infrastructure investment project in question;
- this technique is usually used to implement new investment projects, the so-called *greenfield projects* or *brownfield projects*[9] in the public sector, to conduct projects in cooperation with private entities or to expand, reconstruct and manage the resulting public infrastructure;
- often associated with a high level of external financing in relation to the special purpose vehicle's equity (debt financing may constitute up to 90% of project expenditures);

---

[5]Nevit and Fabozzi [6].

[6]de Nahlik et al. [7], after Pollio [8].

[7]Harries [9].

[8]http://www.uncdf.org/sites/default/files/Documents/uncdf_lfi_project_workshop-21.10.2014daressalaam.pdf, accessed on 11.10.2016 and http://www.eib.org/epec/g2g/annex/1-project-finance/.

[9]*Greenfield* investment projects—one of the types of direct foreign investments (FDI). These are investments created from scratch. They rely on establishing completely new businesses. Such investments are particularly characteristic of developing countries. *Brownfield* investment projects are another type of FDI. They usually occur in highly developed countries. *Brownfield* investment projects consist of the acquisition of already existing companies or take the form of a merger. Source: Górniewicz [10].

- the *ring-fenced*[10] principle does not envision any guarantees to the entity owning the special purpose vehicle;
- the return on debt financing is based primarily on the long-term financial result of the investment project being carried out;
- the most frequently used financial risk hedging instrument by the lenders is contracts concluded by the special purpose vehicle, e.g. contracts with a payer for health services, mining licences, a contract for electricity take-up and motorway tolls.[11]

The presented solution is not modern, as private funds were used to finance public investments as early as in the eighteenth century, for example for the construction of road networks in England. In the nineteenth century, thanks to this organisational solution, other branches of industry are developed, such as gas, water, power and telecommunications industries. Then in the 1930s in the USA, modern *project finance* methods were used to finance the development of the mining industry, and in the 1980s this solution was used in the power industry. In the UK, this formula started to be called *private finance initiatives* (PFIs) in the early 1990s, in connection with a range of road construction projects carried out in the country.[12] It was also in the UK that the term *public-private partnership* (PPP) was used for the first time. This term is often treated as synonymous with the *project finance* process, although PPP projects do not always fulfil all the characteristics of *project finance*. In the source literature, there are many definitions of PPP, emphasising various aspects of this type of cooperation. PPP is a special form of cooperation of the above-mentioned entities, the aim of which is to implement public tasks based on the use of the mutual potential of the parties, including knowledge and capital. A PPP is a cooperation of a public entity with private entities, aimed at obtaining mutual benefits by all of the parties. It is particularly attractive in areas where, on the one hand, there is a high demand for services (transport infrastructure, water supply, sewage disposal and treatment, waste management, public transport, construction of cultural centres, administration buildings, hospitals, schools, even prisons), but, on the other hand, there is insufficient capital to carry out costly investments or modernise inefficient infrastructure.[13] According to Grimsey and Lewis, a PPP is an agreement where a public sector representative establishes a long-term cooperation agreement with a private partner in order to create infrastructure for the provision of public services.[14] On the other hand, A. Sedjar's definition of PPP emphasises the element of solidarity in cooperation as a key element connecting public and private partners, understood as sharing risk, costs and benefits. According to this author, a PPP is a "cultural phenomenon", a process understood by the author as the ability to collectively mobilise the participants of the process, who collectively create

---

[10]Ring-fenced—financing without recourse to sponsors of the project.

[11]Yescombe [11].

[12]Kopańska [12].

[13]Kociemska [13].

[14]Grimsey and Lewis [14].

Table 2.1 Various definitions of the concept of PPP

Institution/person defining the term	Definition of PPP
European Investment Bank	A long-term contractual arrangement for the provision of a public asset and related services in exchange for performance-based payments linked to the asset's availability and/or use and the delivery of the related services
World Bank	Public-private partnerships (PPPs) are a mechanism for the government to procure and implement public infrastructure and/or services using the resources and expertise of the private sector. Such an approach promotes a new solution for improving the financial situation of public entities, as well as guaranteeing the possibility of more effective provision of public services
OECD	Arrangements whereby the private sector provides infrastructure assets and services that traditionally have been provided by the government, such as hospitals, schools, prisons, roads, bridges, tunnels, railways, and water and sanitation plants
European Commission	Cooperation between the public and private sectors with a view to carrying out a project or providing a service traditionally provided by the public sector
Act on PPP in Poland	Joint implementation of a project based on the division of tasks and risk areas between the public entity and private partner

Source Own compilation based on the following documents: *A Guide to the statistical treatment of PPPs*, September 2016, EPEC, www.eib.org/epec/resources/publications/epec_eurostat_guide_ppp, p. 18, stats.oecd.org/glossary/detail.asp?ID=7315, https://ppp.worldbank.org/public-private-partnership/about-public-private-partnerships, European Commission, Act of the 19th of December 2008 on public-private partnerships, Dz. U. [Journal of Laws] 2015, item 696, 1777

the essence and power the implementation of public programmes.[15] Many other authors present different interpretations of the term. It is worth noting that the form of cooperation between public and private entities, defined by various scientists, is of a long-term nature, which distinguishes it from the popular methods of commissioning specific services to the public entity and is connected with the management of the resulting infrastructure also in the long term. Popular views of the PPP phenomenon presented by international institutions and the Polish legislation are presented in Table 2.1.

Each of the definitions above, presented by scientists, institutions or legislators, focuses on the advanced process of implementation of an investment project between two types of partners. Some of the defining entities attach importance to the process of providing public services itself, while others pay attention to the implementation

[15] Sedjar [15].

of investments in a specific way. Both in the case of scientific contributions[16] and in the case of economic practice, each of the presented approaches is reflected in the partnerships being created, although depending on the entity establishing the norms the concept of PPP might be defined in a different way. The lack of conceptual uniformity thus emphasises the essence of the phenomenon itself, which is the result of a conventional consensus developed by public and private parties to achieve mutual goals in the long run. Such cooperation between partners has been functioning in the world for several decades now. As an example of the field of *project finance*, PPPs have developed in the following countries: the UK, the USA, New Zealand, but also in many others, albeit to a lesser extent. For a long time, PPP has been gaining importance in the field of implementation of macroeconomic policies of many European Union Member States. It has become one of the crucial elements in the EU Horizon 2020 Framework,[17] earmarked for financing research and innovation in the economies of individual Member States. It is one of the pillars of this programme, at the same time pointing out the importance of this phenomenon for shaping stable economies and investment programmes of the Member States. A very important aspect of PPP research is the long-standing activity of the Organisation for Economic Co-operation and Development (OECD). For several decades, the organisation has been supporting the efforts of all 35 Member States to achieve the highest economic level and has been developing norms and standards of conduct in international cooperation. Therefore, PPP is one of the important pillars of regulatory activity of OECD, consisting in monitoring the market of public-private partnerships, including international and hybrid legislative solutions facilitating the establishment of such a form of cooperation. OECD[18] runs colleges of experts in the public finance sector in various countries, allowing the experts to exchange experiences and then influence the shaping of the standards in the investment policy on a local scale. The third very important trend in the global practical research on the public-private partnership and its significance for the macroeconomic situation of many countries is the activity of the World Bank within the *Public Private Partnership Infrastructure Resources Center (*PPPIRC).[19] The Center provides access to information on implemented projects, as well as various legal, organisational and management aspects concerning these projects. In addition, it bases its activities on assistance in structuring projects (including appropriate financing) or pointing to key factors of sectors in which partnerships are to be implemented. The phenomenon of PPP is therefore noticed by key institutions that influence the development of the foundations of national economies, and thus constitutes a regular field of scientific research.

From the point of view of the author, the scientific cognitive aspirations enforce the need to deepen the theoretical foundations of public finance and Islamic finance,

---

[16] Cf. Yescombe [16].

[17] The EU Framework Programme for Research and Innovation Horizon 2020, European Commission, 2014, www.ec.europa.eu.

[18] OECD, Principles for public governance of public private partnerships, May 2012.

[19] World Bank [17].

including risk management in public entities capable of implementing PPPs. This will provide an opportunity to place the phenomenon of heterodoxy in the current fields of public finance science as an attempt to reach a consensus between the areas of public finance, finance of privately owned enterprises and Islamic finance, which so far have often been disconnected, based on the example of PPP. A certain shortage of basic research in this area and the deepening of the scientific analysis of the PPP phenomenon in financial theories in connection with the fields of enterprise finance and public finance can be observed, including on the basis of the regulations of the *Quran* and the *Shari'ah* law (deliberations pertaining to this area will be the subject of the subsequent chapters). In conclusion, the following phenomena contribute to the development of PPPs worldwide:

- the growing scale of public service needs, especially in view of macroeconomic, social, demographic and epidemiological changes;
- the scarcity of public funding, both in developed countries and in conventional economies, which have been severely affected by the financial crises in Europe and the USA, as well as in the emerging countries[20];
- obtaining a *value for money*[21];
- the expectation of an increase in the effectiveness of the provision of public service through ensuring conditions of competitiveness in the process of their provision[22];
- the possibility of carrying out the necessary public investments without directly burdening the budget of public entities with debt (applying specific risk management principles in PPP, as well as clean organisational and economic structures, the so-called *ring-fenced* structures, within the *project finance* enables not counting the liabilities of *special purpose vehicles* (SPV)[23] as liabilities of the public entity, and therefore such a structure does not increase the level of public debt);
- challenges faced by public authorities in the use of non-repayable EU funds, where the availability of these funds is conditioned by having own funds for co-financing infrastructure projects;
- the limited ability of officials to manage and operate investment projects, which means the insufficient quality of administrative staff[24];
- politicisation of the privatisation process and using it for current political games (negative connotations).[25]

The adopted methodology defining PPP in different markets makes it a structure used worldwide in different political and economic conditions. The signalled problems of selected economies are a challenge in many developed, developing and emerging countries. The proposed solution to the emerging problems could be a

[20] Sadka [18], Hall [19].

[21] Sciulli [20].

[22] B. Filipak, *Finanse samorządu terytorialnego*, p. 141, after Bailey [21, Kachniarz 22].

[23] SPV—special purpose vehicle, commercial law company, established within the framework of public-private partnership by public and private partners.

[24] Herbst [23].

[25] Boardman [24].

wider use of PPP structures in a heterodox perspective. Therefore, an example of empirical model presented in this monograph will concern the region of sub-Saharan Africa, including, among others, the specifics of emerging or dysfunctional countries, the so-called failed states,[26] requiring a comprehensive policy of regarding shaping public finances and asset management principles, where the use of the heterodox approach based on the example of a PPP project can bring measurable benefits.

One of the important reasons for the development of PPP is the willingness of the public party to obtain a *value for money*. The direct interpretation of this Anglo-Saxon phrase indicates that the appropriate quality/price ratio of the service should be determined. However, both in economic practice and in scientific works, this term means striving to achieve the best possible ratio of all types of outlays in a project to the achieved effectiveness of the project. In this case, outlays are understood as financial resources, human capital and *know-how*. The effectiveness of the project encompasses not only the expected financial result but also broadly understood benefits for the society. The most important manifestations of the benefits of PPP for local communities are:

- ensuring the appropriate quality of public service;
- ensuring adequate access to the public service, understood as the possibility to use the public services of all those who, in accordance with the relevant provisions, are authorised to do so;
- not overcharging for public services, which affects their availability;
- covering the appropriate area with an adequate range of services so that any person entitled to them can use them without any particular territorial restriction;
- employment growth;
- achieving a positive impact on the local and global environment;
- involving local communities in the process of cooperation with private and public partners, for example through social dialogue or participation of local communities in profits obtained from the project;
- development of a social culture in the scope of cooperation between public and private entities, where a key role should be played by the factor of trust in the partner in the project.

Although the listed benefits of PPP for local communities sound like truisms, it is important to highlight them in the process of creating a heterodox approach to PPP. They will become one of the main objectives of establishing public-private cooperation in various socio-economic orders and economic conditions, both conventional and Islamic.

The PPP process is not flawless. For example, in Polish conditions, but not only in Poland, one of the most frequently cited disadvantages is the psychological barrier of the public and private decision-makers, preventing them from forming lasting public-private relationships.[27] Mutual suspicion and reluctance of public and private partners are a result of corrupt behaviours and reports of irregularities in the implementation

[26] Kłosowicz and Mormul [25].

[27] Kulesza [26].

of projects, traditionally undertaken by entrepreneurs within the framework of the Act on Public Procurement.[28] Another area that threatens the success of PPP processes and is visible around the world is the need to maintain long-term mutual commitments between partners, despite the term-based tenure of public authorities and changes in business preferences among the new governing structures. Another flaw, which is frequently cited by practitioners and researchers alike, is the loss of public funding, which is spent on the acquisition of a stake in the *special purpose vehicle (*SPV). There is still a strong awareness of the inseparability of public funding and its owner. The transfer of the legal title to assets to an external company, not in the form of a sale transaction but in the form of acquisition of equity in the form of a contribution-in-kind of assets, raises concerns and often causes strong reluctance on part of public authorities. It is unjustified from the point of view of the substantive course of such an economic and legal transaction. However, a negative assessment of such a move by a public entity is strongly rooted in the decision-making bodies of public administration. To a large extent, this is related to the fears of losing control over the condition and use of assets, which will constitute assets of a public-private entity. Another area particularly associated with dangers causes the lack of social acceptance for the implementation of investments using the PPP approach. It often results from the necessity of paying fees by the community using public services, which were previously free of charge. Another important negative aspect of cooperation within the framework of PPPs is the cost-consuming process of establishing cooperation in the face of necessary purchases of advisory and analytical services for evaluation of thc concept of cooperation at the preparatory stage. It is estimated that the costs of organising the PPP process are much higher and often take more time compared to short-term contracting of public services under traditional public procurement procedures. Unfortunately, higher costs of PPPs are also often associated with raising capital. Market data indicate that the cost of capital of fully public projects tends to be lower than the cost of external financing of the same type of infrastructure but by public-private partnerships.[29] The inability to guarantee a debt obligation, which means that the external financing of investments is secured only by the PPP company's assets and financial flows of the project, was a key factor increasing the risk for lenders and, consequently, increasing the cost of capital. In the author's opinion, apart from the reasons mentioned above, the following factors are reasons for negative assessment of PPP projects in various economic and political conditions around the world:

- spreading over time the effects of a decision to invest in PPP in such a way that the highest costs related to the investment are related to the period of achieving optimum income for the same project. For some industries, this will mean a period of more than 5–6 years, which, due to the term-based tenure of public authorities,

---

[28] Act of the 22 June 2016 amending the Public Procurement Law and other acts, Dz. U. [Journal of Laws] of the 13 July 2016, item 1020.

[29] *Never mind the balance sheet: the dangers posed by PPP in Central and Eastern Europe*, Bankwatch Network 11.2008, http://bankwatch.org/documents/never_mind_the_balance_sheet.pdf, accessed on 10.09.2016.

may generate a risk of recklessness when making a decision on concluding a PPP agreement, given the lack of responsibility for its consequences after the end of their term of office;

- a long period of project organisation and analyses performed before the investment starts, including the period related to the necessity to outsource some of the necessary analyses;
- increasing the scale of investments in PPPs so as to guarantee the partners of SPV the expected profit; the scope of the investment is often greater than the basic investment objective of a public entity, the implementation of which would not ensure the profit expected by a private investor;
- the need to precisely define the quality and availability factors of the public service provided by the SPV in the long-term perspective, i.e. the public entity should identify the determinants of the quality of the public service and its accessibility by a changing society, in terms of demography and epidemiology in the long-term perspective.

The above-mentioned reasons for the expansion of the PPP phenomenon, as well as the benefits resulting from it for the society, shape certain economic and social conditions. The background to this process is formed by positive and negative factors, characteristic of both conventional and Islamic economies. Their understanding and appropriate management, overcoming the shortcomings and barriers, will create the basis for the implementation of the proposed heterodox model in public finance, especially in the PPP formula.

2.2 General Legal, Economic and Organisational Conditions of Public-Private Partnerships in the European Union

The analysis of the provisions of European and Polish law in the field of PPP shows that many regulations of a normative nature differ depending on the legislation of individual countries. No uniform legislation on PPP projects has been adopted at EU level or by other international legislative bodies. On the other hand, there are many public recommendations of a supranational nature concerning the recommendations, standards and golden rules of PPP, which constitute guidelines for voluntary application of the agreement by the parties. The most important legal acts related to PPP are presented in Tables 2.2 and 2.3.

In economic practice, there are countries that create laws and regulations designed for PPPs in order to implement this type of projects. There are also countries where the establishment of cooperation within the framework of PPP did not require the creation of separate legal acts. In Poland, the current acts[30] are based on the following

[30] Act of the 19th of December 2008 on public-private partnership, Dz. U. [Journal of Laws] of 2009, item 696, 1777 and Act of the 9th of January 2009 on concessions for construction works or services, Dz. U. [Journal of Laws] of 2009, No. 19, item 101.

Table 2.2 Summary of the most relevant legislation related to PPPs in the EU

Treaty of Lisbon of 13 December 2007 amending the Treaty on European Union and the Treaty establishing the European Community (OJ C 306 of 17 December 2007)
Treaty on the Functioning of the European Union, as established by the Treaty of Lisbon (consolidated version OJ C 83 of 30 March 2010)
Directive 2014/24/EU of the European Parliament and of the Council of 26 February 2014 on public procurement and repealing Directive 2004/18/EC of the European Parliament and of the Council of 31 March 2004 on public procurement
Manual on Government Deficit and Debt—Implementation of ESA95, Eurostat Methodologies and Working Papers, Publications Office of the European Union, European Commission and Eurostat, Luxembourg, 2012 Edition
Eurostat Decision No. 18/2004 of 11 February 2004 on the treatment of public-private partnerships in terms of deficit and debt
Communication from the Commission to the European Parliament, the Council, the European Economic and Social Committee and the Committee of the Regions on public-private partnerships and Community Law on Public Procurement and Concessions of 15 November 2005
Communication from the Commission to the European Parliament, the Council, the European Economic and Social Committee and the Committee of the Regions of 19 November 2009 on enhancing the role of public-private partnerships
Rules applicable to Institutionalised Public-Private Partnerships. Commission interpretative communication on the application of Community Law on Public Procurement and Concessions to institutionalised PPP (IPPP) 2008/C 91/02
Communication from the European Commission of 29 April 2000 on the interpretation of the provisions relating to the award of concession contracts under Community Law
Commission guidelines on successful public-private partnerships. Guidelines for a Successful Public-Private Partnership published by the European Commission, Directorate General for Regional Policy, January 2003 Communication from the Commission to the European Parliament, the Council, the European Economic and Social Committee and the Committee of the Regions of 19 November 2009—Mobilising private and public investment for recovery and long-term structural change: developing Public-Private Partnerships [COM (2009) 615 final—Not published in the Official Journal]
European Parliament resolution on public-private partnerships and Community Law on Public Procurement and Concessions (20062043(INI)) of 26 October 2006
Green Paper on Public-Private Partnerships. Green Paper on Public-Private Partnerships and Community Law on Public Contracts and Concessions, Commission of the European Communities, Brussels, 30.04.2004, COM (2004)

Source www.ppp.worldbank.org/public-private-partnership/legislationregulation/laws/procurement

Table 2.3 Polish law

Act of 19 December 2008 on public-private partnership, Dz. U. [Journal of Laws] of 2009, No. 19, item 100, hereinafter referred to as the Act on PPP
Act of 9 January 2009 on concessions for construction works or services, Dz. U. [Journal of Laws] of 2009, No. 19, item 101, hereinafter referred to as the Act on Concessions
Act of 22 June 2016 amending the Public Procurement Law and other acts, Dz. U. [Journal of Laws] of 3 July 2016, item 1020, Act of 29 January 2004, Public Procurement Law, Dz. U. [Journal of Laws] of 2010, No. 113, item 759, as amended, hereinafter referred to as the Public Procurement Act
Act of 27 September 2009 on public finance, Dz. U. [Journal of Laws] of 2009, No. 157, item 1240, as amended, hereinafter referred to as the Public Finance Act
Act of 30 August 1996 on commercialisation and privatisation, Dz. U. [Journal of Laws] 2002, No. 171, item 1397, hereinafter referred to as the Privatisation Act
Ordinance of the Minister of Finance of 23 December 2010 on the detailed method of classification of debt instruments classified as state public debt, including State Treasury debt, Dz. U. [Journal of Laws] No. 252, item 1692

Source Own compilation based on http://www.dziennikustaw.gov.pl/

general principles: giving the parties to a PPP agreement as much freedom as possible regarding shaping their cooperation, protecting key public interests, protecting the legitimate interests of private investors, caring for the level of public debt, ensuring compliance with the EU law.[31] Liberalisation of legal requirements in the Public Procurement Act of 2009 contributed to the increase in popularity of PPP solutions in Poland. Thanks to the departure from the requirement to use broad economic analyses in the case of low-value investments (project value up to 211,000 € and construction works up to 5,278,000 €), the introduction of framework assumptions regarding the content of the PPP agreement and various forms of contracting the private partner, the process began to seem much clearer and more comprehensible for all of the potential participants. The above fact is confirmed by market data showing the number of concluded PPP agreements before the new act entered into force (during the period of validity of the act of 2005) and after 2009. After the Act of the 28th of July 2005 entered into force, no PPP agreement was signed in Poland.[32] Between 2009 and 2015, 409 procedures to select a private partner or a concessionaire were initiated, and 101 were successfully concluded.[33] However, the number of notifications does not translate into signed PPP agreements. Eighty-two public-private partnership contracts and concessions were concluded: 1 in 2009, 15 in 2010, 18 in 2011, 15 in 2012, 17 in 2013 and 16 in 2014, which means an average of over a dozen per year with 99 agreements concluded in total until the 10

[31] Poniatowicz [27].

[32] *Raport o partnerstwie publiczno-prywatnym w Polsce*, collective work, ed: Prof. Jerzy Hausner, authors: Dr. Irena Herbst, Dr. Aleksandra Jadach-Sepioło, Tomasz Korczynski, collaboration: Tomasz Jagusztyn-Krynicki, Bartosz Mysiorski, Przemysław Zaremba, Warsaw 2013, p. 18, http://www.centrum-ppp.pl/templates/download/rap_PPP_final_version.pdf.

[33] Zalewski [28].

November 2015.[34] Also important from the point of view of the analysis of legal conditions of PPP is the issue of classification of liabilities under the agreement on PPP to liabilities of the public entity. Fulfilment of certain assumptions makes the project unable to increase the level of public debt in connection with participation in the PPP project of the public entity. The key legal act is Eurostat Decision of the 11 February 2004 on the treatment of public-private partnerships in terms of deficit and debt.[35] In addition, the regulation on budgetary reporting entered into force on 8 February 2010.[36] It is an executive act to the Public Finance Act, regulating the types and rules of preparation of reports by the entities of the public finance sector in the scope of liabilities resulting from PPP agreements concluded by these entities. Unfortunately, the Act on PPP currently in force in Poland lacks continuity of the provisions contained in the Eurostat Decision. Article 17 of the regulation presents the obligation to set in an upper limit for the level of liabilities under PPP contracts which may be incurred in a given financial year in the budget act, but—as the provision envisions—only by government authorities. Therefore, in the Polish act there is no reference to local government units (LGUs), whose obligations are part of the government bodies' obligations; however, the former are not covered by the explicit provision determining the said limit. The Eurostat regulation clearly recommends a specific allocation of risk areas in PPPs depending on whether or not the level of public debt is affected by the planned project. It distinguishes three main types of risk areas, i.e. construction process risk, availability risk and demand risk. If the private partner bears the total risk of the construction process and one of the two remaining areas of risk, i.e. availability or demand, then during the implementation of such a PPP project and the liabilities resulting from it will not have an impact on the increase of public debt and may be treated as *off-balance*—extra-budgetary. This is a positive development from the point of view of individual countries meeting the conditions of the Economic and Monetary Union (EMU) established by the Maastricht Treaty,[37] such as: the upper limit of budgetary deficit in the year preceding the assessment of meeting this criterion not higher than 3% and the public debt in the same period not higher than 60% of the GDP of the evaluated country. Thanks to the application of this rule of classification of risk areas, liabilities resulting from PPP agreements may not constitute a component of public debt. This is an important solution for stabilising public budgets in view of the already high levels of public debt in most EU countries. The level of public debt in selected EU countries is shown in Fig. 2.1.

Comparing the above data on the ratio of the level of public debt in selected countries to their GDP, it is worth recalling the number of PPP projects carried out in the EU in the same period (Figs. 2.2 and 2.3).

---

[34]Report: "Rynek partnerstwa publiczno-prywatnego i koncesji w Polsce w 2014 r. na tle stanu obowiązującego w latach 2009–2013", as cited in http://wartowiedziec.org/index.php/start/aktualnosci/25538-raport-o-stanie-rynku-ppp.

[35]*New decision of Eurostat on deficit and debt: treatment of public private partnership*, 18/2004—11.02.2004.

[36]Regulation of the Minister of Finance of 3 February 2010 on budgetary reporting, Dz. U. [Journal of Laws] No. 20, item 103.

[37]Treaty on European Union, 7 February 1992, www.oide.sejm.gov.pl.

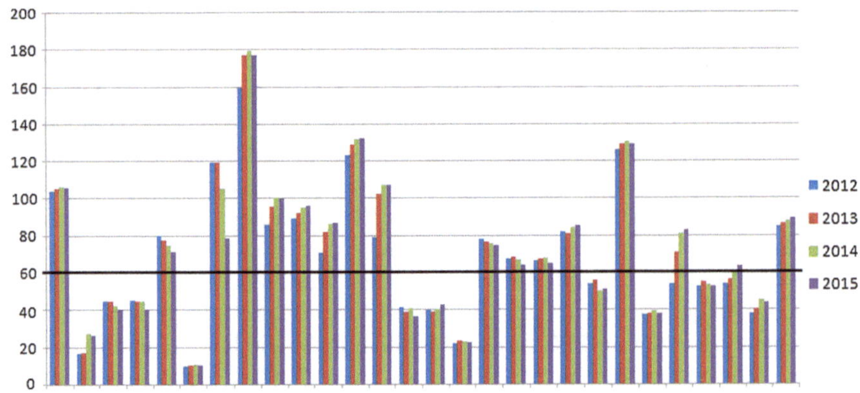

Fig. 2.1 Public debt as a share of GDP in selected EU countries (in %). Countries in order of appearance: Belgium—Bulgaria—Czech Republic—Denmark—Germany—Estonia—Republic of Ireland—Greece—Spain—France—Croatia—Italy—Cyprus—Latvia—Lithuania—Luxemburg—Hungary—Malta—the Netherlands—Austria—Poland—Portugal—Romania—Slovenia—Finland—Sweden—UK. *Source* Own compilation based on data from www.ec.europa.eu/eurostat/statisticsexplained/index.php/File:Public_balance_and_general_government_debt,_2012%E2%80%9315_(%C2%B9)_(%25_of_GDP)_YB16_III.png

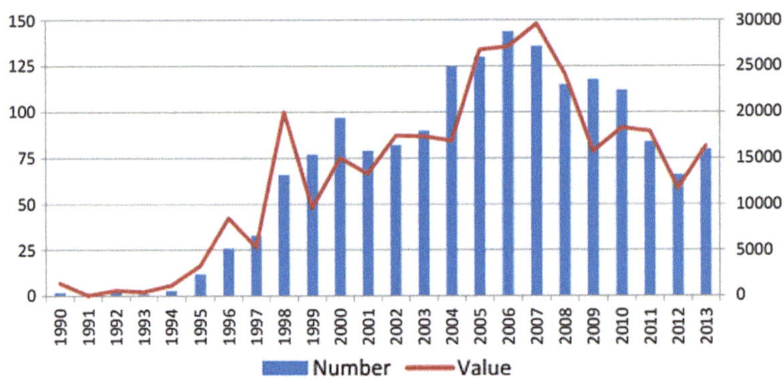

Fig. 2.2 European PPP Market 2004–2013 by value and number of projects. *Source Market Update, Review of the European PPP Market in 2013*, European PPP Expertise Centre

The level of public debt in most EU countries is growing. In many of them, it exceeded the permissible Maastricht Treaty criterion for the maximum ratio of public debt to GDP—60%. At the same time, there has been a clear downward trend in the number and value of PPP projects in the EU since 2007 and 2008. 2012 was the worst year in the last decade in terms of number and value of such projects—11.7 trillion € and 66 agreements concluded. Half of them were concluded in the UK, with the remaining contracts concerning mostly France and the Netherlands.[38] Only in 2013, an increase in the value of concluded PPP agreements was noted, and this

[38]D. Hall, op. cit., p. 9.

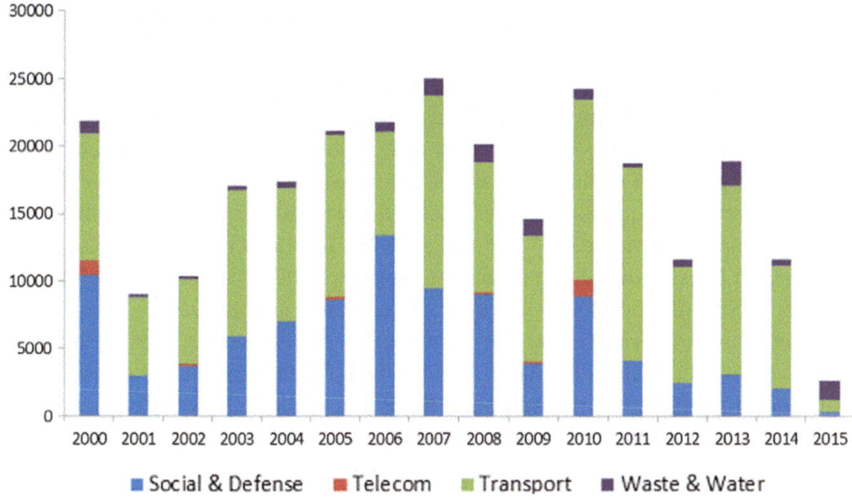

Fig. 2.3 Total value of PPP projects in the EU by industry in millions of €. *Source* Dealogic Projectware database, extraction 07/12/2015 www.ec.europa.eu/economy_finance/events/2016/20160302-pfn/documents/03_tomasi_presentation_on_en.pdf

concerned the transport sector. Subsequent periods of the implementation of PPP projects include a further decrease in the value and number of concluded agreements. According to the EIB, the reasons for this situation can be found in the change of political climate, the inability to provide financial guarantees to SPVs, as well as in austerity measures aimed at reducing public spending, including investment expenditure.[39] In addition, the willingness of public entities to take advantage of transferability of most risks to the private partner may have been an effective deterrent to potential investors. Unfortunately, from the point of view of a private partner, as well as in the light of the implementation of the PPP concept, it is difficult to talk about compromise and long-term partnership relations of partners if one of them has to a large extent, disproportionately larger than a public partner, bear the responsibility for the current and long-term financial situation of the project. Another obstacle to the use of the convenient provisions of the Eurostat Decision of 11 February 2004 for public authorities concerns the complexity of the risk management process, wherein each of these risk areas, much more detailed responsibilities, can be identified. It seems impossible to divide the risk areas connected with, e.g. construction, where some of the key decisions are independent of the contractor or private partner, such as the legal and organisational process of transferring assets in the form of real estate to the special purpose vehicle, used to carry out the investment or to secure it, in a completely one-sided way. Despite the existing shortcomings of the regulations in force in Poland, it is possible to conclude PPP agreements. Thus, an important

[39]EPEC [29].

success factor is the fact that each of the parties in a PPP gives up on some of their expectations or rights.[40]

In many countries outside the EU, there are no specific legal standards pertaining to the classification of liabilities under PPP agreements as public liabilities. In countries with Islamic financial rules in force, there is no problem with the high level of public debt, where governments are looking for extra-budgetary opportunities to develop and implement investments without transferring liabilities to the public entity. The basis for cooperation in the PPP formula is always a contract in writing, reviewed by the *Shari'ah board*[41] in order to determine the compatibility of the planned formulas of cooperation with the provisions of the *Shari'ah law* and the *Quran*.

In sub-Saharan Africa, where, on the one hand, public finance rules are not fully implemented and, on the other hand, the legal and organisational conditions for economic development are still developing; the World Bank (WB), the European Bank for Reconstruction and Development (EBRD) and the Inter-American Development Bank (IDB) play an important role in shaping legal regulations in the area of PPPs. These institutions base their financial involvement on infrastructure projects on compliance with the rules of tender proceedings and anti-corruption proposed by them, or with the rules of securing specific risk areas. The most important sources of recommendations are guidelines concerning public procurement procedures for contracts co-financed by the indicated institutions: *procurement arrangements applicable to public-private partnerships contracts financed under World Bank projects, September 2010,*[42] and *guidelines procurement under IBRD loans and IDA of May* 2004 updated in May of 2010,[43] as well as *Africa's public procurement and entrepreneurship research initiative.*[44] Thanks to the provisions included in these recommendations, the process of establishing public-private cooperation in countries where there is a lack of experience in this area is becoming more transparent. Rules are created to ensure a level playing field between private and public partners, which increases the likelihood of achieving the expected contractual consensus. In addition, the implementation of the regulation increases the legitimacy of the process, which is becoming less prone to political changes. This gives the opportunity to reject the arguments of collusion when concluding agreements and therefore ensures the long-term nature of cooperation, which both partners should care about. The above-mentioned recommendations of financial institutions also put an emphasis on performing reliable analyses of the local market, which the planned investment concerns, so as to ensure the possibility of obtaining the expected *value for money* by the partners in the project.

[40] H. Kociemska, *Public-private...*, pp. 53–58.

[41] For further explanation, see Chap. 3.

[42] www.ppp.worldbank.org/public-private-partnership/sites/ppp.worldbank.org/files/ppp_testdumb/documents/GuidanceNote_PPP_September2010.pdf.

[43] www.siteresources.worldbank.org/INTPROCUREMENT/Resources/ProcGuid-10-06-RevMay10-ev2.pdf.

[44] www.ppp.worldbank.org/public-private-partnership/legislation-regulation/laws/procurement.

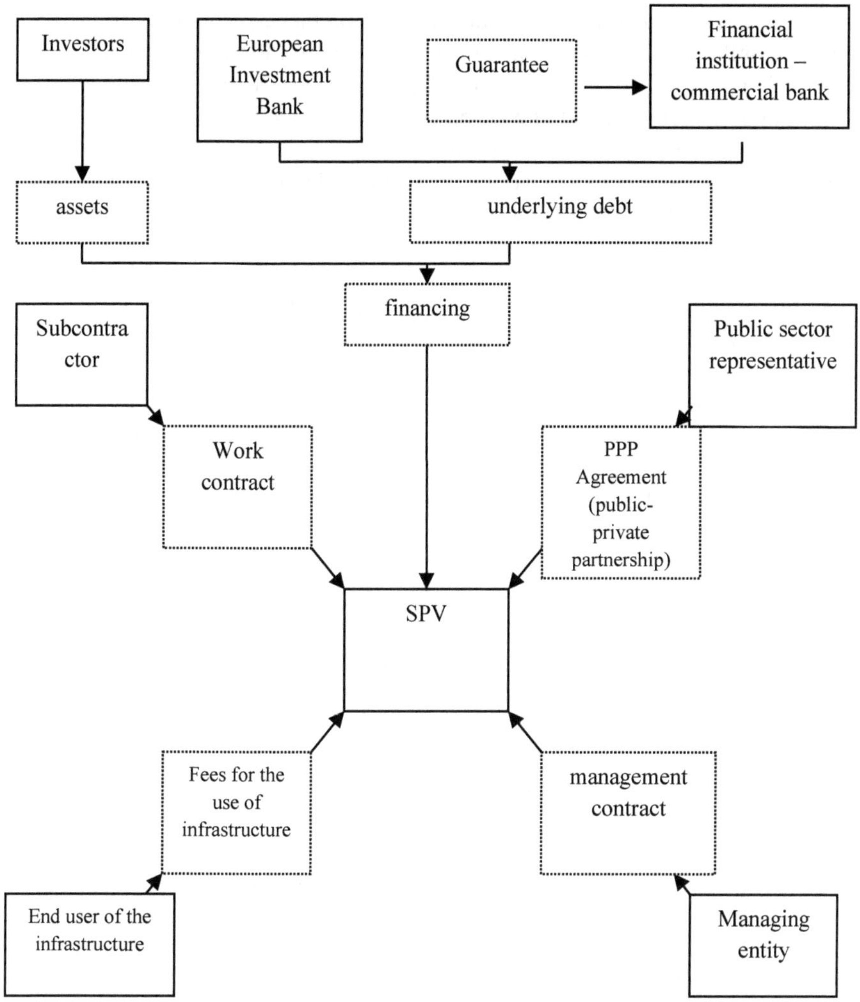

Fig. 2.4 Organisational structure of the PPP process. *Source* Own compilation

Among the organisational conditions, the transparent structure of a typical PPP project meeting the above definitions is critical. For a better illustration, Fig. 2.4 presents an example of an organisation chart of a PPP project.

The key element of the process is the *special purpose vehicle (SPV)*. This entity is established on the basis of local commercial law regulations; for example, in Poland, it may be a limited liability company or a joint-stock company. Public and private partners become partners of the company, the number of which depends on the number of parties interested in the implementation of the investment project. The number of shares of each partner is adequate for their contributions. Such contributions may take the form of tangible and intangible assets and include real estate, movables, cash and *know-how*. Detailed rules of cooperation of partners, particularly in the scope of responsibilities of each of them, are specified in the PPP agreement. The model contract is not generally used, although the business practice has developed many of the standard elements that should be included in such an agreement.[45] In addition, agreements are signed with financing institutions, both commercial banks and global financial institutions, such as the EIB, WB and IDB. Contracts are also signed with contractors and subcontractors in the investment process itself. Outsourcing agreements are often concluded for the management of a special purpose vehicle, especially when it is required by the specialised sector being the subject of the investment. For example, an SPV erects a hospital building but does not itself become a healthcare provider. Thus, the SPV commissions another healthcare provider with appropriate *know-how*—experience and knowledge in this area, to carry out medical activities. The healthcare provider becomes the recipient of services of the SPV with respect to management of medical activities on the basis of the existing infrastructure, and the provider of medical services to an eligible community. The process of organisation of the PPP process, including formal and legal stages, is based on the phases presented in Fig. 2.5.

The organisational and legal structure of a PPP project is closely related to local conditions and the condition of the economies of individual countries. With an ever-increasing global population, rising public expectations for the delivery of public goods and services, and budgetary constraints on public entities, governments in many countries are under increasing pressure to deliver new and improved infrastructure projects, for example in the areas of transport (roads, railways, bridges); education (schools and universities); health care (hospitals, clinics and treatment centres); waste management (collection, use of waste in power plants); water management (collection, treatment, distribution), urban housing, security and defence. Meanwhile, the requirements for financing current and future infrastructure needs are far greater than the financial resources of conventional economies or emerging countries. Meeting societal needs is crucial to ensure continuity of the process of development and economic growth. Budgetary constraints and confirmation of private sector efficiency and know-how are the main reasons why governments around the world are making economic and political decisions to accelerate the use of funds from the private sector and to adopt the model of public-private partnership to ensure the development of public services.

To sum up, the basic argument in favour of a PPP solution is that it provides the possibility of obtaining extra-budgetary funds for the implementation of new investments or the extension of the existing infrastructure. The countries' many years of experience have shown that this form of cooperation provides an opportunity to achieve positive effects, such as

- the possibility of involving extra-budgetary funds in the implementation of investments;
- the possibility of repayment of investment costs from future income obtained from investments;

[45] Cf. Ministry of Economy [30].

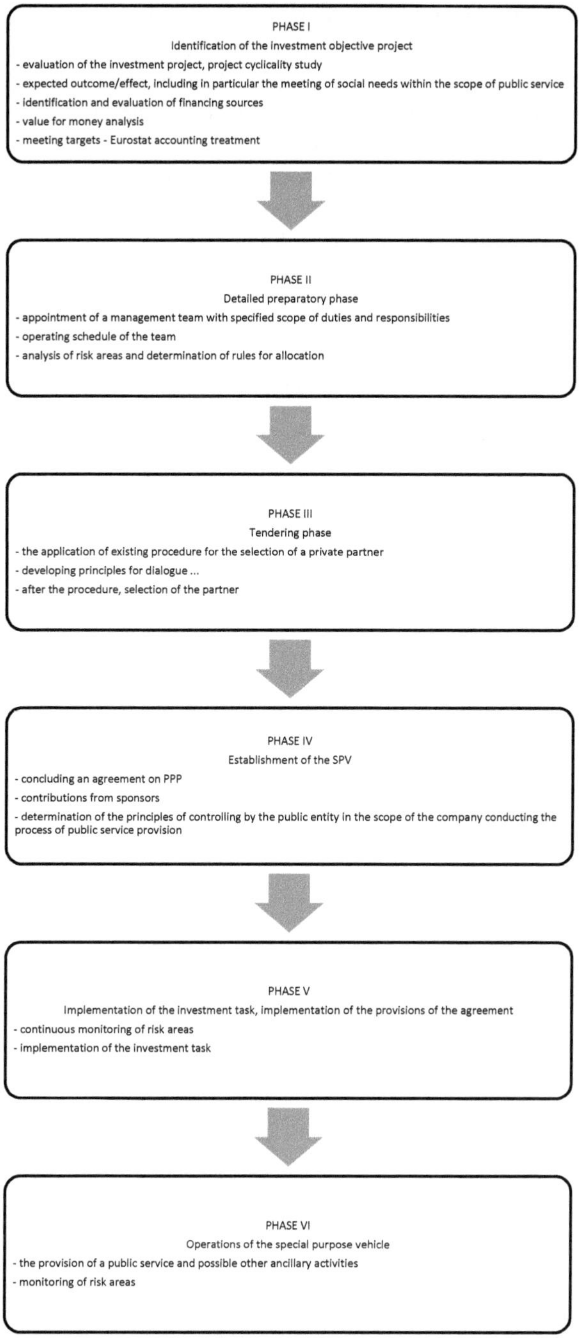

Fig. 2.5 Phases of the PPP process. *Source* Own compilation

- better identification of needs and demand for services[46];
- opening up new areas for economic activity;
- more efficient use of resources held by the public entity;
- encouraging job creation in the local market;
- improving the quality of public services;
- increasing access to part of the public services;
- reducing the unit cost of providing the public services;
- gaining access to new technologies;
- acquiring know-how in the field of modern management.

Although the presented positive effects of PPP seem obvious, it is worth noting them so that they constitute a permanent element of the process of negotiating the objectives of the PPP agreement being concluded between the partners.

2.3 Development of Public-Private Partnerships in Conventional and Islamic Economies

The largest number of PPP projects took place in the EU in 2006 and 2007. Since that time, the number of concluded contracts has been gradually decreasing. There is, therefore, a clear correlation between the public finance crisis in Europe after 2007 and the popularity of PPP cooperation (Figs. 2.6 and 2.7).

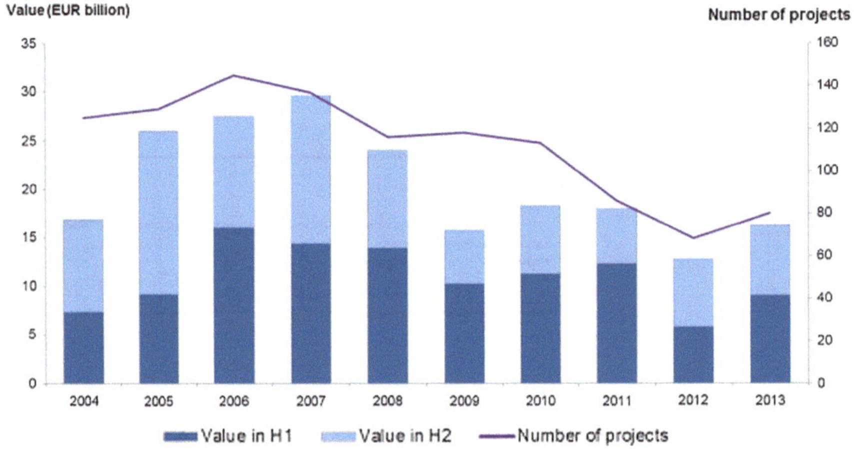

Fig. 2.6 PPPs in the EU—market in 2004–2013 in value and number of PPP projects. *Source Market Update, Review of the European PPP Market in 2013*, European PPP Expertise Centre

[46]European Commission Directorate General Regional Policy, report: Guidelines for successful public private partnerships, European Commission, Brussels, March 2003.

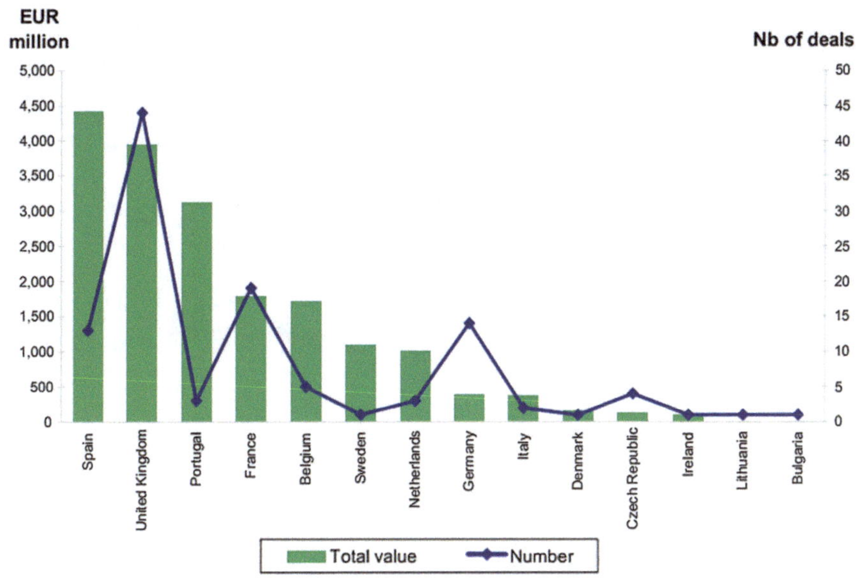

Fig. 2.7 PPPs in Western Europe in 2010. *Source* M. Kollatz-Ahnen, Vice President European Investment Bank, 17 May 2011, www.ec.europa.eu/economy_finance/events/2011/2011-05-17-joint_ec-epec_private_sector_forum/kollatz_en.pdf

The share of particular industries in the total value of PPP projects has changed significantly over the last 15 years. While social and security investments were a key area of investment in 2000, the share of the former in 2012 decreased significantly in favour of transport projects. Other sectors where PPP contracts were implemented to a much lesser extent were water and waste management, and telecommunications. In Islamic countries, the share of PPP projects in the value of GDP did not exceed 1.5% between 2000 and 2010. Similar values were observed in Europe and Central Asia, except in 2000, when they amounted to nearly 2% of GDP. In South Asia, on the other hand, the ratio is much higher, at over 3.5% of GDP in 2010 compared to 0.5% in 2000 in the same area (Figs. 2.8, 2.9 and 2.10).

Despite the initial development of PPPs in Islamic countries in the field of energy, in the following years a clear increase in the implementation of PPP projects in the field of telecommunications and transport can be observed. After 2005, infrastructure investments in water and waste management also appeared. These areas are the greatest challenges for public authorities, which, despite having financial resources to implement these investments, are constantly looking for access to knowledge and specialist skills of external companies in implementing investments in the sectors in question. The desert location of Islamic countries, the wide territorial range and sometimes low industrialisation of the regions have a key impact on the course of these types of investments and require much more knowledge and funding for their feasibility. Examples of PPP projects are given in the table in Annex 4.

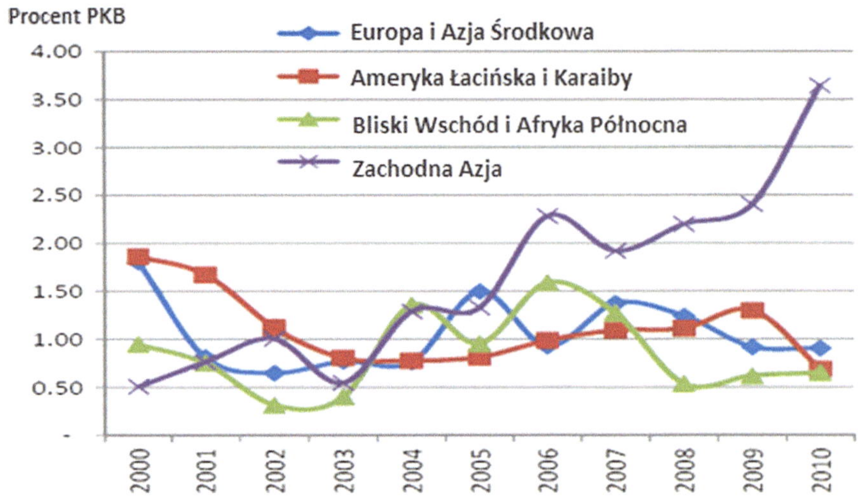

Fig. 2.8 Investments in PPP projects in developing regions as a share of GDP [in per cent GDP]. Blue: Europe and Central Asia, red: Latin America and the Caribbean, green: Near East and North Africa, purple: South Asia. *Source* AFFI Brochure, *Arab Financing Facility for Infrastructure: Developing Infrastructure for Growth and Regional Integration in Arab Countries*

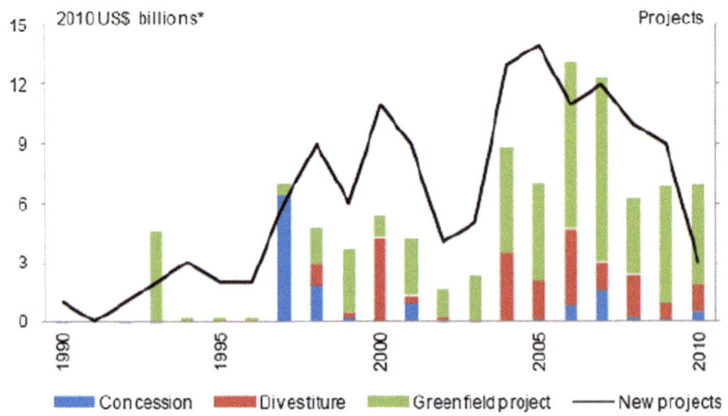

Fig. 2.9 Investments under PPP in countries in the Middle East and Northern Africa in 1990–2010 (in billions of USD). *Source* AFFI Brochure, *Arab Financing Facility for Infrastructure: Developing Infrastructure for Growth and Regional Integration in Arab Countries*

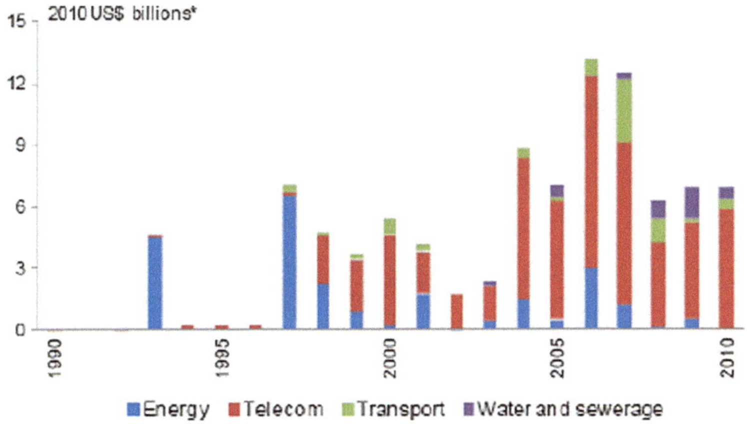

Fig. 2.10 Investments under PPP in the area of the Middle East and Northern Africa in the years 1990–2010 by industry (in billions of USD). *Source* AFFI Brochure, *Arab Financing Facility for Infrastructure: Developing Infrastructure for Growth and Regional Integration in Arab Countries*

2.4 Sub-Saharan Africa as a Region of Interest to Foreign Investors

The sub-Saharan Africa region comprises 47 countries, which can be divided into three groups: low-income countries, lower middle-income countries and higher middle-income countries. Low-income countries include the poorest countries in Africa. Among them are: Benin, Burkina Faso, Burundi, Central African Republic, Chad, Comoros, Democratic Republic of Congo, Eritrea, Ethiopia, Gambia, Ghana, Guinea, Guinea-Bissau, Kenya, Liberia, Madagascar, Malawi, Mali, Mauritania, Mozambique, Niger, Rwanda, Sierra Leone, Somalia, Tanzania, Togo, Uganda, Zambia and Zimbabwe. The group with a lower middle-income includes: Angola, Cameroon, Cape Verde, the Republic of Congo, Côte d'Ivoire, Lesotho, Nigeria, Sao Tome and Principe, Senegal, Sudan and Swaziland. The higher middle-income countries include: Botswana, Gabon, Mauritius, Namibia, Seychelles and South Africa. Equatorial Guinea[47] is the country with the highest income in sub-Saharan Africa (Fig. 2.11).

Sub-Saharan Africa is, geographically, the area of the continent of Africa that lies south of the Sahara. Taking into account geographical, ethnic and cultural criteria, scientists consider over 2/3 of the continent to be sub-Saharan Africa, distinguishing a different number of civilisation regions (among others, H. Baumann divides it into 22 so-called civilisation circles). Polish scientists—B. Hańczka-Wrzosek, Z. Komorowski and A. Rybiński—divide sub-Saharan Africa into nine geographical and ethnic areas, including the following:

[47] World Bank, *World Trade Indicators Country Classification by Region and Income (July 2009–July 2010)*, www.worldbank.org (25.09.2010).

Fig. 2.11 Geographic map of sub-Saharan Africa. *Source* In public domain, https://commons.wikimedia.org/wiki/File:Sub-Saharan-Africa.png

- partly the Sahara (with the Kordofan people, the Kanuri–Teda, the Nubian people, without the Tuareg);
- West African savannah (areas from Cape Verde to northern Cameroon, including the Wolof, Mandetan, Hausa, Fulan and Tukuler populations);
- the coast of the Gulf of Guinea (forests in the south and east, from the Gambia Basin to southern Cameroon, inhabited by the Akan, Ewe, Joruba and Ibo peoples, and others);
- Central Sudan (with the Azande, Kirdi, Sarah peoples);
- the basin of the Upper Nile (inhabited by the Nilotic peoples from the north-western group, including Dinka and Nuer);
- East Africa (from the Great Lakes to the Indian Ocean—areas of Tanzania, Kenya, Uganda, the outskirts of Rwanda and Burundi, inhabited by Nilotes, Kushytes and Bants);
- the wooded area and the humid savannah of Equatorial Africa (Democratic Republic of Congo—former Zaire, with the Bantu peoples);
- savannah south of the equator (Angola, Malawi, Mozambique, Zambia, inhabited by the Bantu peoples);
- South Africa (Zimbabwe, South Mozambique, Namibia, South Africa, Lesotho, Swaziland, with the Bantu and Kojsan peoples).

Sub-Saharan Africa does not include Madagascar, although it belongs to the African continent. According to estimates, between 800 and more than 1200 eth-

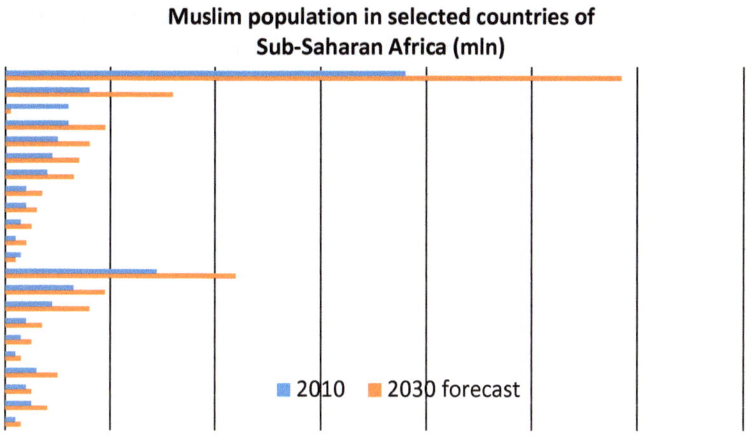

Fig. 2.12 Muslim population in selected countries of sub-Saharan Africa. Legend: y-axis—selected countries of sub-Saharan Africa, x-axis—population in millions of people. *Source Mapping Africa's Islamic economy: A report by the economist intelligence unit*, The Economist, 2015, pp. 5–6

nic groups live in sub-Saharan Africa.[48] On the African continent, both Islam and Christianity are the dominant religions. Most Muslims live in West Africa. Their numbers will reach 257 million in 2030, 67% of Muslims in sub-Saharan Africa and 670 million in 2050.[49] The highest growth in the number of Muslims is forecast in Nigeria. The progressing Islamisation in sub-Saharan African countries is confirmed by the figures in Fig. 2.12.

In most of these countries, the Muslim population will be 100% by 2030. Progressing Islamisation will entail a strong penetration of religious norms into the economic life of these regions. Understanding the functioning of Islamic economies and the shaping of public finances for both internal and external investors in the region will, therefore, be crucial. Conventional countries, as well as developed Islamic countries interested in the stability and development of African countries, can provide a source of knowledge, experience and capital to support the sub-Saharan region in building sustainable pillars for economic development (Fig. 2.13).

Currently, most foreign investments in Africa come from developed countries. In 2008, these countries accounted for 91% of the capital invested. An important partner among developing regions is Asian countries, which provided over 15% of foreign investment in 2000–2008. Among them, China is the country that invests the most. Only 5% of the investments that have arrived in Africa are internal. In this case, the most important investor is South Africa, which accounts for over 50% of investment in the Democratic Republic of Congo, Malawi, Botswana, Lesotho and

---

[48] *Africa Studies Center University of Pennsylvania 2016*, www.africa.upenn.edu/Home_Page/mcgee.html.

[49] *2015 Statistics Regarding Religion Growth in Sub-Saharan Africa, The Future of World Religions Population Growth Projections 2010–2050*, PEW Research Center, www.nairaland.com accessed on 01.09.2016.

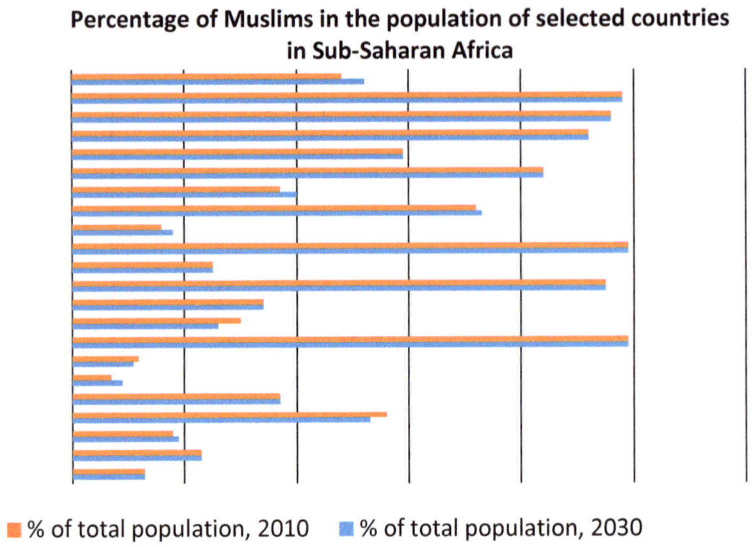

Fig. 2.13 Percentage of Muslims in the population of selected countries in sub-Saharan Africa. *Source Mapping Africa's Islamic economy: A report by the economist intelligence unit*, The Economist, 2015, pp. 5–6

Swaziland. With the exception of South Africa, China was the largest investor among developing countries, having invested approximately USD 2.5 billion in Africa in 2006–2008. The subsequent countries to invest were: Malaysia, India, Taiwan, South Korea, Chile, Turkey and Brazil (Fig. 2.14).[50]

Due to many factors, foreign investors' interest in sub-Saharan Africa is growing. The most important of these is access to numerous rich mineral resources: natural gas and oil, bauxite, copper, cobalt, uranium, tin, gold, silver, iron, diamonds, lead, zinc, nickel, manganese and chromium. In addition, Chinese investors appreciate the flexibility of African contractors: the lack of employment requirements for local workers and the agreement to bring in labour from China. The lack of political pressure to defend human rights or protect the environment is criticised. Thanks to the investments, the countries of the region have access to specialists in both developing and developed countries, their internal market and know-how. Moreover, countries investing in Africa provide capital and develop infrastructure, mainly roads and ports. The most important advantages of investments in sub-Saharan Africa are as follows:

- high demand for infrastructure—roads, transport, logistics, etc.;
- the fact that, despite the widespread opinion that investment in Africa is difficult, countries such as Brazil, Russia, India, China and South Africa (BRICS), as well

[50] M. Krukowska, *Zróżnicowanie poziomu wzrostu gospodarczego w wybranych krajach Afryki Subsaharyjskiej*, Kolegia Szkoły Głównej Handlowej, Warsaw, Kwartalnik Archiwum, pp. 69–73.

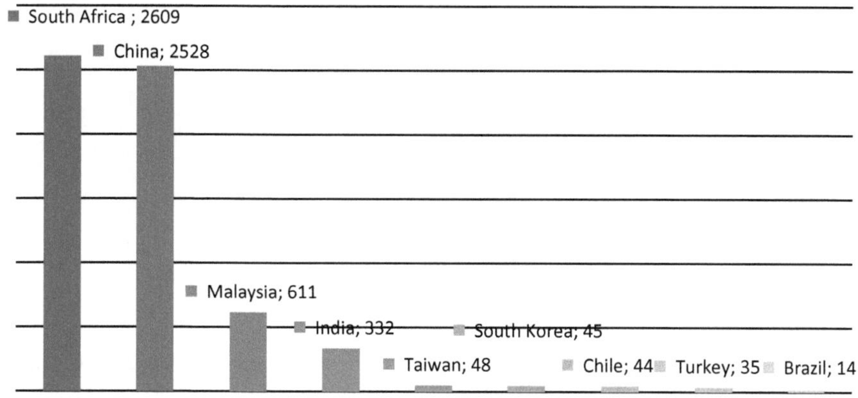

Fig. 2.14 Developing countries investing in Africa 2006–2008 (in millions of USD). *Source* M. Krukowska, *Zróżnicowanie poziomu wzrostu gospodarczego w wybranych krajach Afryki Subsaharyjskiej*, p. 70, as cited in World Investment Report 2010, p. 35

as other Latin American and Asian countries, have been present on the market for many years;

- the trade traditions of conventional countries, such as the EU Member States and the USA, with sub-Saharan Africa;
- liberalisation of foreign trade, removal of barriers to entry for foreign investors;
- the functioning of trade agreements such as America's Africa Growth and Opportunity Act (AGOA), the Trans-Pacific Partnership (TPP), the Transatlantic Trade and Investment Partnership (TTIP);
- numerous natural resources, deposits being an asset from the point of view of foreign investors;
- high unemployment, which in theory gives real chances of finding workers;
- progressive urbanisation—it is estimated that by 2035 half of Africa's population will be living in cities. In 2010, there were 400 million such residents, 60% of whom lived in "suburban slums".[51] In comparison, the population of the EU as a whole in 2016 was 510 million people.[52]

The most important disadvantages of investments in this area are as follows:

- a high degree of economic disparity among the countries of sub-Saharan Africa;
- excessive, poorly controlled exploitation of natural resources, which ultimately leads to the outflow of profit from their sale, mostly to the benefit of foreign countries and entities;
- high levels of poverty, even hunger in particular regions (330 million people in 2012 were living at the poverty level), poor education (2 out of 5 people are illiterate), poor health care, and therefore health, and high crime rates[53];

[51] www.providencemag.com/2016/01/six-challenges-facing-africa-2016/.

[52] www.en.wikipedia.org/wiki/Demographics_of_the_European_Union.

[53] www.providencemag.com/2016/01/six-challenges-facing-africa-2016.

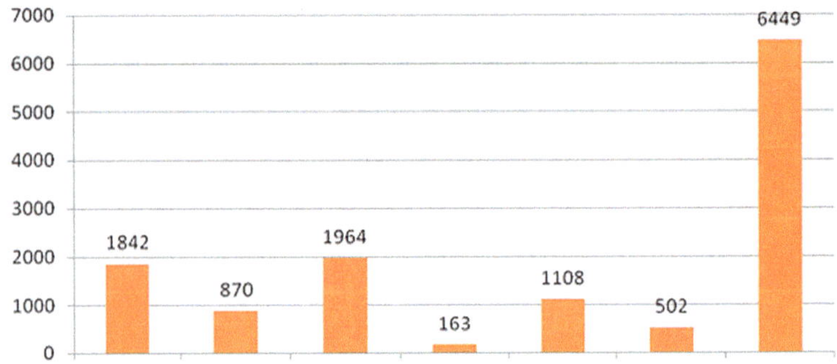

Fig. 2.15 Total number of PPP projects carried out worldwide in the period 1990–2014. Countries in order of appearance: East Asia and Pacific; Europe and Central Asia; Latin America and the Caribbean; Near East and North Africa; West Asia; sub-Saharan Africa, total number of projects. *Source* Own calculations based on DESA Working Paper no. 148, ST/ESA/2016/DWP/148, *Public-Private Partnerships and the 2030 Agenda for Sustainable Development: Fit for Purpose*?, 2016, pp. 8–11

- widespread corruption;
- lack of sufficiently developed transport, logistics, aviation and telecommunications infrastructure;
- limited access to essential public goods such as water, sewage treatment plants, waste treatment facilities, electricity[54];
- lack of qualified staff;
- strong centralisation of management decisions in the public sphere.

PPP projects have also been present in sub-Saharan Africa for many years (Fig. 2.15).

Between 2000 and 2010, 42 African countries implemented 248 PPP projects with a total investment of USD 55.1 trillion. This resulted in the development of mobile telephony in 90% of sub-Saharan African countries, which increased the range of services from 5 to 60% between 1990 and 2010. In addition, it has enabled the development of transport (including the creation of ports—a concession for 30 container terminals), electricity and water. Examples of projects are presented in Table 2.4.

However, among developing countries, only 8% of the total number of PPP projects, worth USD 436 million in total, were in sub-Saharan Africa. For example, 30% of the total value of the project was realised in East Asia and the Pacific region and the same number in Latin America and the Caribbean between 1990 and 2011.[55] The largest number of initiatives was carried out in Nigeria, followed by Ghana and Kenya between 2000 and 2009 (Fig. 2.16).

The region of sub-Saharan Africa is an example of an area in need of strong change. It is inhabited by a huge number of people. It possesses valuable natural

[54] Cf. H. G. Broadman: *China and India go to Africa*, Foreign Affairs, 87, pp. 85–109.

[55] World Bank PPI Database [31]. Private Participation in Infrastructure—by PPP Type.

Table 2.4 Examples of PPP projects in sub-Saharan Africa

Name of the PPP project	Country	Project objective	Cost	Type of contract	Deadline
Dakar motorway—Diamniadio	Senegal	A multidimensional project aimed at creating a new district in the eastern part of the capital, restructuring endangered housing estates and reorganising the waste sector	EUR 485 million	Licence agreement	
Camrail—railway line in Cameroon	Cameroon	1009 km from the main communication axis: (a) north–south in Cameroon, (b) regionally in Chad and the Central African Republic as access to the Atlantic Ocean	EUR 95.3 million	Concession	2002
Bujagali: Uganda power plant	Uganda	Thanks to the construction of this power plant, it was possible, among other things, to increase access to drinking water, reduce CO_2 emissions and create new jobs	USD 872 million	BOT formula	2007

(continued)

Table 2.4 (continued)

Name of the PPP project	Country	Project objective	Cost	Type of contract	Deadline
Songas—Tanzania Processing Plant	Tanzania	The project involves the construction and operation of an integrated gas installation, including the construction and operation of a gas processing plant on the island of Songo Songo, the construction of a 225-km offshore and onshore gas pipeline from the island to Dar es Salaam, and the construction of a 190 MW power plant in Ubungo	Original project—USD 32 million, extension project—USD 60 million		Date of completion: October 2001, the original project, and November 2004, the extension project
Port Maputo in Mozambique	Mozambique	A 15-year concession for the financing, operation and modernisation of the ports of Maputo and Matola. The consortium has the option to continue managing the port for another 10 years	USD 70 million	Concession	April 2003
Lesotho National Hospital	Lesotho	18-year contract for the design, construction, partial financing, furnishing and operation of a national hospital with 390 beds, but also for the renovation and operation of three municipal clinics	USD 107 million		December 2007

(continued)

Table 2.4 (continued)

Name of the PPP project	Country	Project objective	Cost	Type of contract	Deadline
Provision of water and electrical services	Gabon	20-year licence for production, transport and distribution of water and electricity in Gabon. The agreement may be renewed for several periods according to an annexe to the agreement	USD 135 million	Concession	July 1997

Source Own compilation based on the following documents: Yves Boudot, Director African Department AFD: Challenges and Issues of Financing Infrastructures—Case Studies of Public-Private Partnerships (PPP), 2014, and *Attracting Investors to African Public-Private Partnerships. A Project Preparation Guide*, The International Bank for Reconstruction and Development/The World Bank, 2009, pp. 91–101

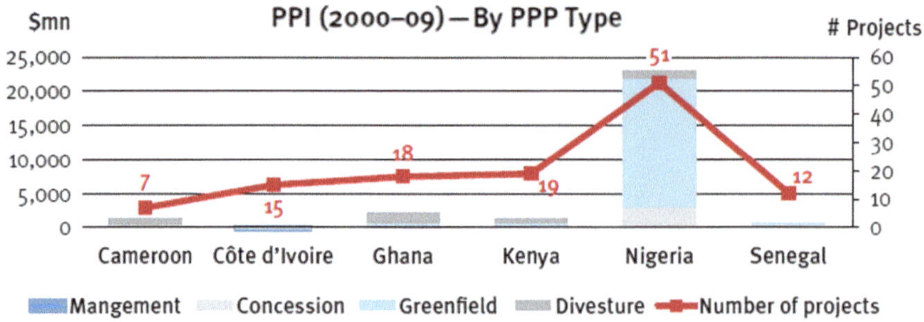

Fig. 2.16 Types and number of PPP projects carried out in selected countries of sub-Saharan Africa. *Source Towards Better Infrastructure. Conditions, Constraints, and Opportunities in Financing Public-Private Partnerships. Evidence from Cameroon, Cote d'Ivoire, Ghana, Kenya, Nigeria, and Senegal*, The World Bank, PPIAF, 2011, p. 6

resources, which can be the basis for economic development. The structures of statehood are relatively young and therefore flexible from the point of view of shaping the principles of public funds management so that the methods worked out guarantee stable, but also safe, long-term development of such countries. Protection of the natural environment, which forms the basis of many world cultures, is also becoming crucial. Demographic and epidemiological changes in sub-Saharan Africa (see Chap. 3 for more details) show a different trend than in the ageing societies of Europe or America. The needs for the development of various types of infrastructure are enormous. These main features of the region provide arguments for legitimate interference by foreign investors and for the creation of a coherent development framework using the potential of conventional and Islamic countries. The heterodox approach to PPPs, which will be presented in this monograph, should be universal enough to meet the specific expectations of emerging and sometimes failed countries (for more details, see Sect. 3.2) in terms of shaping their public economies, establishing forms of cooperation that are beneficial to each of the parties, both domestic and foreign. Importantly, the foundations for heterodoxy in public finances may prove to be an opportunity for real enrichment of the societies in the sub-Saharan Africa region through the permanent inclusion of the local community's share in the profits from the infrastructure investments carried out in its area. This will be a tool to counteract social exploitation and the so-called new colonialisation trends in Africa, which have hitherto been used mainly by Russia and China. It is a common argument in Europe, since the wave of refugees arriving in Europe in recent years has intensified that the best form of support for people in need is to create conditions for development on the ground in Africa, to provide jobs, stable, transparent rules for public administration, better education, communication, etc. The combined attributes and business expectations of investors from conventional and Islamic countries, together with balanced public finance rules developed by those countries and the cooperation of the public and private sectors, can provide such an opportunity for real assistance.

References

1. Hua Jin X, Zhang G, Yang RJ (2012) Factor analysis of partners' commitment to risk management in public private partnership projects. 12(3):298 Emerald Insight
2. Hausner J (2002) Od idealnej biurokracji do zarządzania publicznego. In: Hausner J, Kukiełka M (eds) Studia z zakresu zarządzania publicznego, vol II. Kraków University of Economics, Kraków, pp 64–65
3. Filipak B (2011) Finanse samorządowe, nowe wyzwania bieżące perspektywy. Difin, p 144
4. Sochacka-Krysiak H (2010) Niektóre problemy efektywności w gospodarce finansowej samorządu terytorialnego. In: Wieteska S, Wypych M (eds) W poszukiwaniu efektywności finansów publicznych. Wydawnictwo Uniwersytetu Łódzkiego, pp 192–194
5. Kosikowski C (2011) Naprawa finansów publicznych w Polsce. Wydawnictwo Temida 2, Białystok, p 391
6. Nevit PK, Fabozzi F (1995) Project financing, 6th edn Euromoney Publications, London, p 3
7. de Nahlik DJ, Rutherford W, Montgomerie (1992) Handbook of UK corporate finance, 2nd edn. Butterworths, London
8. Pollio G (1998) Project finance and international energy development. Energ Policy 26(9):688
9. Harries H (1989) The contract law of project financing, vol 6. The Law of International Trade Finance
10. Górniewicz G (2013) Determinanty i konsekwencje bezpośrednich inwestycji zagranicznych, Studia z Zakresu Prawa, vol 4. Administracji i Zarządzania UKW, p 61. http://repozytorium.ukw.edu.pl/bitstream/handle/item/412/Grzegorz%20G%C3%B3rniewicz.pdf?sequence=1
11. Yescombe ER (2007) Project finance, wybrane elementy finansowania strukturalnego. Krakow, Oficyna Wolters Kluwer Business, p 16
12. Kopańska (2006) Partnerstwo publiczno-prywatne: wzory brytyjskie. Czego możemy się z nich nauczyć?. Studia Regionalne i Lokalne 3(25):84
13. Kociemska H (2010) Public-private partnership project success circumstances. J Mod Account Auditing 6(11(36)):53
14. Grimsey D, Lewis MK (2002) Accounting for public private partnership. Accounting Forum 26(3/4):248
15. Sedjar (2004) Public private partnership as a tool for modernising public administration. Int Rev Adm Sci 70(2):303
16. Yescombe ER (2007) Public Private partnerships: principles of policy and finance, 1st edn. Elsevier, pp 1–14
17. World Bank (2015) PPP in Infrastructure Resource Center. https://ppp.worldbank.org/public-private-partnership/
18. Sadka E (2007) Public private partnership: a public economics perspectives. CES ifo Econ Stud 53(3):466–490
19. Hall D (2011) PPP's in the EU: a critical appraisal. pp 1–32. www.psiru.org/publicationsindex.asp
20. Sciulli N (2008) Public private partnership: an exploratory study in healthcare. Asian Rev Account 16(1):21
21. Bailey SJ (1999) Local governmente economics. MacMillan Press Ltd, London, p 298
22. Kachniarz M (2008) Mierzenie efektywności samorządu terytorialnego. Współczesne Zarządzanie (3):57
23. Herbst I, Jadach-Sepioło A (2012) Raport z analizy danych zastanych na potrzeby "Analizy potencjału podmiotów publicznych i przedsiębiorstw do realizacji projektów PPP dla Polskiej Agencji Rozwoju Przedsiębiorczości". p 18
24. Boardman AE (2012) The political economy of public private partnerships and analysis of their social value. Ann Public Coop Econ 83(2): 117–141. CIRIEC Blackwell Publishing Ltd
25. Kłosowicz R, Mormul J (2013) Pojęcie dysfunkcyjności państw: geneza i definicje. Państwa dysfunkcyjne i ich destabilizujący wpływ na stosunki międzynarodowe. Studia nad Rozwojem, Wydawnictwo UJ, Krakow, pp 11–14

26. Kulesza M (2003) Partnerstwo publiczno-prywatne: Uwagi wstępne. Finanse Komunalne, issue 2, extra, Partnerstwo publiczno-prywatne
27. Poniatowicz M (2011) Partnerstwo publiczno-prywatne w sektorze samorządowym a problematyka lokalnego długu publicznego. Optimum Studia Ekonomiczne 3(51):35
28. Zalewski D (2016) Rynek PPP w Polsce: siedem lat za nami. Forum PPP: Magazyn Inwestycji Publicznych 1(31):3–21
29. EPEC (2013) The PPP market European trends and developments. www.eib.org/epec/resources/publications/epec_market_update_2014_en, pp 2–7
30. Ministry of Economy (2014, December) Conclusion of an agreement on PPP: PPP from idea to the selection of private partner. pp 102–106. www.ppp.gov.pl/Publikacje/E_guide/Documents/Raport_MG_umowa_ppp.pdf
31. World Bank PPI Database (2013) Building infrastructure through public private partnership in Sub-Saharan Africa: Lessons from South Africa. Procedia—Soc Behav Sci 143(2014):135

Chapter 3
Public-Private Partnership in the Light of Risk and Public Finance Theories

3.1 Risk and Its Management in Economic and Financial Theory

When looking for areas for the convergence of public finances and Islamic finance, attention should be paid to the concept of risk, one of the key concepts in both sub-disciplines and particularly public-private cooperation. The etymology of the word "risk" leads to the Old Italian word *risicare*, meaning "to dare". In Latin, the word *risco* (*risico*) was used among merchants and meant a danger connected with their business, including when the bill of exchange law was violated. In previous centuries, the dominant accent of the word was a risk, which threatened ships, sailors and merchants. It was expressed in money, particularly in the case of the losses that were associated with the overseas trade. The risk then included negative or positive uncertainty in relation to the actions undertaken. By combining risk and choice, an inextricable link between risk and time was also confirmed.[1] This means that risk is something volatile, a process that evolves rather than a state of the environment. For many years now, economists have been trying to make the concept of risk more specific or general. A coherent element of investigations in this area is the fact that both risk and uncertainty (often understood separately) accompany all aspects of human management. The risk is identified and managed both in private life and in business and public administration. Uncertainty and risk are associated with all types of investments, both private and public. However, the risk always stems from the fact that future cannot be predicted with certainty. It is difficult to determine what the consequences of today's decisions will be, as there may be a lot of additional information or interpretations, which will adversely affect the achievement of the chosen objective.

In the history of economics, risk has already been mentioned, among others, by A. Smith and D. Ricardo, who described it as a cost of doing business. As precursors

[1] Kaczmarek [1].

H. Kociemska, *Public-Private Partnership for Sub-Saharan Africa*,
Advances in African Economic, Social and Political Development,
https://doi.org/10.1007/978-3-030-14753-2_3

to the introduction of the phenomenon of risk into the financial field, they regarded it as an integral part of entrepreneurship. They argued that entrepreneurs should be entitled to a risk premium: "The farmer and manufacturer can no more live without profit than the labourer without wages. Their motive for accumulation will diminish with every diminution of profit and will cease altogether when their profits are so low as not to afford them an adequate compensation for their trouble, and the risk which they must necessarily encounter in employing their capital productively".[2]

According to many authors, the first scientific dissertation distinguishing risk and uncertainty is A. Willet's work.[3] He presented a position that previous achievements of scientists underestimated the impact of risk on business. Humans are not able to change the course of events, but they can predict them and protect themselves against their undesirable consequences. This may be particularly the case with unexpected events. The entity acts differently in the case of foreseeable events, and their actions in unforeseeable situations are different.[4] Willet made a cardinal distinction between risk and uncertainty, stressing that some events are predictable, and others are unpredictable. The uncertainty of the occurrence of future events, treated as accidental, forces humans to change their behaviour.[5] In addition, it recognised that the degree of uncertainty does not coincide with the degree of probability, although the level of uncertainty decreases with the increased probability. As the probability of achieving a loss increases, the uncertainty of the result achieved increases. Another publication, which is considered to be a very important analysis that deepens Willet's opinion in this area, is F. H. Knight's *Risk, Uncertainty and Profit.*[6] To this day, the views expressed in this paper are often used as theoretical sources. Knight defined risk as "measurable uncertainty". In this context, measurability refers to the possibility of using probabilistic methods to determine the occurrence of future events. Uncertainty, on the other hand, is the inability to make a rational decision in the absence of information regarding future events.[7] Another author—K. J. Arrow—used the concepts of risk and uncertainty interchangeably and did not provide their detailed definition. In his work, *Essays on Risk Theory*, he described uncertainty as a state of mind of a given person.[8] The work by M. H. Miller and F. Modigliani is considered the key achievement for the development of risk management processes, especially in large enterprises. In said work, they define uncertainty as well as risk as probabilistic risks, which are calculable using mathematical or statistical methods.[9] Technological progress and the use of IT tools and management support systems have helped to equate uncertainties with quantifiable risks. This view was quite divergent

---

[2]D. Ricardo, 1821, Chap. 6, Paragraph 6.31, http://www.econlib.org/library/Ricardo/ricP.html.

[3]A. Willett, *Economic Theory of Risk and Insurance* (1901), The Committee of the Theory of Risk, S. S. Huebner Foundation for Insurance Education, University of Pennsylvania, 1951.

[4]Bochenek [2].

[5]A. Willet, op. cit., pp. 3–5.

[6]Knight [3].

[7]Ibid., ch. I.

[8]Cf. Arrow [4].

[9]Miller and Modigliani [5], www.jstor.org/stable/1809766, pp. 261–265.

from Knight's theory, which treated these concepts as separate and believed that uncertainty may not be measurable, contrary to risk. Thus, Knight questioned the possibility of estimating the results of all future decisions. The problem of uncertainty was pointed out even more comprehensively in Sect. 3.2 of this agency theory monograph. In the second half of the twentieth century, Jensen and Meckling addressed this issue. The authors emphasised that the lack of full information results in the inability to make a proper valuation of assets, which may constitute the "uncertainty" of the project. It could be limited by obtaining additional information in the process of monitoring and controlling costs. Information on the subjects of management and monitoring of the value of such assets was obtained by insurance companies. They based their activity on estimating potential risks, their impact on the value of specific assets and valuation of possible damages. As a result, risk hedging instruments started being offered in the form of insurance products. Since the issue of risk has become a key area for insurers, one of the concepts of risk definition was developed in the US Commission on Insurance Terminology in 1966. According to the experts of this Commission, the risk is the uncertainty of a specific event under conditions of two or more possibilities. In this sense, the risk is a measurable uncertainty as to whether the intended objective of the action will be achieved. The Commission focused mainly on the determination of the effects of actions taken by the insured entities, providing the second simplest definition of risk, which focused on the fact that the risk is the person or object insured.[10]

The latest source of scientific research on uncertainty and risk issues were the achievements of the new institutional economy, particularly the works of O. E. Williamson. In his opinion, uncertainty means unequal and incomplete access to information and limits the individuals' rationality of management.[11] However, contrary to the agency theory in NIE, the author assumes that the reasoning behind the limited rationality is not only the lack of information on the facts at the time of the conclusion of the contract but also the uncertainty about the events that may occur after the conclusion of the contract.[12] Therefore, NIE deals mainly with theories of resolving conflicts of interest during the period of validity of a contract, rather than focusing, as in agency theory, on the contracting process itself.

The presented concepts of defining the phenomena of risk and uncertainty are based on the delimitation of the possibility of quantifying the risk phenomenon. The unquantifiable uncertainty is assumed to be the subjective risk, while the measurable risk is the objective risk. It is also worth looking at the achievements of the Polish financial or insurance sector. According to Kowalczyk, risk can be defined as the possibility of occurrence of a situation or event having a specific, negative impact on the financial result of the project.[13] The notion of risk formulated in such a way not only gives an opportunity to include potential threats of non-measurable

[10]The Bulletin of the Commission Terminology of the American Risk Association I (1), March 1966, p. 1.

[11]Wiliamson [6].

[12]Klimczak [7].

[13]Kowalczyk [8].

events in the analysis, but also affects the methodology of risk analysis, because the emphasis is placed on qualitative, and not quantitative, approach to events (risks). However, the notion of risk in this sense leads to negative connotations. Unlike the English-speaking scientists mentioned above, *uncertainty* means lack of certainty, but it does not necessarily concern negative results or consequences. "Uncertainty" simply means that the expected outcome will be different from what was originally assumed. According to E. Kowalewski, uncertainty means subjective knowledge of the surrounding world and of the phenomena that govern it, and thus constitutes a source of risk.[14] Elsewhere, the risk is referred to as a threat of not achieving the set objective.[15] According to K. Jajuga, the notion of risk means, first and foremost, that the analysed project will fail or that the outcome of the project is unknown, and secondly, that it may deviate from the expectations, either in a positive or a negative way.[16] The ambiguity of this concept makes it difficult, as we can see, to construct an unambiguous and universal definition. What is a common theme in all of them is certainly a different approach to the rationality of human activity and the choices that they make. Some scientists believe that it is not possible to completely eliminate the concept of behavioural rationality. Others, who take into consideration the rejection of the assumption about the possibility of having full information and the lack of transactional costs or the impossibility of estimating them, suggest abandoning the concept of the rationality of human behaviour.[17] The solution to this dilemma so far has proved to be the search for a consensus between rational decision-making and uncertainty as to its effects in specific actions or economic processes. Uncertainty is never a positive aspect of the organisation of investment projects, but it is virtually impossible to reduce all uncertainties completely. As doubts increase, the risk of project implementation increases, and consequently the chance of failure of the project grows higher. A negative result of an investment initiative may result in the loss of the financial resources invested. At the same time, as the business risk increases, the pressure of project lenders also increases. This pressure stems from the need to safeguard the interests of lenders and to effectively hedge the risks that affect them. This position of a financial institution is reflected in the demand for a higher remuneration for the "borrowed" capital due to the increased risk profile. All of this has an impact on overall project costs. An increase in financing costs in the face of increased risk may have a key impact on the profitability of an investment project or ongoing activities. It is often the case that a high level of risk is the reason why both the financing institutions and the investor abandon the planned project.

Of course, the risk is subject to management processes. The concept of risk management is defined by organisations such as Committee of Sponsoring Organisations of the Treadway Commission [COSO], according to which risk management is carried out by the board of directors, management or other delegated personnel of the

---

[14]Szumlicz [9].

[15]Gruszka and Zawadzka [10].

[16]Jajuga [11].

[17]M. K. Klimczak, *Dylematy*….

company. Risk management is a process, included in the company's strategy, the aim of which is to identify potential adverse events that may have an impact on the company, keep the risk in constant limits and ensure that the company achieves its objectives.[18] There are two main areas of risk management that should be mentioned as the subject of the management process:

- collection of information on the specific risks connected with the project;
- influencing an entity's risk exposure through active action.[19]

The two areas complement each other and form a coherent whole. First, data concerning risk are collected and then, on the basis of the data collected, an assessment is made whether the level of risk is acceptable or whether action is necessary to minimise the risk. In order for such actions to be effective, it is necessary to constantly monitor the effects of the actions and to constantly update the available information. As it can be seen, risk management is not a one-off activity carried out at the planning stage of a project. In addition to risk analysis and the development of risk prevention methods in this phase, it is necessary to monitor the situation throughout the project implementation period, so that an appropriate strategy can be developed due to the situation change.[20] Generally speaking, risk management methods, i.e. methods used in the management process, can be divided into two groups:

- methods used to minimise the risks associated with the project;
- methods transferring the risk to other entities participating in the project implementation.

Both ways of risk management—minimising threats, uncertainties, as well as transferring the risk to other entities—are important because "the primary objective of risk management in *project finance* is to construct a project in such a way that each participant bears the acceptable level of risk while minimising the risk of the project as a whole".[21]

From the point of view of this monograph, risk management in *project finance* is particularly important. In the subject literature, there are many risk classifications in *project finance*. According to R. Tiong, investment risk in the investment (construction) phase is classified as: risk of delay of completion, cost overruns, political risk, the risk of *force majeure* and risk of availability of infrastructure (other than the one planned). The investment risk in the operating (exploitation) phase includes: market risk, supply of materials, risks concerning results, operating risk, technical risk and currency exchange rate risk.[22] Investment risk classification in *project finance* according to C. R. Beidleman is presented in Table 3.1.

---

[18] Committee of Sponsoring Organisations of the Treadway Commission (COSO), www.coso.org/documents/coso_erm_executivesummary_polish.pdf, *Zarządzanie ryzykiem korporacyjnym: zintegrowana struktura ramowa ERM*, 2004.

[19] Frank [12].

[20] Hupe [13].

[21] M. Kowalczyk, op. cit., p. 12.

[22] Tiong [14].

Table 3.1 Classification of investment risk in *project finance* according to C. R. Beidleman

Investment risk		
In the pre-investment (preparatory) phase	During the investment (construction) phase	During the operational phase
– Technological – Tendering – Credit	– Completion – Completion of construction works – Cost overruns – Political	– Concerning the results – Responsibility – Cost overruns – The resale of capital – Object decommissioning

Source Beidleman [15]

Table 3.2 Classification of investment risk in *project finance* according to W. Woody and H. Pourian

Investment risk	
In the pre-investment (preparatory) phase	During the operational phase
– Underestimation of costs (shortages of raw materials and consumables, inflation, technical design and construction) – Shortage of capital – Equipment	– Low efficiency of equipment – Cash flow deficit – Variable prices – Technological – Launch date of the product design – Currency exchange rate – Competitive position on the market

Source Woody and Pourian [16]

Table 3.2 characterises the various kinds of risks classified by W. Woody and H. Pourian.

These authors additionally identified a separate risk group—political risk, including:

- risk of expropriation;
- risk of war;
- risk of nationalisation;
- risk of currency inconvertibility (higher taxes, currency restrictions, suspension of transfers).[23]

D. Woorward divides the investment risk in *project finance* into global and elementary. This division is illustrated in Table 3.3.

C. Walker and A. J. Smith present three main areas of investment risk: financial, political and technical. In terms of financial risk, they point out:

- market risk (changes in prices, sources of supply of raw materials and energy, demand);
- currency exchange and exchange rate risks;

[23] Woody and Pourian [16].

Table 3.3 Classification of investment risk in *project finance* according to D. Woodward

Global risk	Elementary risk
– Legal (scope of the project, types of contracts) – Political (authorities, technologies) – Environmental protection (environmental impact, ecology) – Commercial (market, supply, currency)	– Technical (physical conditions, construction, technology, technical design) – Financial (method of financing, evaluation of project effectiveness, currency, return on investment, ownership) – Operational (operation, maintenance, training) – Market (tariffs, demand, development)

Source Woodward [17]

- risk of construction costs overruns;
- revenue risk.

They also classify the following as political risks:

- risk of instability;
- risk of project sovereignty.

According to the authors, technical risks are:

- risk of delaying the completion of the project;
- risk of construction difficulties;
- operational risk.[24]

J. D. Finnerty presents a different classification of investment risk in *project finance.* Among them, he points out:

- technological risks (non-compliance, obsolescence);
- risk of completion (higher than the expected inflation rate, unexpected delays in construction works, shortages of key materials, technical and environmental problems, underestimation of construction costs);
- currency risk (changes in currency exchange rates);
- financial risk (increase in loan interest rates);
- economic risk (insufficient demand, increase in costs, a decrease in equipment efficiency, a decrease in prices of goods and services);
- political risk (interference of the authorities, problems with obtaining the necessary permits, expropriation);
- environmental risk (delays in implementation works, the need to introduce changes in the technical design, changes in regulations);
- force majeure (fire, catastrophes, strikes, earthquakes).[25]

Classification of risks presented by T. Merna and C. Njiru can be seen in Table 3.4.

The classification of investment risk in *project finance* according to A. Estache and J. Strong is presented in Table 3.5.

[24] Walker and Smith [18].

[25] Finnerty [19].

Table 3.4 Risk classification in *project finance* according to T. Merna and C. Njiru

Investment risk		
In the pre-investment (preparatory) phase	During the investment (construction) phase	During the operational phase
– The validity of the project – Incomplete technical design – The availability of information	– The availability of resources – Natural conditions (weather conditions, ground conditions, etc.)	– Supply of raw materials and energy – Operating conditions – The results obtained – The distribution of production
– Conformity of the project with the standards – New technology – Selection of a technical design compatible with the requirements of the investment project – Reserves to safeguard technological change – The costs of technological change	– Changes in the technical design – The execution of work – Damage – Quality of work – Exceeding the allotted construction time – The nature of the implementing contracts – Omissions – Construction techniques – Construction costs – The nature of the implementing contracts – Insolvencies – Construction insurance	– Interruptions in operation due to damage or negligence – Operating losses – The consumption of materials – Obtaining a licence – Type of contract for operation and maintenance of the project – Reduced efficiency – Underestimation of operating costs – Compatibility of equipment – Availability of spare parts and resources – Sufficient time for maintenance work – Financial: interest, types of interest rates (fixed, variable, with bounds), changes in interest rates, repayment schedules, loan repayment periods, institutional equity support, time and amount of dividends paid – Costs of training of personnel and managerial staff – Revenue: level of charges, demand, charges, currency, changes in tariffs, tariff regulation, development of projects

Source Merna and Njiru [20]

Table 3.5 Classification of investment risk in *project finance* according to A. Estche and J. Strong

Investment risk	
During the investment (construction) phase	During the operational phase
– Cost overruns/delays due to: technical design, construction, engineering works – The acquisition of land – Changes in legislation – Weather – Catastrophes – Environmental protection – Activities of the industry – Transfer of activities – Non-subordination of workers – Force majeure – Confiscates – Insurance – Obtaining approvals, licences, permits – Interest rates – Taxes – Other tariffs and fees	– Operations – Revenues – Maintenance – Catastrophes – Liability for defects – Environmental protection – Activities of the industry – Neglect of employees – Insurance – Confiscates – Force majeure – Taxes – Other tariffs and fees – Interest rates

Source Estache and Strong [21]

The next classification is presented by Lam Ka Chi and Chow Wing Sing. It is shown in Table 3.6.

The presented risk classifications in *project finance* indicate a large diversity and complexity of these processes in the economy. This requires managers to have broad knowledge and experience in identifying risk areas and seeking adequate tools to secure public entities or PPP companies against them. Most of the classifications presented refer to particular phases of PPP projects carried out in the formula of *project finance*. Identified risk areas should be considered as demonstrative. Each infrastructure investment project is carried out under various geographical, demographic, epidemiological, social and economic conditions. Thus, scientific curiosity forces us to search not only for the listed risk areas but also necessary for other proposed new areas of risk and uncertainty, adequate to the forecast social and economic conditions of investments. In addition, in order to simplify the process of identifying the risk area, the authors mentioned above often make a division into individual stages of the investment and long-term cooperation within *project finance*. This simplifies the risk management system, and it seems understandable to proceed in such a way that specific risk areas are identified in the period of pre-investment, investment and joint management in the operational cycle. The risk management process is never a stable, timeless tool. Once identified, the areas undergo changes, as does their impact on the investment or its implementing partners.

Table 3.6 Classification of investment risk in *project finance* presented by Lam Ka Chi and Chow Wing Sing

Investment risk		
In the pre-investment (preparatory) phase	During the investment (construction) phase	During the operational phase
– Fluctuation of inflation – Shortcomings in the technical design – Exchange rate fluctuations – Interest rate fluctuations – Low creditworthiness – Capital shortages – Currency exchange limits – Liquidity – Exceeding the allotted time – Relations with partners	– Shortcomings in the technical design – Shortages of materials/workforce – Slow progress of implementation work – Exceeding the allotted time – Cost overruns – Poor workmanship – Interest rate fluctuations – Fluctuation of inflation – Exchange rate fluctuations – Capital shortages – Currency exchange limits – Low creditworthiness – Relations with partners – Liquidity – Force majeure – Independence of the project	– Defective products/devices – Interest rate fluctuations – Fluctuation of inflation – Exchange rate fluctuations – Capital shortages – Low creditworthiness – Currency exchange limits – Liquidity – Low opportunities to sell capital – Higher taxes – Independence of the project – Competition – Relations with partners

Source Lam and Chow [22]

3.2 Public Finance Functions and Risk

Risk classification in *project finance* processes should be consistent with public functions, thanks to which selected structures of the PPP project will correspond to the tasks and objectives of management of public partners. In this chapter, an attempt is made to investigate the interpretation of the concept of risk and uncertainty in the theory of public finance. Attention was drawn to the basic functions of public finance, which are described inconsistently by key theorists in the field, such as R. A. Musgrave and J. Buchanan. Among the selected streams of science of public finance, risk areas resulting from selected functions of public finance were presented. It is commonly believed that developed risk management programmes in public entities are a relatively new phenomenon.[26] Thus, the search for theoretical risk bases on public finance should begin with an indication of the basic areas of management of public entities, i.e. generation of public revenues and implementation of the system of public expenditures. In Poland, according to the Public Finance Act,[27] public revenue comprises: public levies, other revenues of the state budget, local government units

[26] Williams et al. [23].

[27] Act on Public Finance of 27 August 2009, Dz. U. [Journal of Laws] of 2013. Item 885 as amended, Article 5(2).

and other entities of the public finance sector due on the basis of separate acts or international agreements, revenues from sales of products and services provided by entities of the public finance sector; revenues from property of entities of the public finance sector, inheritances, bequests, gifts in cash to public finance entities, compensation due to public finance entities, amounts obtained by public finance entities due to guarantees and sureties, income from the sale of assets, property and rights, not constituting revenue, within the meaning of the Act. On the other hand, public expenditures are cash flows originating from budgets of public entities, assigned for the implementation of public tasks (assigned for implementation to these entities), the purpose of which is to satisfy public needs. Examples of public expenditure include: infrastructure investments, expenditure on ensuring the external and internal security of the country, expenditure on the maintenance of the state and local government apparatus, the justice and prison system, subsidies for households in the form of pensions and subsidies for the operation of public sector enterprises.

Public expenditure is organised according to different criteria, due to its different nature. One of the classifications is the breakdown of public expenditure by the fund from which the expenditure is made. In such a system, the following elements are distinguished: budget expenditures (including expenditures of the state budget and expenditures of the budget of local government units), social security expenditures, expenditures under special purpose funds, expenditures of the remaining segments of the economy in public finances.[28]

The above-mentioned basic areas of public fund management are connected with the functioning of uncertainty and risk, as in the case of other commercial processes of economic activity of entities or households. The areas of this activity are very similar in each of the countries applying conventional principles of public finance and where the constitutional order of the state is in force. The differences are mainly in the distribution of indicated responsibilities and competencies of public authorities among the lower levels of public administration.

Two different interpretations of the functions of the state are provided by R. A. Musgrave and J. Buchanan. On the basis of the definition of public finance presented by R. A. Musgrave, we can gather that the economic structure of the public sector theory can be based either on the definition of which economic functions should be performed by the public authorities (normative perspective) or on the explanation of why the public authorities carry out such operations with their funds, and not others, and what will be the consequences of the actions taken.[29] Analysing the above definitions, it can be assumed that one of the main areas of uncertainty for public entities is the one concerning the decision on the scope of realisation of the public finance functions to be carried out. In other words, it is the uncertainty of public fund managers about the objectives, opportunities and ways of achieving them. Although the notion of risk or uncertainty is not explicitly defined with the indication of the function of public finance, there is no doubt that there is a type of uncertainty that is measurable or non-measurable. However, the question arises

[28]Owsiak [24].

[29]Musgrave and Musgrave [25].

whether in view of the identified risk of the public entity consisting in the selection of public finance functions to be performed, and—in practice—in the selection of specific management objectives, it may not perform the tasks specified for it for many reasons.

In a constitutional state governed by the rule of law, administrative tasks are defined in the constitution and in laws enacted by Parliament. In carrying out these tasks, the administrative authority may not restrict the rights and freedoms conferred on citizens by the constitution. Public managers are not free to decide what is to be done, but they do have an impact on the shape and scope of the objectives they are asked to achieve.

In a state governed by the rule of law, failure to perform or improper performance of public tasks is subject to legal and political responsibility. The political blame lies primarily with the government and the ministers. The legal liability is of a more complex nature, consisting mainly of criminal liability for offences related to the performance of administrative tasks. It is also possible to be held liable for non-performance or improper performance of the tasks of a representative of public administration in a civil lawsuit.[30] However, it may turn out that failure to perform specific tasks due to reasons beyond the control of the administration, such as lack of public financial means for its performance, will not result in any legal consequences and will not be considered to be a criminal act. This means that it is possible not to carry out a public task and that there will be no direct legal responsibility to do so. The only responsibility in such a situation may relate to the political reliability, as well as the possible loss of credibility towards the voters. The basic result, however, will be that the public will not be satisfied in terms of the type of services or public goods to which they are constitutionally entitled. This type of risk should be identified, which should result in the need to find methods of hedging against its occurrence. Most often, the most effective methods of protection against atrophy of the state, and consequently failure to perform the function of a state, are legal regulations, such as the constitution or public finance laws. In the case of Poland, Article 216 of the constitution stipulates that no loans may be taken out and no financial guarantees or sureties provided, following which the sovereign public debt will exceed 3/5 of the annual gross domestic product.[31] Moreover, the Public Finance Act indicates that the Minister of Finance is obliged to comply with the rule that the state public debt may not exceed 60% of the gross domestic product.[32] The same law provides for a specified remediation procedure in the event of failure to comply with these restrictions. The financial situation of the state, and thus its ability to perform certain functions, is also shaped by the strict need to comply with the criteria set by ERM II in the EU.[33] Theoretically, it is impossible for an EU Member State to "fail" completely. How-

[30] Boć et al. [26].

[31] Constitution of the Republic of Poland of 2 April 1997, Dz. U. [Journal of Laws] of 1997, no. 78, item 483.

[32] Public Finance Act..., Article 69.

[33] www.ec.europa.eu/eurostat/statistics-explained/index.php/Glossary:Exchange_rate_mechanism_(ERM)/pl.

ever, there are many examples of situations which occurred in selected countries that demonstrate a serious crisis in the performance of state functions in Europe (Greece), South America (Argentina) or Africa (many countries of sub-Saharan Africa). The crisis of fulfilling the functions of the state occurred in these countries, despite the fact that some of them have legal acts regulating possible levels of debt and management of public funds. The difficult situation of these countries is illustrated by the *Failed State Index* (FSI). It defines a "failed" state or, in other words, "a state in decay". According to the definitions proposed by G. Helman and S. Ratner, the term refers to a state whose power structures and social infrastructure have collapsed.[34] Although it is still a state under international law, in reality it has all but ceased to fulfil its basic functions. The Failed State Index is developed by analysts from the Foreign Policy periodical and the Fund for Peace NGO on the basis of 12 indicators: demographic pressures, number of refugees (including internally displaced persons), functioning of disadvantaged groups, human flight, developmental disparities, level of poverty and economic recession, legitimacy of state power, quality of public services, respect for human rights, ensuring security of citizens, divisions among political elites and external aggression. The list of "failed" states according to one of the latest reports, published in 2015,[35] is presented in Table 3.7.

The results presented above leave no illusions. Sub-Saharan Africa is the continent most affected by the risk of decomposition of state functions, and the problems are particularly visible in the central part, the eastern part of the Sahel belt and the Horn of Africa. The world's most fragile countries are: South Sudan, Somalia, Central African Republic, Democratic Republic of Congo, Sudan and Chad. As many as 7 African countries are in the second top ten: Guinea, Côte d'Ivoire, Guinea-Bissau, Nigeria, Kenya, Niger and Ethiopia. Every two out of three countries among the top 50 countries with the greatest degree of dysfunctionality are African. With regard to the various components of the FSI, it should be noted that African countries are in the lead in the ranking lists of 9 out of 12 indicators. The region is characterised by the lowest level of economic development and education in the world, the highest rate of poverty and a strong influence of tribal behaviours and conditions. According to the expert in the field of dysfunctional states, this leads to the largest number of armed conflicts in the world, as well as atrophy of state institutions.[36]

Details regarding selected countries in sub-Saharan Africa and their economic trends are presented in Chaps. 1 and 5. They will constitute a premise for building an exemplary PPP model based on the heterodox thought for the provision of public and private medical services. Among the most important factors of the weakness or even complete disappearance of the state functions of these countries, the following are the most important:

[34] G. B. Helman, S. Ratner, "Saving failed states", *Foreign Policy* 1992/1993, no. 89.

[35] www.library.fundforpeace.org/library/fragilestatesindex-2015.pdf.

[36] R. Kłosowicz, op. cit., p. 14.

Table 3.7 *Fragile State Index*—the highest index in 30 countries, 2015

	Fragile State Index 2015	Total	Demographic pressures	Refugees and IDPs	Group grievance	Human flight	Uneven development	Poverty and economic decline	Legitimacy of the state
1	South Sudan	114.5	9.8	10.0	10.0	6.9	8.8	9.0	10.0
2	Somalia	114.0	9.6	9.8	9.5	9.2	9.0	9.1	9.3
3	Central African Republic	111.9	8.4	10.0	9.6	6.9	9.7	8.3	9.5
4	Sudan	110.8	8.7	10.0	9.7	8.8	7.9	8.6	9.6
5	Congo (D. R.)	109.7	9.5	9.4	9.5	7.1	8.8	7.9	9.0
6	Chad	108.4	9.7	10.0	8.2	8.6	9.1	7.8	9.3
7	Yemen	108.1	9.2	9.1	9.4	7.5	8.1	9.3	9.3
9	Syria	107.9	8.1	10.0	10.0	7.4	7.0	7.5	9.9
8	Afghanistan	107.9	9.3	9.1	8.9	8.1	7.2	8.6	9.7
10	Guinea	104.9	9.0	8.7	8.7	7.2	7.6	9.2	9.9
11	Haiti	104.5	9.5	8.2	6.7	9.3	9.3	9.1	9.4
12	Iraq	104.5	8.2	8.9	10.0	8.1	7.8	6.9	9.2
13	Pakistan	102.9	9.0	8.9	10.0	7.0	7.3	7.7	8.6
14	Nigeria	102.4	8.8	7.5	9.9	7.1	8.8	7.6	9.1
15	Ivory Coast	100.0	8.1	9.0	8.7	6.7	7.9	7.1	8.5
16	Zimbabwe	100.0	8.7	8.4	7.8	8.0	8.1	8.0	9.0
17	Guinea-Bissau	99.9	8.2	7.8	5.7	8.5	8.4	8.7	9.0
18	Burundi	98.1	9.2	9.0	8.0	6.8	7.7	8.5	8.4

(continued)

Table 3.7 (continued)

	Fragile State Index 2015	Total	Demographic pressures	Refugees and IDPs	Group grievance	Human flight	Uneven development	Poverty and economic decline	Legitimacy of the state
19	Niger	97.8	9.6	7.9	7.5	6.9	8.4	8.2	7.5
20	Ethiopia	97.5	9.2	9.4	8.5	7.0	7.1	6.9	7.4
21	Kenya	97.4	9.0	8.3	9.0	7.5	8.3	7.5	8.1
21	Liberia	97.3	9.5	9.2	6.2	6.6	8.3	8.6	7.3
23	Uganda	97.0	8.9	8.8	8.7	7.3	7.3	7.0	8.0
24	Eritrea	96.9	8.8	7.8	6.1	7.6	7.2	8.3	9.1
25	Libya	95.3	5.4	7.4	7.8	6.4	6.1	8.0	9.8
26	Mauritania	94.9	8.6	8.5	6.9	6.3	7.1	8.0	7.9
27	Myanmar	94.7	6.8	8.3	9.7	5.7	8.2	6.5	9.0
28	Cameroon	94.3	8.0	7.8	8.1	7.5	7.8	6.2	8.4
29	North Korea	93.8	7.5	4.3	6.3	4.2	8.0	9.0	10.0
30	Mali	93.1	9.1	7.8	7.6	8.4	7.4	8.2	6.0
31	Sierra Leone	91.9	9.5	8.2	6.2	8.4	8.8	8.7	6.9
32	Bangladesh	91.8	8.1	6.6	8.4	7.5	7.2	6.7	8.5
33	Congo (Republic)	90.8	7.8	8.3	6.6	6.8	8.2	6.4	8.7
34	Sri Lanka	90.6	6.0	8.2	9.3	7.8	7.6	5.9	8.0

(continued)

Table 3.7 (continued)

	Fragile State Index 2015	Public services	Human rights	Security apparatus	Factionalised elites	External intervention
1	South Sudan	10.0	10.0	10.0	10.0	10.0
2	Somalia	9.3	10.0	9.7	10.0	9.5
3	Central African Republic	9.9	10.0	9.8	10.0	9.8
4	Sudan	8.8	9.6	9.5	9.8	9.8
5	Congo (D. R.)	9.7	10.0	9.5	9.5	9.8
6	Chad	9.7	9.4	8.8	9.5	8.3
7	Yemen	8.2	9.1	10.0	9.4	9.5
9	Syria	8.2	10.0	10.0	9.9	9.9
8	Afghanistan	9.3	8.6	10.0	9.3	9.8
10	Guinea	9.8	8.2	8.9	9.6	8.1
11	Haiti	9.1	7.4	7.5	9.1	9.9
12	Iraq	7.5	8.9	10.0	9.6	9.4
13	Pakistan	7.9	8.4	9.6	9.2	9.3
14	Nigeria	9.1	8.8	9.9	9.8	6.0
15	Ivory Coast	9.0	7.9	8.3	9.1	9.7
16	Zimbabwe	8.5	8.3	7.9	9.7	7.6
17	Guinea-Bissau	9.2	7.2	8.8	9.6	8.8
18	Burundi	8.3	8.2	7.7	7.9	8.4
19	Niger	9.3	6.8	8.7	8.9	8.1

(continued)

Table 3.7 (continued)

	Fragile State Index 2015	Public services	Human rights	Security apparatus	Factionalised elites	External intervention
20	Ethiopia	8.6	8.5	8.4	8.6	7.9
21	Kenya	7.9	6.5	8.4	8.9	8.0
21	Liberia	9.7	6.7	6.9	8.3	10.0
23	Uganda	8.3	7.9	7.6	8.9	8.3
24	Eritrea	8.7	9.3	7.7	8.1	8.2
25	Libya	7.5	9.0	9.3	9.1	9.5
26	Mauritania	8.9	8.0	7.4	8.8	8.5
27	Myanmar	8.6	8.3	8.3	8.3	7.0
28	Cameroon	8.8	8.0	7.6	9.1	7.0
29	North Korea	8.9	9.7	8.6	8.5	8.8
30	Mali	9.0	6.7	8.7	4.9	9.3
31	Sierra Leone	9.3	5.6	4.8	7.7	7.8
32	Bangladesh	8.1	7.7	7.7	9.6	5.7
33	Congo (Republic)	9.1	7.9	6.7	6.7	7.6
34	Sri Lanka	5.6	8.8	7.9	9.1	6.4

Source www.library.fundforpeace.org/library/fragilestatesindex-2015.pdf

- the consequences of the end of the colonial era;
- the strong influence of tribes, which are far from considering the state system as a superior institution, lack of national identity;
- lack of educated social strata;
- corrupt public administration;
- negative demographic factors;
- negative epidemiological factors;
- negative effects of the policies of external countries, especially former colonial powers, as well as new interest groups from Russia, China or the BRICS countries.[37]

All these factors give rise to the existence of an alleged risk that the state will not be able to perform most of its functions. This risk means that the entire economic and social organisation of the country is dysfunctional. Highlighting the critical situation of "failed" states may answer the hypothetical question asked above about the necessity of fulfilling the functions of the state by its administration. Failure to fulfil constitutional public tasks results in structural crises in various sectors of the country and has a significant impact on the welfare of the community living in a given country. The provision of public services is the core of statehood and is essential for the development of national societies and economies.

A different source of theoretical interpretations of risk may be a model of public authority actions, typical for the positive public finance method, being a part of the school of social choice, including the achievements of J. Buchanan (see Chap. 4). This trend is concerned with explaining how the scope, scale and forms of action of government and local government authorities are shaped by behaviours aimed at achieving goals of the members of society, managing interest groups, politicians and officials, who are mutually dependent.[38] In social choice theory, the process of identifying uncertainties and risks should, therefore, focus on the study of "government malfunctions". As a consequence, this would mean verifying the impact of decisions taken against previous pressure from stakeholders or politicians.[39] J. Buchanan has identified three basic methodological assumptions of the social choice theory connected with the issue of risk (see also Chap. 4):

- methodological individualism;
- behavioural *homo oeconomicus* model;
- analysis of politics as a process of exchange.

This means that individuals act rationally in the public sphere, based on maximising their own usefulness in making public decisions. Moreover, it proves that it is possible to interpret political phenomena from the standpoint of the market by presenting the objectives of interest groups, politicians and voters (where maximising the sense of usefulness among voters translates into supporting a specific party).

---

[37] www.kulturaliberalna.pl/2014/07/09/afryka-panstwa-kruche-czy-upadle-failed-states-index and Rotberg [27].

[38] Walasik [28].

[39] Filipowicz and Opawski [29].

Therefore, uncertainty regarding the implementation of particular, often short term, objectives of a public decision-maker or an elector faced with the choice of a political party emerges. It is understood that representatives of the parties always strive to maximise their usefulness function. The maximisation of one's own usefulness function is not necessarily connected with fulfilling the social function of the business. Moreover, the perspective of the impact of the choices made may be so distant in time that it will not be significant for the decision-maker maximising its usefulness in the short term. Such assumptions partly contradict the proposed pillars of the heterodox approach to PPP, where a consensus should be sought between the particular interests of public and private parties in shaping a long-term, contractual form of cooperation. The intersection of these two views clearly indicates an area of uncertainty (not necessarily measurable risk) related to the impact of politics on the course of economic processes and the stability of long-term cooperation within the framework of PPP. This area is widely explored in the subject literature. Political risks in public decision-making were discussed by [30–32]. These scientists defined the concept of political risk and searched for possible forms of security. The majority of them related political risks to the level of domestic and foreign investment and trade.

The research conducted by G. S. Becker was an important element of risk in social choice theory.[40] He points out the realisation of the redistribution function of public entities. This function is based on instruments such as taxes and social transfers to society, which are used to improve the well-being of interest groups (the so-called more powerful ones). This makes it possible to identify another field of uncertainty, even though the author does not explicitly call it an immeasurable risk area. This uncertainty lies in the design of public tax and social policies so that the positive effects are felt by a specific group of stakeholders. It can also be a calculable type of risk, based on the mismatch of the system of redistribution of public funds by the state with the actual needs of society, which translates into measurable losses for the general public and the benefit of specific interest groups. The mismatch between the objectives of financial transfers and the real and verified needs of the community can contribute to an increased sense of social injustice and diversification of the level of both economic and social developments. An example of such activities is the risk of insufficient financing of health needs in one medical area, despite the clear demand of patients for this type of services, and public financing in other medical areas, despite the lack of clear demographic or epidemiological indications in this respect. The redistribution of resources is not always based on real needs; sometimes it is based on local political or business circumstances of public decision-makers. Moreover, the redistribution of public funds does not always take into account the availability of selected public services on a macroeconomic scale. Such actions lead to an excessive underestimation of the level of decision-making in the field of redistribution of public financial resources, without taking into account the possibility of using such services or goods at the level of the region or the whole country. An example is again the poor saturation of selected medical services, which are exces-

[40]Becker [33].

sively available in communities or voivodeships, such as access to haemodynamic laboratories in the voivodeship. This may result in inefficiencies in the use of existing medical infrastructure, where the supply of the services offered exceeds the demand or availability of qualified personnel to operate specialised medical devices. In PPPs, this could mean a key risk area where a mismatch between the financial transfers due to the SPV for providing public services would significantly affect the ability to provide the expected access and quality of public services to the local community. The reduction of the planned public revenues is also reflected in the failure to achieve the planned level of profit of public and private partners. As a result, in the heterodox model constructed, it may translate into the failure to perform the function of social responsibility in managing financial surpluses and disposing of them partly back to the indicated social groups.

Another approach to risk in the performance of the redistribution function of public finance may be an excessive tax burden on certain types of financial or material transfers within the framework of a PPP investment and the current activity of a special purpose vehicle. This would have a negative impact on the level of financial flows in the special purpose vehicle and would have reduced the expected level of profit. Conversely, it can be assumed that the tax burden or the public financial transfers to the SPV will result in higher cash flows and higher than expected profits as a result of the activities of the interest groups. Such uncertainty as to the effects of lobbying on national governments and how they implement their redistributive policies can be reduced within the framework of the heterodox approach to public finances. Financial expectations of investors acting in PPP on the basis of heterodox approach are limited by the predetermined profit level. At the same time, achieving a higher than expected level of profits obliges the partners to jointly perform and carry out the redistribution of financial surpluses above the level of *Niṣāb* to the society, especially to potential users of the constructed infrastructure. Users of assets managed under PPP are not business groups, but most often the opposite—they are selected parts of the local communities (excluded or with clear restrictions on access to universal public services, e.g. persons uninsured with the National Health Fund (NFZ)). The scope of such consumers using the services of a public-private company is much wider than that of a potential interest group. Changes in tax systems as well as in social transfers are an important risk area. They will always have a key impact both on the profits achieved by an investment project and on the financial capabilities of the recipients of the goods. However, the idea of limited maximisation of investors' profits, as in the proposed heterodox approach to PPP, will not reduce the negative impact of tax rate fluctuations on the investment project. Mandatory performance of the corporate social responsibility function by public-private investors, as part of a heterodox approach, will be a factor preventing the public administration from excessive tax burdens of PPP transfers. The tax burden would result in a decrease in the expected profit and, consequently, in a decrease in the planned financial or material transfer above the agreed value of *Niṣāb* to the local community (described in more detail in Chap. 2). Ultimately, therefore, the negative effects of the tax burden would not only affect the special purpose vehicle itself but would also affect the public, who would thus have limited access to the public benefits to which it is entitled.

Continuing Becker's concept, it is worth noting a different approach to the redistributive function of public finance. In some circumstances, the risk area is theoretically generated by society itself. Buchanan points out the dependence based on the fact that individuals forming the majority required in a democracy, through political processes, may obtain a significantly higher share in the redistribution of public expenditures or significantly reduce the amount of taxes paid by themselves, thus reducing participation in the costs of financing public spending that benefits everyone.[41] This indicates the significant role of public opinion and views in democratic countries as a determinant of public spending. A majority vote in favour of a given political group may influence the allocation of public spending and the level of funding costs that are favourable to the supporting group. This makes it possible to identify further areas of risk in the framework of the redistributive function of public finance:

- the risk of the lack of continuity of the rules regarding financing of the public service in view of the term-based tenure of public authorities;
- the risk of a change in the approach to the management of the process of providing public services—from one that is favourable towards public-private partnerships to one that assumes only public management of the processes of creating and providing public services.

The lack of continuity of the rules for redistributing public funds may have a negative impact on many areas of economic activity, not only public activity. With a continuing need for public services, changes in the amount of financial transfers for the provision of public services will reduce the availability or quality of these services. Social pressure to reorient redistribution objectives will benefit some while being detrimental to others. Awareness of this type of risk forces entrepreneurs to monitor changes in social preferences and to constantly adjust their services to the real needs of the market. Another manifestation of uncertainty in the performance of the redistributive function of the state is the influence of public opinion on the goodwill or lack thereof towards public-private cooperation in the provision of public services. A way to minimise such a risk area, often of an immeasurable nature, is to involve local communities in the process of investment planning or management of public funds. Clear rules and objectives for the management of public funds should be known to all, and as a result, the public should not be dissatisfied with the fact that they are managed by private, public or public-private bodies. Conducting social dialogue becomes an essential element of any economic activity aimed at providing public services.

When interpreting the approach to risk in public finance theory, Musgrave demonstrates a broader approach to public finance functions than Buchanan in the so-called conceptual public finance theory. In addition to the redistribution function described

---

[41] Buchanan and Tullock [34], cf. A. Walasik, op. cit., p. 18.

above, it indicates a sequence of two consecutive financial functions, namely: the function of allocation and stabilisation.[42] These areas also provide an explanation of the phenomena of uncertainty or risk. He proved that the identified successive functions of public finances are consistent with the proper objectives of the use of fiscal instruments. The allocation function is responsible for meeting individual needs and collective requirements (public goods) by allocating resources. The stabilisation function is to achieve the objectives of economic equilibrium.[43] Musgrave proposes a clear separation of the three public finance functions. He presupposes the need to preserve the sequencing of public authority action in the materialisation of these functions. Arrangement of the fiscal authority is supposed to include actions initiated by the establishment of payments resulting from the different level of income of the society. In any case, tax transfers and the payment of social transfers for the purpose of achieving the desired distribution of income in society must then be determined. The achievement of the objectives of stabilising public finances is to be based on the principle that taxes and charges must reflect in their structure, rather than in their amount, the monetary operations established in connection with the realisation of the redistributive function. Musgrave assumed, however, that the performance of particular functions is separate; i.e. the redistribution function is determined on the assumption that the distribution of income is made with full employment and all collective needs (public goods) satisfied.[44]

When pointing out different approaches to the definition of risk within the field of public finance, it is worth referring to the social choice theory (presented in Sect. 2.3). An important area of risk in the framework of the financial function is the *free rider problem*, which is related to the public choice theory and social choice theory. This issue is consistent with the implementation of the principles of the allocation function of the state. It was described, among others, by M. Olson, who described the logic of collective choice, referring to property rights and the theory of transactional costs.[45] In Polish subject literature, the most comprehensive discussion of the theory of interest groups can be found in a paper by B. Klimczak entitled *Teoretyczne podstawy badania działań grup interesu na rzecz ładu rynkowego*.[46] According to the basic thesis of this theory, in large social groups, even a very obvious common interest of group members does not usually lead to collective actions, which are beneficial for all members of the group, because there will always be *a free rider*. This justifies the interference of the state carrying out the allocation and stabilisation functions. Positive or negative stimuli, which are manifestations of the state carrying out these functions, are to cause people to act collectively in order to gain mutual benefits. Buchanan emphasised that people who are guided by their selfish interests are not able to communicate on their own. Therefore, state interference in market relations is necessary. Under the above assumptions, the concept of

---

[42]Musgrave [35].

[43]Ibid.

[44]A. Walasik, op. cit., p. 11.

[45]Olson [36].

[46]Klimczak [37].

free rider is related to the efficiency of resource allocation in the markets of mainly public goods, which are characterised by very high costs of excluding someone from their consumption. This allows to define the *free rider* as such an entity, which uses the public goods or services to the extent exceeding their share in the cost of their production or provision.[47] Such a situation most often occurs in transitioning economies and societies. This is connected with the emerging legal and institutional order typical for a market economy. This type of risk is particularly relevant in the case of public-private partnerships. If the SPV introduces a price for the provision of public services, there will certainly be a group of *free riders*, who will not want to voluntarily finance the production of public goods. The most illustrative example is the person who uses public transport for free. Said person benefits from the use of the public service but does not bear the cost of maintaining it. The service may be provided because the vast majority of users bear the cost of tickets and access to public transport services as a public good should be unrestricted and inclusive. In 1920 A. Pigou and later A. Marshall reported on the effects of the transfer of part of the cost of or benefits from the operations of one group to another.[48] Moreover, in his work *The Economics of the Public Sector* J. E. Stiglitz[49] pointed out that if the public is aware that public goods will be provided to those who will not pay for them, then some of them will go for the free riders' tactics. From the point of view of public and private investors, it would be important to find effective tools for monitoring and controlling users' payments of public fees. When the SPV finances the provision of public services by an external payer (e.g. a PPP hospital in which payments for services are financed by the National Health Fund), the problem of *free riders* may be of marginal significance, because the users of the infrastructure do not bear the direct cost themselves.

3.3 Internal and External Risk Determinants in Public-Private Partnerships

The author wonders why the concepts of risk and uncertainty in the field of public finance have not previously been widely recognised and analysed in depth by scientists. On the other hand, theoretical foundations of risk management in private entities, in particular corporate companies, have been very popular and are still being intensively developed. Many methods of risk identification and management in enterprise finances have been developed. Their usefulness for the functioning of public entities proves to be negligible. In public administration, the subject of risk management is services and public goods, which are received by society as a whole. Moreover, the exclusive provision of a public service does not always involve profit-making activities and the generation of various types of financial risk. The management of

[47]Galor [38].

[48]Ibid., pp. 63–78.

[49]Stiglitz [39].

public funds from the point of view of society argues in favour of a specific approach to the problem of risk management in public entities.[50] As a result, in the area of public finance, many different risk areas can be identified, which do not exist in private entities (for more details, see Chap. 5). Some of the risk areas are the same for private and public partners, but the management process itself is different in these entities. Often, the risk management process in public entities is only a formal, static procedure, necessary for the annual filling in of management control reports. It is not a dynamic tool for the day-to-day management of the public sector or infrastructure investments as in the case of private investors. The risk management process is a key element for any cooperation between private and public entities in the PPP formula. It is also a formal and legal requirement to begin such cooperation. It is worth noting that the period of development of PPP in Europe is similar to the period of appearance of the first works on the perception of risk and methods of managing it in public administration. Perhaps, therefore, the wider use of project finance solutions, forcing the implementation of risk management procedures in public administration, contributed to the greater attention paid to this process in the public sector. Business practice has developed a number of standards in risk management systems commonly used in public entities in most countries. These include, for example, the principles of management control in Poland,[51] *Orange Book Management of Risk* developed by the UK Treasury,[52] *Principles of Good Corporate Governance and Best Practice Recommendations in* Australia,[53] *Enterprise Wide Risk Management* in Botswana and many others. Such studies provide a model and practical guidance for public employees on how to conduct the risk management process and what the exemplary risk areas and methods of protection are. In addition, they provide a factual basis for carrying out control activities in public entities. Using the example of Poland, it can be pointed out that the purpose of management control over public administration is:

- a faster response to crisis situations;
- accelerating innovation;
- better project management;
- efficient, effective and economic use of the organisation's resources;
- taking advantage of opportunities that appear in the environment;
- improving the quality of public administration services.[54]

In the Public Finance Act, Article 68 contains other objectives of exercising management control, i.e. risk management, promotion of ethical conduct and reliability of financial statements, in addition to those mentioned above.

---

[50] Dylewski and Filipiak [40].

[51] Act on Public Finances... from art. 68 to art. 71 and Regulation of the Minister of Finance of 2 December 2010 on the model statement on the state of management control, Dz. U., no. 238, item 1581.

[52] www.gov.uk/government/uploads/system/uploads/attachment_data/file/22067/orange_book.pdf.

[53] www.anao.gov.au/sites/g/files/net616/f/McPhee_risk_and_risk_management_in_the_public_sector_2005.pdf.

[54] Kumpiałowska [41].

It is, therefore, worth identifying the internal determinants of the slow development of risk management in the public sector. In the case of public administrations in different countries, there is still little awareness among public employees of the existence of risk areas and the need to adequately protect against them. Unfortunately, the perception and active management of risk in public administration are rarely the subjects of broad scientific exploration. Available research results in this area include a survey of risk perception in municipalities in Poland. They show that in 355 of the investigated municipalities, there is no significant conviction as to the importance and positive role of risk management in the management of local government units (LGUs).[55] In another study conducted in 366 municipalities in Poland, only 30% of the surveyed municipalities declared their knowledge and understanding of the notion of "risk appetite" in the public sector, i.e. a reference point to the level of risk which LGUs are able to accept and take.[56] Of course, such selective theses regarding awareness of the existence of risk in the public sector and skilful management of it should be contrasted with those economic systems for which the notion of risk or uncertainty is crucial. The best example, based on highly advanced methodologies of risk identification and management, is the system applied by the state administration in the USA, covering all categories of risk areas together with a wide range of hedging instruments, mainly by insurance entities. Selected atypical examples of the analysed risk areas are presented in Table 3.8.

The presented unconventional selected risk areas prove a high awareness of the responsibility of public entities in all areas of public fund management and public service provision.

Another important reason why risk management is still a relatively new area in the management of public funds and in the theory of public finance itself is the contestation of innovative solutions by public employees. In its Europe 2020 Communication, in the Innovation Union chapter, the European Commission highlights a better understanding of public sector innovation by identifying and presenting successful initiatives. It is also important to carry out benchmarking of progress in this area on a scale of all countries in the EU.[57] Access to technology and innovation is often limited, albeit procedurally, by the public procurement system. The rules of making purchases or services contracted in this way do not allow for support of the absorption of innovative solutions. The presence of public entities on innovative markets is also negligible, as the trend of creating innovative tools for public administration entities is slower than for commercial entities. On the other hand, the introduction of modern solutions does not translate into an increase in the employee's specific objectives, which are the initiator of such solutions. Motivational systems in the public sector are unlikely to focus on motivations for process changes, the

---

[55]Report from the study "Risk management in the activity of local government units with particular emphasis on catastrophic risk", MRC Consulting, Qualifact, Market Research & Analysis, University of Gdańsk, May 2013, Gdańsk, http://www.wzieu.pl/zn/794/ZN_794.pdf.

[56]Jastrzębska [42].

[57]Communication from the Europe 2020 Commission. A strategy for smart, sustainable and inclusive growth, European Commission 2010, p. 20.

Table 3.8 Risk related to US public sector financing

Level of risk ****	Risk subject matter	What is the risk/what phenomenon or factor can be associated with?
***	Airports	Normal and operational risks associated with large concentrations of people
***	Medical transport	Carrying out of medical tasks, accidents related to fast-track driving
***	Amusement parks	Breakdown of equipment, inadequate supervision, inadequate licence
***	Athletic facilities and structures	Incorrect supervision, dangerous or inappropriate equipment
*	Tax collectors	Threat of fraud
**	Car parks	Inappropriate supervision, criminal acts
***	Beaches	Incorrect supervision, incorrect bottom formation
**	Stages	Incorrect evacuation plans, overcrowding
**	Botanical gardens	Pesticide use, volunteer work
***	Bridges	Poor design or maintenance, exceeding width and height limits, damage due to flooding
***	Building inspections	Accidents or damage due to incorrect recommendations of inspectors, accidents of the inspectors themselves at work
***	Construction sites	Accidents, destruction, explosions
***	Maintenance of buildings	Unsuitable maintenance
***	Operation of bus routes	Driver errors, kidnappings
***	Bus and rail terminals	Risk related to the public utility building itself, crowd problem
***	Waterworks	Explosions, floods, pollution
***	Police units	Civil and constitutional rights, safeguards against threats of weapons of mass destruction, public security

(continued)

Table 3.8 (continued)

Level of risk ****	Risk subject matter	What is the risk/what phenomenon or factor can be associated with?
***	Rehabilitation facilities	Errors while proving care or maintaining facilities
**	Recycling centres	Pollution, inadequate maintenance standards
*	Risk management managers/insurance administrators	Errors in obtaining or maintaining insurance disadvantageous to employees
***	Roads and bridges	Errors in construction, maintenance and repair, traffic control, engineering repairs, construction explosions
***	Road maintenance	Car accidents related to bad signage, traffic lights, road surface maintenance
***	Schools	Maintenance, protection, faults in evacuation and safety systems
**	Sport shooting ranges	Errors in supervision or in the equipment made available
***	Cycling paths	Poor signage, incorrect condition of the surface
***	Ramps for skateboarders	Maintenance and monitoring of correct use
**	Snow overhangs	Destruction of parked cars and other objects
***	Stadiums	Crowd control, inadequate evacuation systems, destruction due to armed robberies
***	Swimming pools	Errors in construction, supervision, contamination, random accidents
**	Tennis courts	Maintenance and monitoring
**	Theatres	Crowd control, inadequate evacuation systems
**	Environmental nurses	Liability of own medical practice with all personal properties
***	Water and waste management	Pollution, flooding, storage
***	Zoo	Injuries by animals

—Low, **—Medium, *—High

Source Own compilation (selected examples) based on the following documents: T. W. Rynard, *Insurance and Risk Management for State and Local Governments*, Matthew Bender & Co., Inc., Lexis Nexis

effects of which are often of a long-term nature, but on motivations for achieving short-term results, quick measurable effect, and on the short-term responsibility of a public administration employee. Another obvious obstacle to the implementation of innovative solutions, including tools for permanent and effective risk management, is the cost of such implementation. Due to the difficult financial situation, many public entities do not have the possibility to purchase unconventional and often cost-intensive solutions. In a survey of public entities in 27 states of the European Union and Norway, as many as 78% of all public organisations (3699 feedback questionnaires were obtained) indicated the lack of financial resources as a basic barrier to innovation.[58] IT limitations and classified information constraints are also an obstacle to the implementation of new technologies. Managing public data involves much higher risks and the need to ensure the security standards in this area.

A critical reason for limited interest in the advanced level of risk management in the public sector is the aspect of a lack of awareness of the existence of a threat, together with the identified uncertainty or risk. There is a clear trend in behaviour, in which the lack of direct impact on the unit of identified risk does not cause it to be averse. The aspect of the impact of the danger on society or on public property is far removed from the individual sense of security and private property of a public employee. The issue of public ownership does not translate into care and avoidance of exposure to risk among managers of such assets. This is often due to the very limited real legal and financial responsibility for the consequences of decisions taken in the risk management process. Another dimension of the difficulty in taking on risks is the insufficient ability to quantify using predictive methods and to estimate the effects of uncertainty, even in the case of non-measurable processes. Therefore, the problem concerns not only the awareness of the existence of the effects of certain errors or omissions in the management of public funds, the lack of direct responsibility for the result of their occurrence, but also the proper ability to estimate the value of potential consequences. This means limited access to risk management knowledge and forecast IT tools to calculate risk.[59]

Another obstacle to the implementation of a continuous risk management process in the public sector may be the sustainability of policy decisions in the face of policy changes by public authorities. Political terms and the existence of political conditions in decision-making often hamper risk management processes, especially in long-term projects such as PPPs. The lack of continuity of responsibility of the public authority as such, towards partial, periodic responsibility (already negligible) of individual employees, may constitute a significant problem in the implementation of long-term objectives of public-private investment projects. The short-sightedness of the decisions taken may prevent a continuous process of identifying and managing risk areas in PPPs. However, the stable shape of several decades-long PPP agreements may be an element of counteracting the short-sightedness of public decisions. Thus, it increases the chances of adaptation of innovative solutions in public-private

[58]European Public Sector Innovation Scoreboard: Methodology report, PRO INNO Europe, Inno Metricks 2012, p. 7.

[59]Cf. Nagji and Tuff [43].

structures through wider access to knowledge and faster decision-making processes in special purpose vehicles of PPP. Meanwhile, a much longer period of decision-making in the public sector is a significant barrier to innovation in public administration and the processes of providing or producing public services. Frequently, formal and organisational rules resulting from legal regulations of public finance make it impossible to react quickly to identified risk areas. Making a binding decision may require much more time for formal reasons than the duration of the risk situation itself or related to the implementation of processual or organisational innovations in public administration.

Apart from presenting internal determinants of development in the area of risk management in the public sector, attention should also be paid to the wider context of this process, i.e. external determinants. Changes of a macroeconomic or even global nature may be fundamental to progress in risk management in public entities. The economic, social, demographic and geopolitical situation may give rise to many new areas of risk for public entities. Although the literature rarely refers to the economy of public entities in the context of changes in global markets, this seems to be an increasingly important factor in performing the function of public finance. Although the objective of the management of public entities is not profit, the public entity is an entity in a market game. It should monitor the situation on the global market with full commitment and adapt its economic activities accordingly. This is best demonstrated by the effects of the financial crises on conventional markets, which have affected governments and local authorities across Europe in general, despite the fact that public entities are not, by their very nature, the primary profit players in these markets. Turning points in the economies of countries all over the world, affecting the development prospects on a global scale, are presented by the results of the research conducted by [44] (Table 3.9).

The turning points in the development of the world's economies presented by the authors are important for the perception of risk in the conventional public sector. The fact that emerging countries[60] have high foreign exchange reserves proves the high

[60] An emerging country is a nation's economy that is becoming increasingly advanced and has some form of market exchange and a regulatory authority. Not all agree on which countries belong to this group, but some institutions have chosen to classify them. The International Monetary Fund, for example, classifies 23 countries as emerging markets. The same number is reported by Morgan Stanley Capital International. Standard and Poor, and Russell rank 21 emerging markets worldwide, and Dow Jones lists 22 countries. The following is a list of countries that each of the above organisations has classified as emerging markets since 2016, but also a list of countries that are classified as such by only some of these institutions. The following countries are included in the classification of all organisations mentioned above: Brazil, Chile, China, Colombia, Hungary, Indonesia, India, Malaysia, Mexico, Peru, Philippines, Poland, Russia, South Africa, Thailand and Turkey. The other countries on the IMF list are: Argentina, Bangladesh, Bulgaria, Pakistan, Romania, Ukraine and Venezuela. The Morgan Stanley Capital International classification also includes: Bangladesh, Czechia, Egypt, Greece, Qatar, South Korea, Taiwan and United Arab Emirates. The S & P list also includes: Bangladesh, Czechia, Egypt, Greece and Taiwan. The Dow Jones also classifies the following: Czechia, Egypt, Greece, Qatar, Taiwan and United Arab Emirates. The other emerging market countries according to Russell are the following: Czechia, Greece, South Korea, Taiwan and United Arab Emirates (www.investopedia.com/terms/e/emergingmarketeconomy.asp). Developing countries are countries with low levels of material wealth. However, there is no generally

Table 3.9 Turning points in economics and business—key drivers and implications for the twenty-first century

Turning points in economics and business	Key drivers of sustainable change	Main consequences
Emerging and developing economies account for almost half of the world's economic output. Three-fourth of global economic growth comes from Asia, Latin America, the Middle East and Africa [IMF 2011]	Differences in GDP and population growth rates	– Redistribution of geo-economic market powers – Evolution of consumer markets
Emerging and developing economies hold 75% of foreign currency reserves	Large surpluses on the current account of the balance of payments	– Possible further disruption of global financial markets – Poverty reduction
Nearly 30% of the total number of international companies are international companies in emerging markets, and their level of foreign direct investment in the total number of investments amounted to 41% in the years 2006–2010	Searching for new markets, entry methods and strategic assets; large current account surpluses	– Increased competition in the global industry – New decision-making centres

Source Guillen and Ontiveros [44]

security of the country's payment balance operations, guaranteed convertibility of the country's currency and possible interventions on the currency market.

In Poland, the central bank's foreign currency reserves amounted to USD 98 billion at the end of 2015, in China to USD 3.8 trillion at the end of 2014,[61] in Saudi Arabia to USD 732 billion[62] and in India to USD 320 million.[63] Operations in foreign currency reserves are a key instrument of monetary policy, especially exchange rate policy. An adequate level of reserve assets supports the credibility of entire economies. They need to be carefully allocated to ensure their security and liquidity, as well as an adequate level of income.[64] The two most important benefits of increasing the amount of foreign currency reserves are the possibility of obtaining income from investments and reducing the perceived risk of the country's insolvency.[65] This could

accepted definition of a developed country. The level of development of these countries may be at different levels (www.pl.wikipedia.org/wiki/Kraje_development%C4%85ce_si%C4%99; www.iugg2015prague.com/list-of-developing-countries.htm).

[61] Snapshot for China Monthly Foreign Exchange Reserves CNGFOREX, Bloomberg L.P., accessed on 24.04.2015.

[62] International Reserves and Foreign Currency Liquidity, 24.04.2015.

[63] India International Reserves and Foreign Currency Liquidity, 24.04.2015.

[64] Karwowski [45].

[65] Konopczak [46].

mean that some BRICS (Brazil, Russia, India, China and South Africa) and MINTS (Mexico, Indonesia, Nigeria, Turkey, South Africa), while accumulating reserves and stabilising their economies, would act as providers of finance to countries that were previously considered wealthy, with sustainable economies, e.g. from the EU, but often in crisis with public finances and high indebtedness. The Persian Gulf countries and selected Asian countries, where transactions based on Islamic finances play a decisive role, will also play an important role in the role of capital providers. Paradoxically, another risk area for the system of conventional public finances of developed countries may be the lack of interest in traditional markets on the part of investors from new economic centres of the world (India, the Persian Gulf, China) in view of the growing attractiveness of new investment areas, as in sub-Saharan Africa. Despite the very poor economic situation in most countries in sub-Saharan Africa, the trend towards recovery from the structural crisis has been slow. Investment opportunities in this region have been confirmed for many years by the business involvement of China and Russia in particular. Having high foreign currency reserves and convenient balance of payments base puts emerging and developing countries at the forefront of the race to win new markets. On the other hand, limited resources of assets, including financial resources of developed countries, high current level of debt, often limiting the possibility of additional debt financing for development, will contribute to a worse competitive position of the economies of these countries in relation to emerging stars. Another source of threats to the situation of conventional public finances is changes in the demography and development of societies presented in Table 3.10.

Negative demographic changes in developed countries are mainly based on the progressive ageing of the population. Falling birth rates, as a result of, among other things, rising costs of living and increasing life expectancy are causing significant problems for the performance of proper social policy and social security by public administration (the so-called reversed age pyramid). Increasing deficits of financial resources available in the budgets of developed economies, as a result of a decreasing number of economically active people, limit allocation functions and various types of transfers, including people of retirement age. A smaller number of economically active people will also contribute to a decrease in tax revenues and, consequently, to problems of public entities with the proper performance of the redistributive function. As a result, both the financial base and the human capital, which shape the well-being of societies in developed countries, are significantly shrinking. Reverse trends in demographic change can be seen in emerging and developing countries. A key area of mitigating the risk of negative effects of demographic changes is the growing number of people along with the growing lifespan (although the lifespan in these countries is much shorter than in developed countries). An increasing number of active people, together with a gradual improvement in the quality of life, including health care, may contribute to the transition to a stable demographic situation in emerging and developing countries. This will once again give these countries a competitive advantage in other markets and a stable basis for further development, including, for example, the development of public health systems and investment in human capital. Such factors can also have a significant impact on access to skilled

Table 3.10 Turning points in societies and demographics—key drivers and implications for the twenty-first century

Turning points for societies and demographics		
An ageing population—reversing the age pyramid	– Declining birth rates due to the new role of women in society	– Changes in consumer, social and political behaviour – Growing income disparities – The increasing level of government debt
More people live in cities than in the countryside	– Relative prices and changes in productivity of sectors	– Growing challenges in cities – A decrease in the birth rate – Sedentary lifestyle
Africa and Asia will be the fastest growing continents in terms of population	– High, although decreasing, birth rates are still higher than in other parts of the world	– Global redistribution of consumption and geo-economic power
More people suffer from obesity than from hunger	– Growing income, an abundance of inappropriate food, sedentary lifestyle	– Changes in consumption and social behaviour – Improving life chances/perspectives
Income disparities between communities in different countries are growing (stratification of societies)	– Skill shortages, urban–rural duality, lower tax revenues and lower public transfers	– Growing social unrest and political protests
Falling poverty rates	Economic growth in emerging and developing countries	– Improving living conditions

Source Guillen and Ontiveros [44]

workers and on the development of knowledge-based societies. So far, it has been mainly the countries of the old continent that have provided a base for part of the human resources for developing countries. It can be expected that with such dynamic development, based on real high tangible and financial assets of emerging and developing countries, new scientific, research and educational centres will be created. Also, the investors themselves, discovering new investment areas in these markets, can be a source of knowledge and experience for new forms of cooperation. The location of the largest concentrations of people will also change. It is estimated that in 2030 the largest metropolises will be: on the African continent, Lagos, with a population of 25 million; in China, Chongqing, with more than 32 million people; in Europe, London, with a population of 16.7 million; in North America, New York, with 20.4 million people; in Asia, Jakarta, with 37 million. According to the highest level of income for household expenses in 2030, the first place will be taken by the inhabitants of New York—USD 434 billion, then Shanghai—USD 433 billion, the next two cities are also Chinese metropolises, and the fifth place is taken by Jakarta—USD 274 billion.[66] This indicates positive demographic and economic trends in those countries where the major metropolises are emerging. At the same time, it may mean a high interest in migrating workers from other locations to new social and economic centres. For the inhabitants of conventional economies, this may contribute to an outflow of human resources towards developing markets. This means that the situation of the social security system is getting worse in the face of a shrinking number of people actively financing the social security or pension system. Population migrations will also result in a decrease in tax revenues for local government units, which will further worsen the situation of public and local government finances in countries such as the EU. The awareness of the existence of such areas of risk for the system of conventional public finance should result in already seeking the possibility of creating assets of these economies, which may determine their competitive position. The knowledge and experience of staff, including public administrations, can make a real contribution to shaping public-private partnerships in the new emerging markets. The transfer of knowledge and experience, in a formalised manner and based on a long-term PPP agreement, may provide an opportunity for the development of conventional economies and contribute to the acquisition of long-term private partners for cooperation and implementation of joint infrastructure investments in new markets. The purpose of such cooperation from the point of view of public entities would be to transfer the profit to the budgets of the countries of origin of public entities. It is worth noting, however, that this return would be obtained from investments of a social nature and always related to the provision of public services or the production of public goods, which is in line with the provisions of legal norms governing the management of public funds. Until now, such a form of activity of public entities, at least in Polish conditions, has not been considered as a way out of the difficult financial situation of the public sector. However, in view of the sensitive international developments, this form of activity should be considered, especially as it increasingly encourages the generation of tangible fixed assets and the generation of a positive financial result from the actual activity and production of public goods (Table 3.11).

The presented forecasts of disposable household income levels of inhabitants of selected cities may deepen the outflow of the population (migration) towards new economic centres of the world from the conventional economies of many already developed countries. If migration of personnel:

- has an even more pronounced negative impact on public finances, mainly as a result of falling tax revenues, both for individuals and for businesses;
- further highlights the problem of ageing populations, e.g. in Europe;
- contributes to a reduction in tax revenues and an increase in social spending, which will further aggravate the crisis in conventional public finances in many countries.

---

[66] *Future trends and market opportunities in the world's largest 750 cities: How the global urban landscape will look in 2030*, Oxford Economics, p. 3. https://www.oxfordeconomics.com/Media/Default/landing-pages/cities/OE-cities-summary.pdf.

Table 3.11 Households disposable income in 2030

Household disposable income (change 2013–2030)			
Rank (2030)	City	Country	USD billion
1	New York—Newark—Jersey City	US	434
2	Shanghai	China	433
3	Beijing	China	368
4	Chongqing	China	279
5	Jakarta	Indonesia	274
6	London—metro	UK	255
7	Los Angeles—Long Beach—Anaheim	US	243
8	Tokyo	Japan	236
9	Riyadh	Saudi Arabia	234
10	Tianjin	China	231
11	Houston—The Woodlands—Sugar Land	US	231
12	Dallas—Fort Worth—Arlington	US	230
13	Guangzhou, Guangdong	China	225
14	Istanbul—metro	Turkey	222
15	Shenzhen	China	198
16	Sao Paulo	Brazil	196
17	Chicago—Naperville—Elgin	US	177
18	Dongguan, Guangdong	China	175
19	Doha	Qatar	175
20	Moscow—metro	Russia	168

Source Future trends and market opportunities in the world's largest 750 cities: How the global urban landscape will look in 2030, Oxford Economics, p. 8. https://www.oxfordeconomics.com/Media/Default/landing-pages/cities/OE-cities-summary.pdf

Then, the question is: how far can the crisis go? Indeed, as Guillen and Ontiveros predict, can there be a crisis in the functions of the state in many countries? At this point, it is worth analysing the level of GDP and public debt in selected countries (Table 3.12).

The data presented in Table 3.12 show most of the countries surveyed have already achieved very high levels of debt and their assets are insufficient to stimulate further growth. Italy has the highest public debt in terms of GDP among the selected countries. In 2015, the debt level was as high as 132.7% of GDP. In the USA, the debt level was at an equally high level, reaching 104.17% of GDP in 2015. In Islamic countries, the highest level of public debt in relation to GDP is observed in the United Arab Emirates; however, its level is much lower than in the USA or Italy, and in 2014 it

Table 3.12 Level of public debt and public debt-to-GDP ratio in selected countries in 2011–2015

Country	2011		2012		2013		2014		2015	
	Public debt (USD bln)	% GDP	Public debt (USD bln)	% GDP	Public debt (USD bln)	% GDP	Public debt (USD bln)	% GDP	Public debt (USD bln)	% GDP
Poland	2635157.14	54.40	2460772.44	54.00	2524357.20	56.00	2735616.00	50.50	3255858.06	51.30
Italy	2655630.00	116.50	2556470.00	123.30	2748969.00	129.00	2837947	132.50	2409469.00	132.70
Spain	1034994.00	69.50	1144405.00	85.40	1282999.00	93.70	1373321.00	99.30	1189587.00	99.20
Germany	2946630.00	78.30	2817898.00	79.60	2892375.00	77.20	2893121.00	74.70	2388690.00	71.20
USA	14790340.00	99.40	16066240.00	100.83	16738180.00	101.17	17824070.00	102.98	18150620.00	104.17
United Arab Emirates	61199.00	17.61	63575.00	17.04	61459.00	15.87	62626.00	15.68		
Kuwait	13171.00	8.55	11811.00	6.79	11319.00	6.44	12177.00	7.08		
Saudi Arabia	36149.00	5.40	26331.00	3.59	16036.00	2.15	11810.00	1.57	37942.00	5.81
Kenya	15860.00	47.10	17560.00	38.20	19460.00	39.80	24900.00	44.20	31500.00	52.80
South Africa	159428.00	38.20	162399.00	40.90	161760.00	44.20	164828.00	47.10	156650.00	50.10

(continued)

Table 3.12 (continued)

Country	2011		2012		2013		2014		2015	
	Public debt (USD bln)	% GDP	Public debt (USD bln)	% GDP	Public debt (USD bln)	% GDP	Public debt (USD bln)	% GDP	Public debt (USD bln)	% GDP
Ethiopia	12209.00	38.19	14124.00	32.76	17577.00	36.88	22580.00	40.69	29958.00	48.62
Zambia	4883.00	20.80	6349.00	24.91	7440.00	26.53	8532.00	35.14	11589.00	52.95

Source own compilation based on
http://www.finanse.mf.gov.pl/zadluzenie-skarbu-panstwa/-/document_library_display/a7KU/view/4079196
http://ec.europa.eu/eurostat/tgm/table.do?tab=table&init=1&language=en&pcode=tsdde410&plugin=1
http://countryeconomy.com/national-debt/italy
http://countryeconomy.com/national-debt/spain
http://countryeconomy.com/national-debt/germany
http://www.statista.com/statistics/187867/public-debt-of-the-united-states-since-1990/
http://www.tradingeconomics.com/united-states/government-debt-to-gdp
http://countryeconomy.com/national-debt/united-arab-emirates
http://countryeconomy.com/national-debt/kuwait
http://countryeconomy.com/national-debt/saudi-arabia
http://www.tradingeconomics.com/kenya/government-debt-to-gdp
http://www.statista.com/statistics/531654/national-debt-of-kenya/
https://www.focus-economics.com/country-indicator/south-africa/public-debt
http://countryeconomy.com/national-debt/south-africa
http://countryeconomy.com/national-debt/ethiopia
http://countryeconomy.com/national-debt/zambia

Table 3.13 Turning points in policy area—key drivers and implications for the twenty-first century

Policy		
Budget deficits and local government debt are more of a problem in rich countries than in emerging or developing countries.	Falling competitiveness, an ageing population, political paralysis	– Further budget cuts – A decrease in the capacity to perform the functions of the state – Financial tensions
Decrease in legitimacy and capacity of the state	Social unrest, political revolts, reduction of state functions, social inequalities	– Less ability to efficiently counteract local and global problems, the phenomena of the "failed" state

Source Guillen and Ontiveros [44]

amounted to 15.68%. Among the countries of sub-Saharan Africa, the level of public debt is at a similar level as in the other countries mentioned above, reaching the level of about 30-50% of GDP. The lowest level of public debt is observed in countries that base their economies on capital and real assets, and not on the creation of debt and virtual money. The vast majority are systems based on Islamic finance. Conventional economies present such a high level of debt that they do indeed authenticate the forecasts of the presented authors about the real threat of atrophy of state functions in many countries.

In view of these turning points, it would, therefore, be important for societies and demographics to actively seek opportunities to develop and move away from consumer forms of economies towards economies that stimulate growth and production, based on assets rather than debt. A possible path to development and elimination of macroeconomic risk is a heterodox approach to PPP proposed in public finance. Its implementation will help prevent the loss of legitimacy of the state function. Material assets held by public entities may determine their competitive position in relation to private entities. They will be translated into shares in special purpose vehicles and then, in accordance with the principle of profit and loss sharing, into shares in profits and/or losses of the investment project. The undertaking fulfilled in the PPP formula in a heterodox approach will be based on providing public services actually related to the possessed special purpose vehicle assets and planned in advance return on the long-term investment. The projected profit must not come from speculation with financial instruments, but from a public service that is genuinely profitable. Moreover, the allocation of free financial resources above a certain amount to the local community will strengthen the role of the public entity in the perception of the society. This will contribute to calming down fears about the performance of state functions and will provide an opportunity to even out large disproportions in the development of the community.

Another risk area in the performance of conventional public finance functions is changes in the political and geopolitical nature, as projected in Tables 3.13 and 3.14.

Table 3.14 Turning points in the geopolitical field—main carriers and consequences in the twenty-first century

Geopolitical turning points		
Decreasing inequalities in state income	Rising interest rates in emerging and developing countries	Redistribution of geo-economic forces
The spread of the phenomenon of failed states, exceeding the number of those with dictatorial regimes	Income inequalities, civil wars, the "curse of natural resources"	– Risk of delivery and forwarding – Illegal trade – Terrorism
According to key scientists, without corrective action, climate change will become irreversible at some point in the twenty-first century	Greenhouse gas emissions	– Food shortages – More frequent and more drastic natural disasters – Floods in coastal areas
By 2030, food prices will be twice as high as in 2011, and more than half of the world's population will be affected by severe water shortages	Climate change: pollution, changing eating habits, urbanisation	– Social unrest and political protests – Lack of geopolitical stability
India will be the country with the largest population, China will be the largest economy, and the USA will be the richest among the largest economies	Changes in global demography, higher economic growth in emerging countries, technological innovation	– Global redistribution of power – Multipolarity – Geopolitical instability – A "G-zero" world

Source Guillen and Ontiveros [44]

The new world order, called the "G-zero world", is being presented by scientists with increasing frequency. This concept was put forward by Ian Bremmer,[67] on the assumption that no country is strong enough to lead the world in the face of the changes taking place from the level known as G-zero, and a new balance of power will emerge. The EU countries, which are in stagnation, should see the risk of the emergence of new conditions for development in the world, so as to create the basis for the competitiveness of their economies in modern conditions. One of the expansion models, especially in the context of stabilisation and creation of development perspectives for public finance, will be the proposed heterodox approach in PPP. Stronger interference of private entities in the redistribution and allocation function of the state may turn out to be a real chance to emerge from the crisis. Basing the principles of management of public and public-private funds on actual tangible and financial assets (held or acquired in countries where they are still available) may provide a stable basis for assuming a competitive position after the G-zero period. The joint expansion of public and private entities may be one of the possible exit routes from the crisis situation of conventional public finances and provide an opportunity to react in the face of forecast geopolitical changes. Removing the risk implications

[67] Bremmer [47].

for conventional public finances in geopolitical and political areas through the use of heterodox accounting in PPPs should be based on the following:

- reducing the risk of disproportions in the income of the society by applying the principles of corporate social responsibility, which means involving private entities in the redistribution of public income from PPP companies to local communities;
- promoting environmentally responsible infrastructure projects in PPPs;
- improving the quality of public services and their profitability through the implementation of processes of long-term cooperation with private partners within the PPP, based not only on the implementation of infrastructure investments but also on joint management of the generated infrastructure in the long term;
- mitigating the negative effects of political changes in the course of infrastructural investments by applying long-term PPP agreements in a heterodox perspective, where, in addition to the objective of maximising the partner's profit, maintaining a long-term, politically resistant partnership brings measurable financial benefits to society through real financial transfers of the above-mentioned *Niṣāb* value;
- perceiving changes in the formation of new economic and social centres in the world, as well as directing public investment to new markets;
- counteracting permanent migration of the population by offering opportunities for development in own previously conventional economies through obtaining measurable financial benefits, e.g. from knowledge transfer and innovations in emerging markets, within the framework of the implementation of PPP projects based on the heterodox approach.

3.4 Risks and Functions of Islamic Public Finances

The concept of risk in Islam is present in various aspects of the economic life of Muslims, such as religion, psychology, mathematics, statistics and history. The history of risk, based on all these conditions, is described extensively by P. L. Bernstein in his book *Against the Gods: Remarkable Story of Risk.*[68] He pointed out that the concept of risk was contrary to the provisions of many religions, especially in the context of speculation and usury. It has evolved over the centuries in different ways, depending on the political, economic, social and religious situation of the countries, so that all threats could be managed. He divided the history of the risk into three stages. The first one covered the period from antiquity to the Renaissance and was characterised by the recognition of future fate as dependent only on gods of different religions. At that time, the study of finances focused only on describing current phenomena and behaviours of consumers in the economies of those times. Rationalism in the approach to risk analysis was the next stage in the development of this field. Thanks to mathematical tools, the probability of the occurrence for specific future events was started to be determined. Results of scientific work, such as Pascal's, have

[68] Bernstein [48].

led to the development of innovative risk management solutions. The third stage in the evolution of this field began after World War I and was associated, according to Berlin, with uncertainty, which was not always measurable. In his work, the author advocated a reasonable approach to risk, especially in the sphere of public spending, claiming that the reason for contemporary financial crises is the propensity to risk and speculation. Thus, although not explicit, this confirmed the fact that the Islamic financial system, based on capital and not on debt, and free from financial speculation, protects public finances against many areas of risk and uncertainty. The author presents his reflections without giving a clear answer, basing his analysis mainly on historical analysis, trying to indicate how to achieve a balance between the security of financial resources of states, the performance of their functions and development opportunities.[69] The heterodox approach to PPP proposed in this work may be one of the responses to Bernstein's problem.

Like all other financial matters, risk in Islam is based on the *Quran* and is interpreted according to the provisions of the *Shari'ah* law. Although it is an inseparable element of management in the conventional financial system, it is interpreted differently in accordance with the provisions of the *Quran* in Islamic finance. Risk (*gharar*) and gambling and speculation (*maysir*) are prohibited. However, since risk is inevitable, only excessive risk is prohibited.[70] The definition of risk focuses on the primacy of the real economy, based on assets (mainly property, plant and equipment, property rights and knowledge) and the principle of *profit and loss sharing*. Thus, the risk is not the subject of the transaction but is always linked to specific assets and monetary value. The benefits and or disadvantages of an asset cannot be separated from the actual ownership of the asset or the right of disposal over it. The most important principle related to risk management in Islamic finance is the *al.-kharaj bi-I-daman* principle, which means that profit *follows* responsibility.[71] Any reasonable profit (*kharaj*) must result from real responsibility of the entity undertaking business activities. It is therefore important, as emphasised in the provisions of the *Quran*, to make all agreements between partners clear and transparent, defining the scope of responsibilities and duties in an understandable and legible manner. In order to avoid risks in the contract, the following conditions must be met:

[69]Ibid., pp. 15–16.

[70]Obaidullah [49], www.islamiccenter.kau.edu.sa/english/publications/Obaidullah/ifs/ifs, p. 29.

[71]Cattelan [50].

- Each party must be certain of the existence of the object of the transaction and of its price.
- The contract must clearly indicate the characteristics of the subject of the contract and the quantities involved.
- The contract must specify quality indicators for the product or service and the date of delivery.[72]

The subject of the contract cannot be a potential, unspecified object, the occurrence of which is uncertain. For example, the potential harvest of apples on the following day may not be a subject of a purchase agreement; however, hiring of a farmer to harvest apples the following day can be a subject of a contract.

The subject literature rarely analyses risks in the functioning of Islamic public entities. The risk of Islamic financial institution functioning is much more frequently the subject of research. However, from the point of view of the purpose of this monograph and the possibility of using the proposed heterodox approach in selected countries, especially developing countries of sub-Saharan Africa, the functions of public finances in Muslim countries will be first identified. The specific role and functions of the state are key elements of the proposed approach. It is also justified to search for risk areas in the activity of the state, despite the fact that this problem is rarely mentioned in the field of Islamic finance. The beginnings of the science of Islamic statehood date back to the period between the eleventh and fourteenth centuries.[73] As a result, Islam has formed two large groups with different theological visions of the nature and functions of the state. The most numerous group—almost 90%—are the Sunni people. According to them, the state structures result from the logical provisions of *the Quran* and the principles of Islam. The whole of social life remains within the reach of a state which deals not only with religious matters but also with economic, social, political, etc. Most Sunni countries apply the law of Islam administered exclusively by the state. There is also a second group, the Shiites, who reject public authority, and they consider the Prophet Muhammad and imams as the only authorities in Islam. The Imams are the descendants of the Prophet from his daughter Fatima and his uncle brother Ali. At present, they are mainly religious leaders of Muslim countries or individual religious communities. They often have a significant impact on economic policy and an irrefutable authority in the evaluation of religious, social or economic phenomena.

The functions of the state in Islamic finance include:

- functions resulting from the provisions included in the *Quran* and *Sunnah*;
- functions based on *Ijtlhad*;
- functions conferred by the society.[74]

The scope of the objectives in the public economy of Islamic states, based on the provisions of the *Quran*, is to supervise the observance of all the rights set forth

---

[72] Visser [51].

[73] Cf. Lapidus [52].

[74] Nejatullah Siddiqi [53].

by the *Quran*, to apply the law in everyday life, and to administer the affairs of the populace, including the issues of security and defence of the country. *Ijtlhad*, on the other hand, means legal interpretations regarding the creation of new rules, which were not explicitly included in the *Quran*.[75] In a modern approach, scientists within this function deal with legal interpretations of environmental protection, price stability and development of economic activity, promotion of scientific development, building sustainable assets in national economies or providing public services.[76] The state functions conferred by society are based on broad public consultations in the public decision-making process[77] and the promotion of the functions of social well-being as a key objective in management. It is worth to pay attention to the *fard kifaya* function. It includes a set of tasks, the performance of which the state assigns to specific, elected representatives of the society. If they fulfil these tasks, the rest of the society is released from the obligation to carry them out. This applies, for example, to education, defence and environmental control. The most important role in the proceedings of representatives of public administration is to be played by maximisation of social utility, instead of individual one.

The above functions of the state can be interpreted more broadly on the basis of the conventional functions of public finance described earlier and the *Islamic Moral Economy.* This will contribute to a better understanding of similarities and differences in the system of organisation of public administration between the two legal systems. At the same time, it will make it possible to identify specific risk areas in the management of public funds in Islamic countries. Interpenetration of these areas is essential in order to establish long-term cooperation between Islamic entities and conventional ones. The mere understanding of the principles of *Islamic Moral Economy* is insufficient to build a model of cooperation between public and private entities, coming from diverse social, economic and religious orders. The definition of risk management principles in Islamic finance is a key complement to the proposed approach, which can in practice contribute to wider investor cooperation in emerging or developing markets.

Categorising the functions of public finances, Islam presents the three basic functions mentioned above. In modern Islamic economies, each of them is connected with the proper allocation of financial resources, their distribution, stabilisation of economies and development of societies in individual countries. Therefore, the generation of public revenues and the execution of expenditures are subordinated to these activities. We should pay attention to the primacy of the religious principles of *the Quran* and the *Shari'ah* law, which determine the conduct of public administration. Such a basis for public decision-making does not exist in conventional economies, wherein the vast majority of countries the separation of public administration from taking into account the influence of religion on the management processes in the public sphere is observed. A key paradigm in public governance in Muslim countries is also the observance of principles of just distribution and control over the

[75] *Nowoczesność, Europa, Islam. Religia a dylematy obywatelstwa i wykluczenia*, p. 245.

[76] Siddiqi [54].

[77] Quran, XLII: 38.

disparities of income redistribution and the wealth of members of society.[78] This is achieved through a sound fiscal policy, which allows for an adequate allocation of state resources for the creation of public and private goods. At the same time, the fiscal function protects the economies of individual countries against inflation in situations of reduced demand as a result of high taxes. The basic type of tax income is the *zakat* tax. It is based on the principles of *the Quran*, and it concerns believers in Islam. Those who do not believe in Allah are also obliged to bear the tax burden, but in other forms (it is not a tax in the sense of conventional finance). These are, among others, taxes paid for avoiding the *zakat*, taxes imposed as a result of the necessity of changes in the macroeconomic trends, taxes on harmful consumption of specific products, taxes aimed at preventing environmental pollution, taxes on defence improvement.[79] If the tax and fee revenues are insufficient to meet the needs of the community, it is assumed that the sources of public revenue may also be:

- public loans for specific investments;
- PPP agreements using the BOT formula, i.e. build, operate, transfer, where the public is operated, and public services are provided together with a private partner;
- *Waqf system*—two types of *waqf* are known: foundations for religious or public purposes—mosques, libraries, hospitals, cemeteries, bridges—and family *waqfs*, which include provisions for the poor.[80]

Funds as part of *zakat* are often generated obligatorily, for example in Saudi Arabia, Libya, Malaysia, Yemen and other countries; it also forms the basis of activities of *zakat* government agencies, for example in Lebanon, Bahrain, Egypt, Saudi Arabia or the United Arab Emirates. For example, in 2011, the zakat fund of the United Arab Emirates distributed the equivalent of USD 229 million, including USD 55 million to the poor, USD 45 million to students, USD 29 million to the sick, over USD 23 million to university students.[81] In the light of the analysis for this monograph, it is important to point out that *zakat* funds can be managed both by public and by private entities. It is often pointed out that the effectiveness of redistribution of funds within the framework of *zakat* by private entities is higher, as evidenced by such funds organised in the USA, UK or Indonesia.[82] This would thus be one of the areas for the attractiveness of the heterodox approach, where the redistribution of public funds by public-private partnerships is more advantageous than their direct distribution to the public.

[78] R. Kłosowicz, op. cit., p. 15.

[79] Dr. A.-R. Yousri, *The Role of Taxation, Expenditure and Debt in an Islamic Economy*, University of Alexandria, Egypt, pp. 33–35.

[80] Elements of civil law, with particular reference to property law, in the light of Islamic law, cf: *Problemy własności w ujęciu historyczno-prawnym*, E. Kozerska, P. Sadowski, A. Szymański (eds.) Opole 2008, pp. 47–56.

[81] J. Bremer, *Zakat and Economic Justice: Emerging International Models and their Relevance for Egypt*, Takaful 2013, 3rd Annual Conference on Arab Philanthropy and Civic Engagement, June 4–6, Tunis, Tunisia, p. 58.

[82] J. Bremer, *Zakat and Economic Justice...*, p. 69.

From the point of view of the Islamic entity, the risk of gaining less and less income from *zakat* and the risk of lower redistribution of the funds to the needy are negligible. This is mainly due to the fact that the *zakat* imperative is based on the *Quran* and the *Shari'ah* law, which constitute an unquestionable basis of management for every follower of Islam. Moreover, the avoidance of such a levy has unpleasant consequences in terms of serious penalties and the exclusion from the community of the believers.

The rule that at least 51% of shares in companies must be owned by nationals of many Islamic countries, including the UAE, is also significant in terms of public revenue. Thus, the majority of profit levels are retained in the country and constitute the source of subsequent investments. As the market data show, this rule does not limit the possibility of influx of foreign investors in: the data of the Ministry of Economy of the United Arab Emirates from January 2014 show that foreign direct investments increased by 20% in relation to the previous year and reached the level of USD 12 billion, which accounts for nearly 40% of all foreign direct investment in all Gulf countries.[83] In addition, there is income tax, but it is imposed only on branches of foreign banks (20% of taxable income) and all companies in the gas and fuel industries. This represents a significant source of budgetary revenue. Income tax rates in these industries range between 55 and 85% of operational profits of such companies; however, they vary depending on individual agreements.[84] VAT has not been introduced yet, although its introduction is under consideration for 2018.[85] Duties on imported products are generally applied at a rate of 5%, with the exception of tobacco and alcohol, the import of which is much more expensive.[86] However, the largest group of income in the budget is constituted by different types of fees related to registration and licensing of business activity, constituting in total nearly 62% of the total revenue.[87] The risk of significant changes in tax income is therefore not high. Conservative behaviour of the authorities in retaining the majority of the profits from investments in the hands of the state and its citizens guarantees stable levels of budget revenues. The attractive tax system in most Islamic countries generally excludes the application of personal income tax, which makes it more resilient to the adverse risks of demographic change. The local community operates in optimal "tax" conditions so that they do not need to migrate to other areas. To sum up, it must be said that the performance of a fiscal function in Islamic finance countries is not the main activity of the state. The instruments of this policy include various types of fees and selected types of taxes, with particular emphasis on the *zakat* fee. The risk of erroneous fiscal policies resulting in the deterioration of the country's economic situation and population outflows to other countries is insignificant. It should, therefore, be noted

[83]UAE Ministry of Economy, The Annual Economic Report 2014, 22nd edition, p. 34.

[84]www.quora.com/How-does-the-UAE-government-generate-revenue-without-any-income-tax.

[85]www2.deloitte.com/content/dam/Deloitte/global/Documents/Tax/dttl-tax-unitedarabemirateshighlights-2016.pdf.

[86]www.gov.uk. Accessed on 04.09.2016.

[87]www.oxfordbusinessgroup.com/analysis/income-breakdown-look-government's-main-revenue-streams.

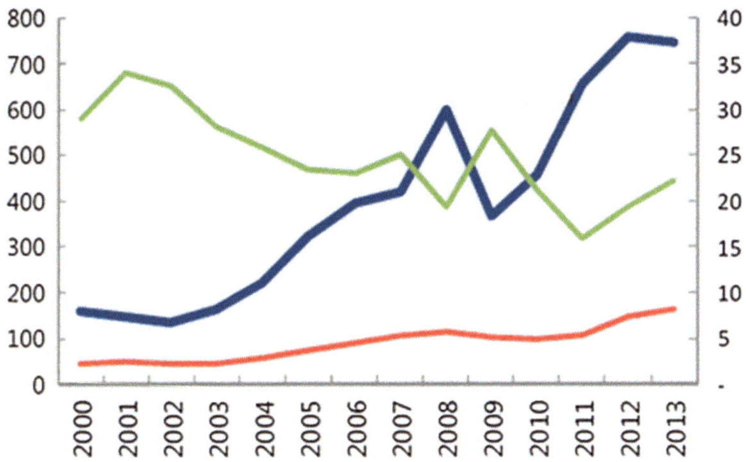

Fig. 3.1 Fiscal revenues of GCC countries. Legend: blue—GCC countries, red—revenues without oil industry, green—the stake of revenues without oil industry in total revenues. *Source* T. Callen, R. Cherif, F. Hasanov, A. Hegazy, P. Khandelwal, *Economic Diversification in the GCC: Past, Present, and Future*, IMF Staff Discussion Note, December 2014, SDN/14/12, p. 17

that perhaps the conventional system of tax revenue could be replaced by other sources of revenue. In the case of Islamic countries, these are mainly different types of fees associated with the production of certain types of goods and proceeds from shares in companies in key industries. Again, the income of the state budget depends on the actual products or services produced and the economic result of the companies involved in their production. The multiplication of state resources takes place through production activities based on generating an increasing value of real assets and not mainly through the fiscal system. Investment needs are then met with their own material resources and often within the framework of sustainable cooperation with private investors. This contributes to a small share of external financing, including debt financing, in the development of state infrastructure. This is evidenced by the levels of public debt of countries based on Islamic finance indicated in the previous chapter.

The level of public income of selected countries based on Islamic finance is presented in Figs. 3.1 and 3.2.

The data presented in Figs. 3.1 and 3.2 show a key risk area for the Gulf states' government revenue collection, which is the lack of diversification of their revenue sources to a greater extent. The share of non-oil industry government revenues in Gulf GDP is on average 30% of total GDP, and in some countries, such as Bahrain and the United Arab Emirates, it is below 20% of GDP. Fiscal revenues in all Gulf countries are between USD 700 and 800 billion in 2012 and 2013. These include income from non-oil processing industry, which represents less than USD 200 billion

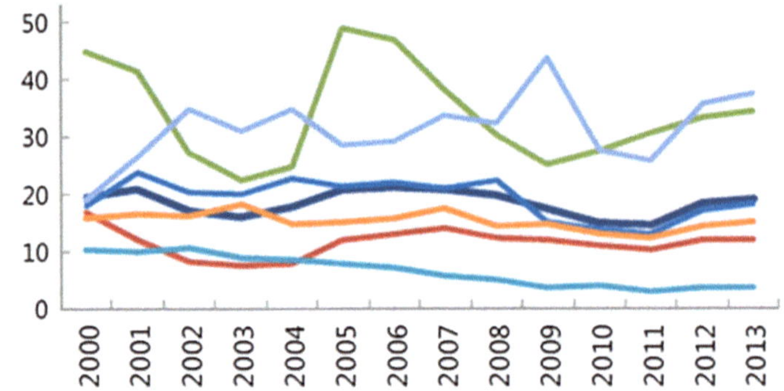

Fig. 3.2 Revenue of GCC countries excluding oil industry. Legend: dark blue—GCC countries, green—Kuwait, light blue—Qatar, darker blue—Saudi Arabia, ocean blue—Bahrain, orange line—Oman. *Source* T. Callen, R. Cherif, F. Hasanov, A. Hegazy, P. Khandelwal, *Economic Diversification in the GCC: Past, Present, and Future*, IMF Staff Discussion Note, December 2014, SDN/14/12, p. 17

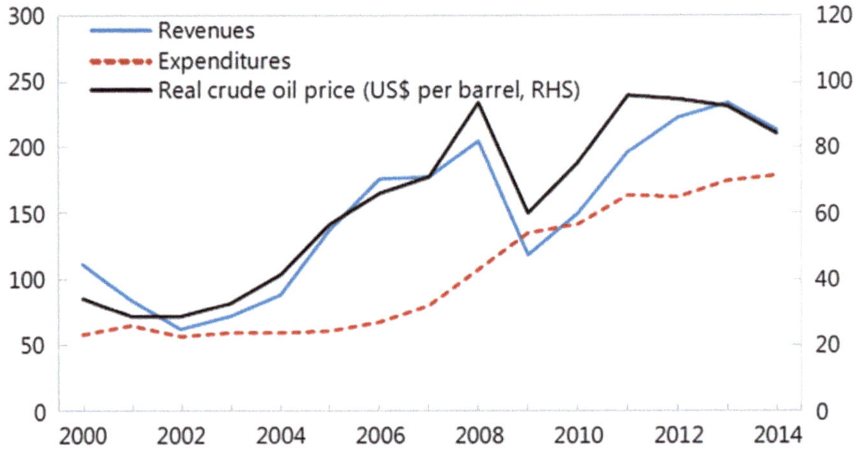

Fig. 3.3 Total revenue, expenditure and oil price in 2000–2014 (in real AED billions). Legend: blue—revenue, red—expenditure, black—oil per barrel in US dollars, *Y*-axis: billions of AED. *Source Qatar. Selected Issues*, IMF Country Report No. 15/87, March 2015, p. 4

in all Gulf countries.[88] In the vast majority of these countries, the manufacturing and processing of oil and gas are the main sources of income. It is worth noting, on the example of the United Arab Emirates (UAE), that the fall in oil prices has had exactly the same impact on public spending in 2009 (Fig 3.3).

[88] The Gulf Cooperation Council (GCC) was established in May 1981 to facilitate cooperation in the fields of economy and security. The GCC controls 45% of the world's oil reserves and 20% of the world's gas reserves. The Council comprises the following states: Saudi Arabia, United Arab Emirates, Bahrain, Qatar, Oman and Kuwait. www.persiangulffund.com/gulf-area/gulf-cooperation-council/.

It is therefore a sign of the key importance of this mining and crude oil processing industry in shaping the state budget. In the following years, observing this threat, attempts were made to diversify income sources.

It is also worth emphasising the specificity of the redistributive function in public Islamic finance. It is based, like a fiscal function, on the records of the *Quran*, but also on the second pillar of the state function in Islam, i.e. on the *Ijtlhad*. This is the name for the interpretations of the *Quran* by Islamic scientists, which allow for the development of a proper policy for the distribution of funds to the public. The funds to be distributed by the state come from all public revenue, including that from participation in undertakings, *zakat*, taxes, charges and penalties. The manner of their distribution is subject to the provisions of the *Quran* described above, preferably in the highest possible amounts for each of the entitled social groups. A significant risk in the performance of this function can be seen in public-private structures. A private investor, especially one from a different economic system, would be interested in clearly defining in advance the groups of persons and entities entitled to receive financial transfers, even if in amounts above the value of *Niṣāb*, the maximum expected profit from the activity. From their point of view, the risk may consist of an indirect participation of a conventional private partner in financing often broadly understood military or religious goals in Muslim countries. The effects of such financing are not always consistent with the beliefs or principles of management of conventional entities in their countries of origin. The main types of public expenditure, as well as the manifestations of the distribution function, which may be financed from the previously presented sources, are as follows:

- covering the needs of all recipients of *zakat*;
- direct or indirect investments in favour of the poor, needy and pilgrims;
- subsidising micro- and small enterprises in financial difficulty or with high levels of debt;
- ensuring and maintaining internal security and the rule of law;
- maintenance and operation of the *hesba* system—this system ensures that market actors do not engage in unauthorised operations contrary to *Shari'ah* law, but in no way interfere with private business or market mechanisms (it is often based on the activity of individuals, who are supposed to perform the function of quasi-police, observing impropriety or violation of religious rights, and inform the authorities about this is the case).[89]

A specific area of state function in Islamic countries is the function of growth. The literature on the subject of conventional public finance does not distinguish between the functions of stimulating development. However, from the point of view of emerging and developing countries, this function should be highlighted. It is also a key aspect of public finance management for public administrations in Islamic countries. This is due to the limited role of the fiscal function in the light of the small number of fiscal instruments that are a tool for shaping the welfare of Islamic

[89] B. Whitaker, *Arabs without God: Atheism and freedom of belief in the Middle East*, self-published, 2014.

economies. Other stimuli for development are being sought, which are mainly considered to be investments by private entities. These investments are treated as an essential element of the state's function to ensure the efficiency of the economy.[90] In order to perform the growth function and due to the insignificant importance of the fiscal function, a policy of wider state intervention in market relations is also called for. A manifestation of such a policy is the fact that the state has control over strategic industries, mainly those based on deposits and other natural resources, which are key assets of the state budget. Moreover, government subsidies for innovative entrepreneurs and micro- and small enterprises are also applied. Creating favourable investment conditions for foreign investors is an important element of this function of states and building developing economies. This is often done through the creation of special economic zones, offering tax breaks and exemptions, but also the possibility of conducting business activity by entities fully owned by a foreign investor. A key condition for foreign investors to gain access to these zones is that the value of their investments must be maintained and that the employment of local workers must be maintained over the long term. It is important for investors to demonstrate long-term financial and operational plans of such an undertaking and manifestations of innovativeness of solutions beneficial for the local community or the whole country. The conditions of capital outflow from such investments are also precisely defined, where it may be partially limited by the necessity of further reinvestment in the infrastructure and constant transfer of knowledge to the enterprise located in the zone. In the United Arab Emirates alone, 17,000 companies operate in 34 special zones, Saudi Arabia has 5 such zones, 6 can be found in Oman, and 6 can be found in Bahrain.[91]

Another function of Islamic public finances is to allocate and stabilise the economy. The former, as in the case of conventional finance, is related to the proper allocation of public funds and was analysed in this publication as part of the presentation of the theory of public and social choice. The most important tool for the stabilisation function, on the other hand, is a balanced state budget. It is worth to draw attention to the issues of approaching the budget deficit in Islamic finance in the face of the so-called *maslaha* (public interest), which generates further risk areas in the functioning of public administration. Islamic economies seek to finance the debt budget deficit, but on the basis of the principle of profit and loss sharing. Fiscal gaps are not expected to be covered by tax revenues, which are low in both source and value. A loan to finance public expenditure is justified if it is linked to a specific investment which, in the long term, will bring tangible benefits to society, such as the construction of irrigation systems, dams, roads and hospitals. These benefits are often demonstrated in terms of increased social welfare and not in terms of tangible positive financial flows, as in the case of private investment. Such financing does not entail any cost for the state budget in the form of interest (*riba*). The maintenance

[90] R. Kłosowicz, op. cit., p. 17.

[91] Assessing Investment Policies of Member Countries of the GULF Cooperation Council, MENA OECD Investment Programme, presented on 5 April 2011 at a conference in Abu Dhabi, http://www.oecd.org/mena/competitiveness/PreliminaryassessmentGCCinvtpolicies.pdf.

of debt levels in the budgets of Islamic economies must be based on the following principles of *Shari'ah* law and real market conditions:

- Interest on issued bonds must be retained.
- All contractual debts have to be repaid.
- It is not possible to repay debt immediately.[92]

A private bondholder should have the option of accepting the return on a public investment based on profit and loss sharing. Otherwise, lenders have to wait until the loans have been repaid in accordance with the provisions of the agreement, but no interest is paid to them. Thus, when loans to the public sector appear, they are repaid either by the return on investments made in cooperation with private entities (profit due on shares held in companies) or by the repayment of debt within a predetermined period of time, without this being linked to profits from a specific investment project. This is similar to the income bond instrument, but relatively rarely used by conventional public entities. These tools generate specific sources of risk for the public entity within the framework of *sukuk*. In order to identify them, it is worth paying attention to the course of the transaction on *sukuk* and the most important risk areas for each of the parties (Fig. 3.4).

The course of the *mudarabah sukuk* process:

- The SPV issuer issues a *sukuk* certificate, which constitutes an indivisible share in the underlying assets of the project. These shares also represent the right to periodically pay out the expected return on *mudarabah* profit to the issuer of the certificate.
- Investors buy *sukuk* certificates and pay the SPV issuer the so-called amount of the principal. The issuer of the SPV certificates makes a declaration of confidence in the revenues (and in any assets or shares of *mudarabah*) and thus acts as a proxy on behalf of the investor.
- The issuer of the certificate in the SPV (as *Rab al Maal*) and the originator (as *mudarib*) enter into a *mudarabah* agreement. On the basis of the agreement, the issuer of the SPV certificate pays back the principal amount due to the *mudarabah* enterprise for a purpose in accordance with *Shari'ah* law.
- The originator (*mudarib*) agrees on the basis of the *mudarabah* agreement to contribute their management know-how to the *mudarabah* company, operated in accordance with *Shari'ah* law and responsible for the management of the ready-made contribution-in-kind.
- The issuer of the SPV certificate brings to the *mudarabah* company cash, knowledge and skills of managing the company in order to generate profit from the main amount.
- The profits generated by the *mudarabah* company are distributed between the issuer of the SPV (*Rab al Maal*) and the originator in accordance with the profit distribution proportions set out in the *mudarabah* agreement but calculated for the duration of the *mudarabah* company.

---

[92]M. Siddiqi, op. cit., p. 58.

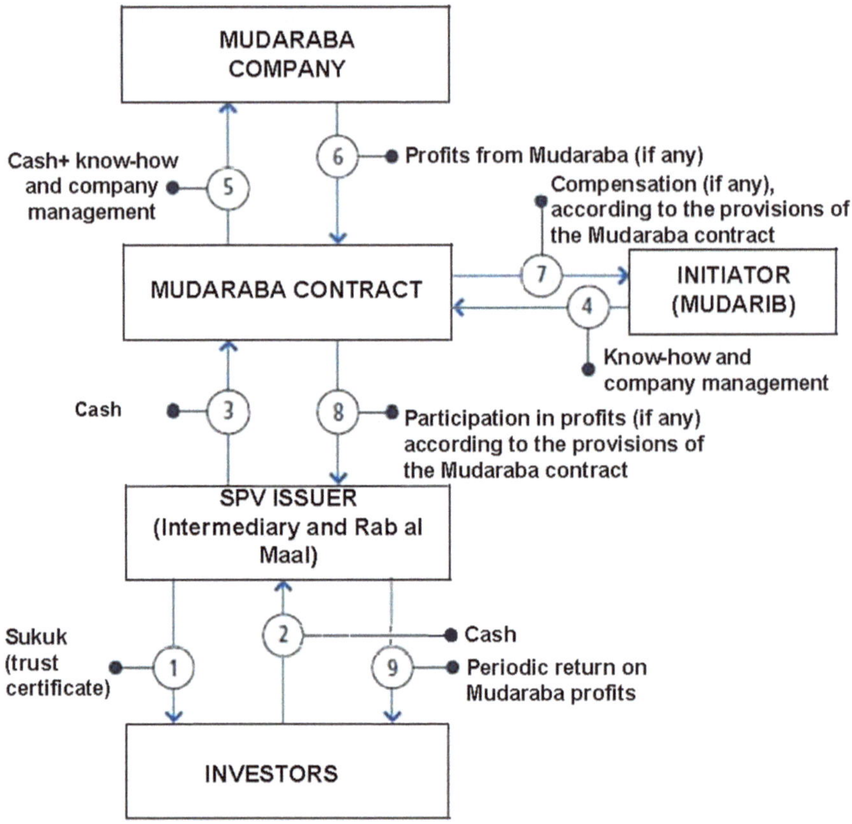

Fig. 3.4 Structure of a *mudaraba sukuk*. *Source* www.islamicbanker.com/education/sukuk-al-mudaraba; *Dubai International Financial Centre Sukuk Guidebook*, Clifford Chance, pp. 28–29; *Handbook of Islamic Banking*, ed. K. Hassan, M. Lewis; Edward Elgar, Original Reference, Cheltenham, p. 230

- In addition to the profit-sharing component, the originator (*mudarib*) may be entitled to remuneration for providing its management knowledge and skills if the profit realised by the *mudarabah* company exceeds the expected return.
- The issuer of the SPV certificate receives the *mudarabah* profits and retains them as a proxy on behalf of the investor.
- The issuer of the SPV certificate, as a proxy, pays any periodic rate of return to investors using the *mudarabah* profits received under the agreement.

As part of the *sukuk* emission, the following risk areas should be taken into account. The risk of the rate of return is significantly limited due to the use of Islamic financial instruments and the predetermined level of the rate of return on investment, which is based on the level of return on assets held. According to *Shari'ah* rules, the certificate issue rules should not contain references to fixed or variable percentages,

LIBOR, etc., but only indicate the expected rate of return on investment and its distribution to investors and managers. Another risk area is the risk of loss, which is highlighted more strongly in the case of the *sukuk* certificate. Holders of such financial instruments are closely connected with the course of the investment, without any particular possibility of influencing its course, and therefore they are exposed to the risk of failure of the project. Within the framework of lawful *Shari'ah* rules, there is no possibility of using guarantees, e.g. government guarantees, return of the base amount to the investor. Therefore, certificate holders expose themselves to market risk, where in case of failure of the investment project, the underlying assets can be sold at a price lower than the initial investment value.[93] In *sukuk* transactions, there is also an exchange rate risk, manifested in adverse changes in exchange rates, in currencies in which, on the one hand, assets of an investment project may be valued and, on the other hand, certificates may be issued. However, it is considered that the use of a *sukuk* emission can provide good protection against exchange rate fluctuations in the currencies when several issues of a certificate use different currencies for their valuation.[94] Another area of risk in the process of issuing the *sukuk* certificate is the lack of compliance with *Shari'ah* law.[95] The sanction for non-compliance with *Shari'ah* rules concerns the investor's reputation loss and may be a significant obstacle in future potential development of such investor's projects.[96] A particularly important area of risk is liquidity risk, especially when it is not possible to use, for example, short-term current loans in Islamic finance. Only Malaysia uses short-term loans between banks, applying the principle of profit loss sharing; however, this construction is not used in any other country.[97] The solution to the liquidity problem, with the use of the instrument in question, has been proposed by the Bahraini government, which has issued a certificate in a specific investment project, based on various payback periods of these certificates in, e.g., 3-month and 6-month periods.[98] Another risk is the assets, on which the investment and the issuance of certificates are based. Due to the need to observe *Shari'ah* rules, some types of assets will be excluded as impossible to use. The most frequently accepted source of income is real estate, which in the current situation of significant fluctuations in the value of real estate on the real estate markets, especially conventional ones, makes it difficult to use it as a base for investment projects and issuing *sukuk* certificates.[99] The inability to insure such assets is another source of risk and potential loss for investors in natural disaster situations. Another risk, this time legal, may be broadly understood

---

[93] Tariq and Humayon [55].

[94] M. R. El Shazly, *Sukuk Structures, Profiles and Risk*, Columbia College, 2004, www.isfin.net, p. 8.

[95] A. Tariq, D. Humayon, op. cit., p. 210.

[96] AAOIFI Standards 2008.

[97] Cf. M. R. Ab Aziz, "Islamic Banking and Finance in Malaysia", *System, Issues and Challenges*, University Sains Islam Malaysia, 2013, pp. 147–173.

[98] J. Karwowski, "Sukuk—islamskie certyfikaty inwestycyjne", [in:] *Finanse: nowe wyzwania teorii i praktyki. Rynki finansowe*, ed. K. Jajuga, Wrocław University of Economics, Wrocław 2011, p. 233.

[99] Al Bitar [56].

within the framework of a *sukuk* emission. On the one hand, the investment and issuance of a certificate must be in compliance with the law, but at the same time, such compliance should also appear in all contracts used as part of the investment financed in the issue of a certificate. Hence, it is difficult to interpret the provisions of individual agreements and their compliance with *Shari'ah* law, on the one hand, and the law of the country of origin on the other hand.[100] Other areas of risk under the issue of a *sukuk* certificate are the following:

- risk of lack of qualified staff in the use of Islamic financial instruments;
- risk of limited comparison data in transactions of *sukuk* certificate issue;
- risk related to the proper application of tax rules in a situation when investment assets are located in one country, investors come from another country and the SPV special purpose vehicle is located in yet another country;
- lack of standardisation of the issue certificates within the *sukuk* framework may create the risk of higher costs of the initial organisation of the issue itself;
- risk of lack of diversification of transactions within *sukuk*, where most of the process is related to real estate and takes place mostly in Gulf countries and Malaysia.

Despite the presented area of risk, issues of *sukuk* certificates are dominated by public, government and local government institutions, mainly in Malaysia and the Gulf countries. Their share in the total number of issues is over 50%, and in 2009 it rose to nearly 54%.[101]

In addition to the identified risk areas, selected environmental and demographic factors, as described by M.F. Guillen and E. Ontiveros, should also be taken into account in the performance of state functions in Muslim countries (for more details, see Sect. 2.3).[102] Both the types and the impacts of ecosystem factors, in countries such as Gulf, on public finances will be different than in conventional public finance countries. The most important environmental risk areas are: sufficient water extraction and desalination, stable power supply, wastewater treatment and waste disposal. All of these are the dominant spheres of activity of public administration, which is responsible for their provision. Economic policies in these areas have not kept pace with the strong and rapid development of the Gulf countries. It is estimated that water resources, e.g. in the United Arab Emirates, from local sources of water and from the desalination system would last for 4 days.[103] Moreover, together with the strong urbanisation of the country, the development of the mining industry and the continued operation of desalination systems, insufficient energy is an important problem for the administrative authorities. Supply disruptions are not very acute at the moment, but the problem is growing. These countries will most probably be forced to develop nuclear energy sources, which, in the face of the current terrorist

---

[100] Zawya report on Sukuk www.zawya.com. December 2016.

[101] Ibid.

[102] *Global Turning Points: Understanding the Challenges for Business in the 21st Century*, Cambridge University Press, Cambridge, 2012.

[103] Report on water management in the world, www.unic.un.org.pl, prepared by the UN Information Centre, March 2003, accessed on 10.06.2016.

Table 3.15 Imbalances in demographic and national wealth resources

Country	Population in 2010 (in millions)		Labour force		National wealth resources (per capita of the country)		
	Citizens	Non-citizens	Citizens (%)	Non-citizens (%)	Oil (in millions of barrels)	Gas (in billions of m^3)	SWF (in USD per inhabitant of the country)
Bahrain	0.51	0.54	36.1	63.9	…	0.00037	16.852
Kuwait	1.04	2.43	16.9	83.1	0.98	0.00173	284.615
Oman	2.39	1.02	28.7	71.3	0.02	0.00029	3.431
Qatar	0.22	1.46	5.7	94.3	1.18	0.11500	386.364
Saudi Arabia	20.94	7.75	50.5	49.5	0.13	0.0038	22.818
United Arab Emirates	0.95	7.24	4.2	95.8	1.03	0.00632	759.053
Gulf countries	26.05	20.45	38.3	61.7	0.19	0.00161	61.313

Source For the population: Al Khouri; for the workforce: the Kataru—the Qatar Statistics Authority; access 2011, for the year 2009. For UAE, the authors made calculations on the basis of "The UAE's National Bureau of Statistics Labor Force Figures for 2005" and its latest population forecast for 2010, all others—Routledge (2009) compilation from official sources from 2002 to 2006; for energy reserves: BP Statistical Review (2011); for an estimate of the value of state assets under active management: SWF Institute (2011)

movements, may represent another risk area in their economies. Another environmental threat for most of the analysed countries is the production of waste and its disposal. Existing entities dealing with this area accept twice the amount of waste every day, compared to the maximum amount they are able to process per day.[104] Thus, these difficulties pose a major challenge to public authorities, where private investors are increasingly providing solutions to them by proposing certain types of long-term economic partnership in order to operate in these areas and mitigate the risk of these escalating problems. Another aspect of a proper public economy in Islamic countries is the identification of and protection against demographic problems. Again, they have a different course than in conventional economies. Current trends are best illustrated by the data presented in Table 3.15.

These figures show that there has been a rapid demographic change in many of the countries of the region, which are characterised by a majority share of the foreign population in relation to the inhabitants of these countries. Already, the rates of foreigner participation among the employed, e.g. in the United Arab Emirates,

[104]*New York Times*, October 28, 2010, page B1 of the New York edition with the headline: "Rapid Growth in Dubai Outstrips Its Resources".

are reaching the level of 95%. From the point of view of the performance of the state function, this may be a key risk area. This threat results mainly from the loss of national identity, especially religious identity, and multiculturalism of society as a consequence of such strong globalisation, as well as the loss of competitiveness of their own human resources in the face of much cheaper labour from outside the region. Another significant demographic risk in the region is the increasing life expectancy of the population and the growing number of elderly people.[105] This is another challenge for economic policymaking, especially in the area of social security, including medical care, for the growing group of elderly people. It is therefore difficult to predict the demographic trends of such a diverse society in the long term. This is a particular phenomenon on a global scale, where over 90% of the employees in the economy are immigrants. Thus, the development of a sustainable pension system could prove significantly hampered. The lack of national affinity of the employees to the country in which they are employed makes it impossible to predict the scope of migration of this population or their willingness to remain in the existing pension and healthcare system until retirement.

Summarising the presented public financial functions in *Islamic Moral Economy* and the turning points in global economies, presented in Chap. 2.3, one can mention the following areas of risk in the management of public funds of states based on Islamic finances:

- risk of dependence of the state budget revenues on revenues from strategic sectors: production and processing of crude oil, gas and other natural resources;
- risk of avoidance of *zakat*, as well as other levies and fees;
- the risk of excessive state interference in the market by maintaining majority shareholdings in companies in key industries;
- the risk of difficulties in attracting private investors for minority shareholdings in companies with increased state ownership;
- the risk of creating too many economic zones;
- risk of over-subsidisation of selected companies;
- risk in *sukuk*;
- environmental risks, such as large water shortages, insufficient cultivated land and environmental pollution;
- risk of a shortage of qualified staff and basic staff;
- the risk of excessive stratification of society and the emergence of significant inequalities in household income and in their access to public products and services;
- the risk of excessive bureaucracy in the face of an extensive system of state offices and agencies and the participation of state partners.

From the point of view of both the Islamic public administration and private investors, the proposed heterodox approach to PPPs can provide an important security for many of the identified main areas of risk for the implementation of state

[105]"Aging in the UAE and Services Available for the Elderly: Structured Interviews with Experts in Field", *Policy Brief* 34, Dubai School of Government, February 2013, p. 3.

functions based on Islamic finance. The heterodox model of PPP, by combining public and private management objectives, introduces transparent co-responsibility for the outcome of management at each stage. It disseminates the idea that those who receive measurable benefits also bear the risk associated with their lack (profit loss sharing). Since many of the areas of public activity that have hitherto been carried out under the new approach can be transposed onto a public-private entity, the latter will mainly bear the risk. At the same time, the provision of public services or their production will have to ensure that the public interest is safeguarded, but at an acceptable level of return for investors. Investors will optimise their profits to a predetermined value, and the public entity will maximise the welfare function of society by redistributing to the public and private financial surpluses in excess of the planned financial results. The interpretation of risk areas in the performance of the functions of the state of the conventional and Islamic systems, as well as in the structures of PPP, enabled the creation of a PPP model in a heterodox perspective, based on the interpenetration of selected principles from each of the orders.

References

1. Kaczmarek TT (2006) Ryzyko i zarządzanie ryzykiem: Ujęcie interdyscyplinarne 2nd edn. Difin, p 51
2. Bochenek M (2012) Ryzyko i niepewność w naukach ekonomicznych. *Ekonomia* [Economics] 4(21). Wrocław University of Economics, Wrocław, p 51
3. Knight FH (1921) Risk, uncertainty and profit. Hart Schaffner & Marx Houghton Mifflin Co., Boston, MA. https://www.econlib.org/library/Knight/knRUP.html?chapter_num=2#book-reader
4. Arrow KJ (1979) Eseje o teorii ryzyka. PWN, Warsaw, pp 15–97
5. Miller MH, Modigliani F (1958) The cost of capital, corporation finance and the theory of investment. Am Economy Rev 48(3):261–297
6. Wiliamson OE (2000) The new institutional economics: taking stock, looking ahead. J Econ Lit 38:597
7. Klimczak MK (2008) Dylematy ujęcia ryzyka w teorii ekonomii. Acta Universitatis Lodziensis, Folia Oeconomica, Lodz 221:364
8. Kowalczyk M (2001) Zarządzanie ryzykiem w project finance. National Bank of Poland, Department of Analysis and Research, Warsaw, p 17. www.nbp.pl/publikacje/materialy_i_studia/137.pdf
9. Szumlicz T (2016) O niedostatecznej ochronie prawnej jako ryzyku społecznym. Wiadomości Ubezpieczeniowe [Insurance News] 1:54
10. Gruszka B, Zawadzka Z (1992) Ryzyko w działalności bankowej: Zabezpieczenia systemowe. SGH, Warsaw
11. Jajuga K (2007) Zarządzanie ryzykiem. PWN, Warsaw, p 13
12. Frank H (1986) Project financing: ein Verfahren zur finanziellen Absicherung des Unternehmenswachstums. Service Fachverlag of the Vienna University of Economics, pp 86–87
13. Hupe M (1995) Steuerung und Kontrolle internationaler Projektfinanzierungen. Peter Lang, Frankfurt am Main, p 47
14. Tiong R (1990) BOT projects: risk and securities. Constr Manage Econ 8:316–320
15. Beidleman CR (1990) On allocating risk: the essence of project finance. Sloan Manage Rev 1:48–51

16. Woody W, Pourian H (1992) Risk assessment and options in project finance. Project Manage J 23(4):21–28
17. Woodward D (1992) Risk management of BOOT projects. Project 3:10–11
18. Walker C, Smith AJ (1995) Privatized infrastructure: the build operate transfer approach. Thomas Telford Ltd., London, pp 143–158
19. Finnerty JD (1996) Project financing: asset based engineering. Wiley, New York, pp 40–50
20. Merna T, Njiru C (1998) Financing and managing infrastructure projects. Euromoney Publications, Jersey, pp 111–117
21. Estache A, Strong J (2000) The rise, the fall, and the emerging recovery of project finance in transport. World Bank Working Papers no 2385, pp 8–9
22. Lam KC, Chow WS (1999) The significance of financial risks in BOT procurement. Building Res Info 27(2):84–95
23. Williams CA Jr, Smith ML, Young PC (2002) Zarządzanie ryzykiem a ubezpieczenia. PWN, Warsaw, p 51
24. Owsiak S (2001) Finanse publiczne: Teoria i praktyka. PWN, Warsaw, pp 202–206
25. Musgrave RC, Musgrave PB (1980) Public finance in theory and practice. McGrew Hill Book Company, p XVII
26. Boć J, Błaś A, Jeżewski J (2013) Nauka administracji. Kolonia Limited, Wrocław
27. Rotberg RJ (2003) When states fail: causes and consequences. University Press Princeton, New Jersey
28. Walasik A (2008) Redystrybucyjna funkcja finansów publicznych w ujęciu teoretycznym. UE Katowice, p 12
29. Filipowicz L, Opawski K (1992) Teoria wyboru publicznego wybrane koncepcje badawcze. Ekonomista 3:378–379
30. Jensen N (2008) Political risk, democratic institutions, and foreign direct investment. J Politics 70:1040–1052
31. Cole H, English W (1991) Expropriation and direct investment. J Int Econ 30:201–227
32. Thomas J, Worrall T (1994) Foreign direct investment and the risk of expropriation. Rev Econ Stud 61:81–108
33. Becker GS (1983) A theory of competition among pressure groups for political influence. Q J Econ 98(3):371–400
34. Buchanan JM, Tullock G (2004) The calculus of consent: the logical foundation of constitutional democracy. University of Michigan Press, Ann Arbor, p 190
35. Musgrave RA (1959) The theory of public finance: a study in public economy. McGraw Hill, New York, p 5
36. Olson M (1977) The logic of collective action: public goods and the theory of groups. Harvard University Press, Cambridge, MA
37. Klimczak B (2001) Teoretyczne podstawy badania działań grup interesu na rzecz ładu rynkowego. In: Klimczak B (ed), Samorząd gospodarczy i zawodowy w procesie powstawania ładu rynkowego, Wrocław, pp 11–64
38. Galor Z (2010) Socjologiczno-własnościowy sens "problemu gapowicza": stosunki lumpenwłasności w Polsce. In: Galor Z (ed), Odmiany życia społecznego współczesnej Polski, instytucje-polityka-kultura. Naukowe WSN Humanities and Journalism in Poznán, Poznań, pp 63–78
39. Stiglitz JE (2000) Economics of the public sector, 3rd edn. W.W. Norton &Company, pp 154–155
40. Dylewski M, Filipiak B (2010) Ryzyko w finansach i bankowości. Warsaw, Difin, p 31
41. Kumpiałowska A (2011) Skuteczne zarządzanie ryzykiem a kontrola zarządcza w sektorze publicznym. CeDeWu, p 17
42. Jastrzębska M (2015) Zarządzanie—odejście normatywne do zagadnienia pod względem procesów decyzyjcyjnych i ryzyka. Finanse Komunalne [Regional Chambers of Accounts Monthly] 1–2:72–78
43. Nagji B, Tuff G (2012) How to manage an innovation portfolio. Harvard Business Review Polska, p 46

44. Guillen MF, Ontiveros E (2012) Global turning points: understanding the challenges for business in the 21st century. Cambridge University Press, Cambridge pp 150–152
45. Karwowski J (1997) Operacje zagraniczne banków centralnych. Wróclaw University of Economics, Poznań, pp 53–54
46. Konopczak M (2014) Ocena wpływu zmian poziomu rezerw walutowych na premię za ryzyko kredytowe Polski: wykorzystanie metody roszczeń warunkowych. Bank i Kredyt 45(5):469
47. Bremmer I (2012) Every nation for itself: winner and losers in a G-zero world. Penguin-Portfolio
48. Bernstein PL (1996) Against the Gods. Wiley, Hoboken, New Jersey
49. Obaidullah M (2005) Islamic Financial Services. Islamic Economics Research Center at Kind Abdul Aziz University, Jeddah
50. Cattelan V (2014) In the name of God: managing risk in Islamic finance. Oxford Center for Islamic Studies, eabh Papers 14-07
51. Visser H (2009) Islamic finance principles and practice. Edward Elgar Northampton, USA, p 45
52. Lapidus IM (2002) A history of Islamic Societies, 2nd edn. Cambridge University Press, University of California, Berkley, pp 197–218
53. Nejatullah Siddiqi M (1992) Teaching public finance in Islamic perspective. Center for Research in Islamic Economics, Kind Abdulaziz University, Jeddah, Saudi Arabia
54. Siddiqi M (1992) Teaching public finance in Islamic perspectives. Center for Research in Islamic Economics King Abdulaziz University Jeddah, Saudi Arabia
55. Tariq A, Humayon D (2007) Risk of Sukuk structures: implications for resource mobilization. Thunderbird Int Business Rev 49(2):203–205
56. Al Bitar B (2015) Risk management under Sharia Law: products, techniques and competitiveness. Anchor Academic Publishing, Hamburg p 26

Chapter 4
Heterodox Approach to Public-Private Partnership (PPP)

4.1 Main Schools of Thought in Public Finance and Rules of Islamic Moral Economy (IME)

The proposed heterodox approach to PPP is an attempt at describing cooperation between public and private sector entities originating from different legal, economic and religious systems that witness an interpenetration of selected management standards/standards of economic activity which have so far been frequently considered to be mutually exclusive. Hence, when analysing potential interdependencies between public and Islamic finance, it is worth beginning by recalling the key features and the most important trends in both sciences. The conventional public finance has been an important element of the majority of world economies since the eighteenth century. It forms a basis for public funds management in the majority of countries. It reflects different social and economic conditions in the respective countries, with religious influence being a less frequent phenomenon. It should be emphasised that, apart from the achievements of the Antiquity and Middle Ages, the verification of public finance foundations leads to cameralists. Representatives of that school were the first ones to clearly link the fiscal activity of the state with the well-being of the society. Moreover, they pointed out that it was necessary to set an upper limit on public expenditure and, consequently, to define the limits of taxation.[1] At the same time, they outlined the methodology for the development of state budgets that should match income to the identified types of expenditure. This historical period also witnessed the scientific achievements of mercantilist (nation's economy must be protected by taxes and customs duties) and physiocrats (who developed a concept of "single tax" to be paid by landowners).[2] The era of capitalism began with liberal financial thoughts of Adam Smith that have played an important role in the shaping of both governments and economies since the eighteenth century. They referred not

[1]Loughlin [1].

[2]Owsiak [2].

H. Kociemska, *Public-Private Partnership for Sub-Saharan Africa*, Advances in African Economic, Social and Political Development,
https://doi.org/10.1007/978-3-030-14753-2_4

only to classical economics, but also to finances and theory of tax.[3] In Adam Smith's opinion, the role of the state was limited to the issues of defence, property protection and justice. In the liberal doctrine, the aspect of taxation was based on three pillars:

- neutrality of tax policy;
- economic activity unrestrained by excessive tax burdens;
- indirect taxes imposed in such a way that the tax burden can be allocated among various users in the economy.

From the nineteenth century until the middle of the twentieth century, an orthodox public finance theory developed by J. B. Say had been in place, emphasising the need for a small state budget to be constantly balanced. A characteristic feature of this doctrine was its search for management platforms common to public entities, households and enterprises. Its strongly conservative views called for the ethical and religious evaluation of state's activities.[4] This was, however, one of the few schools of thought in the public finance science to include religion as an evaluative factor in the decision-making process relating to public funds management. It was approximately around the same time that the concept of social well-being and a school of thought based on Wagner's law, the so-called law of increasing state spending, were developed. This school relied on a thesis that as social development progresses, public authorities raise demands for an increasingly higher income due to the even faster growing public expenditure needs. It also gave rise to the emergence of the first state pension systems in Europe. Unfortunately, it has never established itself in the economic history of some continents, e.g. the sub-Saharan Africa discussed herein. Social welfare instruments have not been used since the beginning of the twentieth century, and in some countries, they are still not in place at all. The Keynesian Revolution which, through the introduction of the notion of state intervention, revolutionised the role of public finance in economy became the milestone in the evolution of public finance theory. The purpose of state intervention with respect to economy was to stimulate demand and mitigate economic cycle fluctuations. Both income and expenditure tools were used to that end. For conventional public finance, the importance of Keynes' theory consisted in the departure from the orthodox fiscal doctrine and proved that higher spending out of the income accumulated in the state budget was possible.[5] This theory was further developed by a number of schools. J.M. Buchanan's works turned out to be an important achievement in that regard. In 1986, Buchanan was awarded the Nobel Prize for his development of the contractual and constitutional bases for the theory of economic and political decision-making.[6] According to Buchanan, the Keynes' theory was the main reason why the unwritten principle of the balanced budget that had been in place before the 1930s was breached. According to this theory, the incurrence of public debt is undesirable, among other things, for reasons that stem from:

---

[3] Stiglitz [3].

[4] Eatwell [4].

[5] S. Owsiak, op. cit., p. 46.

[6] www.nobelprize.org/nobel_prizes/economic-sciences/laureates/1986/.

- reduced investment;
- increased interest rates;
- extra taxation that is required to fund higher interest payments;
- possibility of falling into a debt trap;
- for moral reasons.[7]

The subsequent achievements of public choice theory underlined also the consequences of public debt for future generations. This issue was dealt with, among other things, by the Virginia school of political economy (researching the processes of rent-seeking and special interest groups); the Chicago school of political economy (the *homo oeconomicus* concept of a self-maximising man, deprived of any ideology); and the Rochester school (enhanced the theory of choice by adding the issues of conflict resolution). In addition to the public choice theory, a social choice theory was also developed. The foundations of those theories will be cited and confronted with the interpretations of *Quran* and achievements of Islamic economics. It will be used by this author to propose a heterodox approach to PPP in public finance built upon the common platform of ideological and economic agreement between the systems of conventional and Islamic finance.

The Islamic financial system is based on religion. The holistic nature of Islam and its legal provisions makes it possible to state that Islam is both a faith and a state; hence, the Muslim law (*fiqh*) is a religion and a law simultaneously. There are no economic schools of thought or theories of finance in Islam that would stem from a discussion or contestation of *Quran* or that would operate independently of *Quran*. This law and the commands of prophets have remained constant and unchanged for hundreds of years. The religion is one of the few in the world to regulate the system of management/economic activity of both individuals and enterprises in such a thorough and detailed way. None of the developed economic systems based on multiple schools of economy and theories of finance is so closely related to religion. It is rather the contrary: a very small number of scientific theorems in economics or finance are related to any religion or behaviour of its followers. "*Islam, therefore, determines the nature of the legal system which regulates the entire lives of its followers in accordance with an ideal defined in the teachings of God and Prophet Muhammad. Just as the norms of the natural law exist in the nature itself and are only discovered by men, so the law of Allah has existed for centuries and has only been revealed to humans through Muhammad.*[8]" This law is contained in the original "Mother of the Book"—*Umm al-Kitab*, i.e. in nature. The contents of *Umm al-Kitab* were provided to the Prophet in separate revelations that were gathered together in one book here on earth.[9] The Sunnah (*hadith*, i.e. the practice of the Prophet himself and of his companions), based on tradition and experience, forms an equally important source of Islamic law, as well as of the rules of financial management. Further sources include the following: *ijma* (consensus), *qiyas* (analogy), *ijtihad* (individual interpretation), *ray* (expert interpretation). All of the above, and more than a dozen of others, are the

---

[7]Buchanan [5].

[8]Sadowski [6].

[9]Visser [7].

interpretations of *Quran*, and they rely all the time on the religious and social order imposed rather than created on earth. The basic duties of a Muslim that in a sense also influence the method of management of funds as a constant element of everyday life or economy are as follows:

- Profession of faith (*shahada*)—there is no god but God.
- Prayer (*salat*)—recited five times a day while facing in the direction of Mecca.
- Charity (*zakah, zakat*)—Muslims have an obligation to spend a portion of their wealth for the benefit of the poor; it is a kind of donation.
- Fasting (*sawm*)—during the ninth month of the Muslim year, i.e. Ramadan, Muslims must refrain from eating and drinking from sunrise to sunset.
- Pilgrimage to Mecca (*hajj*)—Muslims must make the pilgrimage at least once in their life, if their financial situation enables them to do so.[10]

The most important prohibitions, in turn, include the following: prohibition of usury (*riba*—increase, addition, growth); prohibition of gambling, acquisition of wealth without effort at the expense of others (*maysir*); prohibition of uncertainty in contracts (*gharar*); prohibition of the accumulation of wealth solely for oneself (*ihikar*); prohibition of fraud (*tatfief*). The set of economically important orders, prohibitions and guidelines has been described most extensively in the longest surah of the Holy Quran.[11] In addition to the aforementioned prohibitions, the main ethical and economic rules are based on the following core assumptions included in the Hadis of the Prophet Muhammad:

- All business activities (other than the prohibited ones) are allowed, provided that they do not cause harm either to individuals or to the society.
- Even the slightest doubts as to the perpetration of offence or crime in that sphere benefit the defendant, thus protecting him/her against punishment provided for in *Quran*.
- The right of pre-emption in trade transactions is vested in business partners, relatives and neighbours.[12]

It should be emphasised that the economies of the majority of Islamic countries have already in the past been governed by mandatory rules, each time with a strong influence of political factors that have frequently been destructive to economic processes. Over the centuries, several attempts have been made to develop a theory of Muslim economics; among other things, in the eighth century, the kadi Abu Yusuf wrote a book on the organisation of Caliphate economy. His work was, however, more religious than economic in nature. Another important attempt at creating the theory of Muslim economics came in the form of an excerpt of the *Muquaddimah* of Ibn Chaldun.[13] The authors who attempted to interpret *Quran* to develop theoretical

[10] W.R. Schumm, A.L. Kohler, *Social cohesion and five pillars of Islam: a comparative perspective*, American Journal of Islamic Social Sciences, 23(2), p. 128.

[11] Karwowski [8].

[12] www.encyklopedia.pwn.pl/haslo/ekonomia-muzulmanska;3897007.html.

[13] Erdem [9].

Table 4.1 Five principles of the system of Muslim economy

Five principles of Muslim economy
Obligation to abide by the provisions relating to economic activity contained in the *Quran* which is a divine law
Obligation to abide by the principles of permanence and flexibility in the economic sphere, consisting in the fact that any economic activity which is in line with the religious law or regulated in accordance with the unanimous opinion of scholars on issues not provided for in the *Quran* or *Sunnah* is allowed
Obligation to abide by the principle of balance between the well-being of an individual and the interests of the entire society, which entails the issue of private ownership. According to Islam, land and everything that is situated thereon belong to God; God, however, gave the man free will to use all provisions in such a way so as not to infringe other people's rights. The essence of social ownership is that it is for everyone to enjoy
Obligation to abide by the principle that the Muslim society is obligated to maintain those who are vulnerable: the unemployed, the disabled, orphans or those whose wages are not enough to sustain themselves; funds for these objectives come, among other things, from the *zakah* "tax"
Obligation to abide by the principle of economic freedom relating to free choice of work and method of earning money and freedom of possessing and spending the same; this must, however, remain in line with the divine law and social solidarity

Source Compiled on the basis of El-Gamal [42]

bases of Muslim economics include Abu al-Ala al-Maududi who authored numerous publications in which he called for the Islamisation of all spheres of life, including also the economy. The same trend was followed by other Muslim thinkers, such as Sayyid Qutb of Egypt, Muhammad Baqir al-Sadr of Iraq, or Muhammad Taleghani of Iran.[14] They all shared the same assumption that Islam was a universal and timeless religion upon which a coherent system of modern Muslim economics should be based. The said interpreters, however, were theoreticians rather than specialists in economics or finance; therefore, the approach that they represented was expressly religious. They referred to the basic sources of Islam: the *Quran* and *Sunnah* and to the period of the first Islamic state. Thus, taking into account the Islamic values and norms presented above, five principles were formulated around which the system of modern Muslim economy should be developed (Table 4.1).

Economic systems based on religion and interpretation of its rules for the purposes of trade turn out, in many Muslim countries, to be very advantageous for the economies in those regions. It is worth emphasising that this economic style is predominant in the following countries: Indonesia, Pakistan, India, Bangladesh, Saudi Arabia, Oman, Morocco, Sudan and many others, especially in Asia or the Arabian Peninsula. The countries which rely on Islamic economics include those that are characterised by high economic growth, such as the Gulf Cooperation Council (GCC) states of the Persian Gulf (Kuwait, Qatar, Bahrain, Saudi Arabia, United Arab Emirates, Oman) (Table 4.2).

---

[14] Nejatullah Siddiqi [10].

Table 4.2 Persian Gulf States at "global level"

The Persian Gulf States control more than 40% of global oil reserves and almost one-fourth of global natural gas reserves
By the end of 2006, foreign assets of those states had reached USD 1.9 trillion, to further increase in 2007 and 2008 before the financial crisis
Investors from those states currently hold, or have held for a long time, majority interests in renowned global corporations …
In 2006 alone, net capital outflow from those states amounted to USD 200 billion, to be surpassed only by China
In 2006, GDP per capita amounted to USD 19,000, i.e. 5 times more than in India, and 3 times more than in China
GDP per capita in Qatar in 2008 reached almost USD 86,000, being 1.8 times more than in the USA in the analogous period; 2.6 times more than in the European Union; 14 times more than in China; and 31 times more than in India
McKinsey Global Institute has estimated that the overall level of Persian Gulf States' foreign assets will be USD 8.3 trillion by 2020
Currently, almost all major banks that have so far only offered conventional instruments, now also offer Islamic instruments; those banks include, among other things: HSBC, Citigroup, Deutsche Bank

Source Rehman [43]

It is further estimated that the resilience of economies of the aforementioned states to economic crises is significantly higher than in traditional economic systems of European states. Despite the fact that they did suffer in the crisis after 2009, their budgetary surpluses and high assets enabled them to emerge from the crisis much faster than traditional economies are able to do. Hence, this author's attempt at showing the possibility of convergence between both financial systems, i.e. the conventional and the Islamic, based on the example of PPP. A heterodox approach to PPP is presented through the interpretation of major schools of thought in public finance and rules of Islam. This will ensure further development of conventional finance and enable more PPP projects to be implemented in business practice in mixed capital structures or in emerging or developing markets that are totally new to investors.

One of the key features of Islamic finance, as mentioned hereinabove, is the waiver of interest and a different interpretation of the notion of risk (*gharar*). Financial institutions have their sources of income not in interest or generation of loan-related debt, but rather in the creation of assets and sharing in profits from the sale thereof. The profit is always related to assets on which it is generated. Financial institutions provide funds for the development of manufacturing and service sectors. They do not apply derivative instruments. Funds are allocated to specific projects and assets generated thereunder. Therefore, they are invested directly in the economy, and, by definition, there is no "artificial" creation of money or speculative activity. To that end, Islamic finance has developed some properly structured financial instruments, adequate for both private and public entities. Economic behaviour of those entities is always determined by the interpretations of *Quran*. Therefore, the common prohibition of *riba* (interest) means that the budgetary policy of Islamic states must be more creative because of the need to rely on other financial instruments and rules of their structuring that do not use interest products. In conventional finance, central banks develop monetary policies relying on interest rates that are not related to assets. They may also act as lenders or depositors. Islamic finance, just as conventional finance, identifies public goods, such as water supply systems, road infrastructure and educational services. Their management or creation must serve social welfare. Public authorities may play the role of financial institutions' clients based on the principles of profit and loss sharing. This principle provides for an active participation of each party in the performance of the agreement. Moreover, it necessitates fair cooperation between the partners in the spirit of solidarity both in the generation of profits and incurring of losses.[15] Such is the case with public utility companies or other activities that ensure a specific profit.[16] For instance, solutions to finance public transport or real property include *ijjara* or *ijara waiqtina*, where in the case of PPP projects, public authorities decide upfront to buy back the real property from a special purpose vehicle, at a predefined price, at the end of long-term cooperation or lease agreement. Ongoing expenditures may be financed through *sukuk*, implemented for the first time by the government of Malaysia in cooperation with HSBC.[17] Another feature important from the point of view of these considerations is the joint and several distributions of credit risk in Islamic finance. It finds its reflection in the distribution of future profits or losses from the funds invested between the financing entity and the client in proportion to their shares in the company. The financing entity operating on the basis of the Shari'ah law does not multiply funds through the creation of debt but rather uses real capital originating from deposits. The deponent thus bears a real risk, which gives him the right to share in the profit earned by the entity that finances the investment. The level of profit does not need to be predetermined, as it only results from the real profit generated in the economic process. Thus, partners act together, sharing both profits and losses, which fully implements the idea of partnership under PPP and the principle of profit and loss sharing. Direct investments in the manufacturing sectors of the economy are connected with the aforementioned important rule of Islamic finance, i.e. being guided by the interests of and support for the community. There are also restricted areas of economic activity such as, among other things, gambling, production and sales of pork and alcohol, or usury. Moreover, each of the proposed financing structures must be consulted with the Shari'ah Advisory Board whose legal opinions, even if sometimes ambiguous, are absolutely binding for each of the parties.[18] The notion of risk is accepted in the Islamic finance, but its nature is specified somewhat differently than in the conventional finance. Hence, in the previous chapter, differences in the theoretical approach to risk were noted to

[15] Khoutem and Hichem [11].

[16] H. Visser, op. cit., p. 122.

[17] Karwowski [12].

[18] Alexander [13].

reconcile the foundations underlying the activities of both types of investors in PPP, i.e. the conventional and the Islamic ones.

How can then economic terms adopted in Islamic finance affect risk management in international investment projects where conventional and Islamic finance overlap? As a thesis for further considerations, this author assumes that risk is a term operating in Islamic finance but defined differently than in conventional finance. The term takes on a different meaning in view of the applicable Islamic rules that prohibit: *riba*—interest, *gharar*—uncertainty, speculation and *maysir*—gambling.[19]

4.2 Agency Theory Versus Islamic Finance

With reference to conventional public finance and the neoliberal trend, and based on the agency theory, M. C. Jensen and W. H. Meckling define dependence as a contract under which one or more parties (principal) engage another party (agent) to carry out certain activities on their behalf.[20] This activity is connected with principals delegating a certain part of their decision-making independence to the agent. The agency theory refers to two entities: the principal and his agent; hence, it is worth being analysed here in the context of relationships between PPP participants. The principal commissions the agent to perform a task and relies on the agent's knowledge and will. The principal-agent relationship always entails the asymmetry of information. The agent has more information than the principal does about possible terms and conditions of transactions or the status of economic environment. As a result, the agent can undertake activities characterised by high level of his own benefits, while at the same time exposing the principal to excessive risk of losses. This is when moral hazard occurs. Moral hazard, i.e. the transfer of risk of possible losses caused by the agent's activities onto the principal, can occur when[21]:

- The usefulness of the principal and agent depends on the agent's activities.
- The principal is not fully capable of controlling the agent's actions, as a result of which the principal can only watch the results of the agent's activity.
- The agent's activities are not Pareto-optimal.[22]

---

[19] Kabir and Lewis [14].

[20] Eisenhardt [15].

[21] Salanie [16].

[22] According to Pareto, a situation is optimal only if no individuals can be made better off without making someone else worse off. The Pareto theorem identifies the well-being of a society with the well-being of its individual members. Such a position can be sustained, although there are such ethical systems where the society or certain groups thereof are given a moral dimension that differs from the one assigned to individuals. In such ethical systems, the Pareto criterion is at best considered to be inadequate or at worst treated as irrelevant. Is there, however, any system that would meet all of the criteria? The answer is provided by Arrow himself who formulated the so-called impossibility theorem. There is no system that would meet all of the Arrow's axioms. There are, however, such systems that do not contradict these axioms but rather mitigate them [www.politykaglobalna.pl/2010/01/teoria-wyboru-publicznego-a-proces-podejmowania-decyzji-w-radzie-unii-europejskiej/2/].

According to the agency theory, the agent is appointed to pursue the goals set by the principal. However, in his activities, the agent may also take into account his own objectives. The principal, while being aware of the conflict between his own goals and the goals of the agent, can implement some preventive measures to regulate these issues in an agreement. And while it is theoretically possible to draft a contract that will take into account all possible variants of market situation or agent's behaviour, in practice, however, such a contract does not exist, not even in Islamic finance. Thus, the principal remains to a certain extent dependent on the agent's will. In turn, the agent's activities cannot be controlled due to the amount of costs which should be incurred for that purpose. A detailed and frequent inspection would also undermine trust in an honest agent. In view of such limitations, a dishonest agent, guided by egoistic reasons and presenting opportunistic behaviour, can strive to carry out his own plans that are not optimal from the point of view of the principal's effectiveness. Losses suffered by the principal as a result of an excessive risk taken up by the agent can distort mutual trust, and, at the same time, they would then also contradict the principles of Islamic finance. In Islamic finance, responsibility for an activity rests with the person who performs it. This is a special relationship between the principal and the agent. It is a significant interpretation of the agency theory where, with the transfer of rights and obligations, such transfer also refers to risk. Islamic finance does not allow freedom with respect to individual speculation or distribution of principals' responsibility among agents. The role of office control in the interpretation of the principles of Islamic finance could unambiguously suggest that the only supervision is *Quran* and *Shari'ah* law. Hence, in the Islamic reality, the problem of moral hazard in the agency theory seems to be much more serious.[23] Islamic banks have fewer instruments at their disposal to restrict moral hazard, including a reduced possibility of imposing penalties under the *Shari'ah* law. They use the profit and loss sharing formula mainly to obtain deposits.

In the event of credit actions, Islamic banks act as principals who are afraid that the funds will not be used as planned or that the reported profits will be understated.[24] With PPP, the direct involvement of partners in a joint, long-term contractual cooperation can mitigate this risk. In conclusion, it should be stated that the risk of moral hazard in the agency theory and its link with the principle of partners' profit and loss sharing in Islamic finance seems higher than in the interest-based conventional finance. The availability of financial instruments eliminating *gharar* is limited, but the avoidance of speculation undoubtedly facilitates sustainable cooperation under PPP.

[23] H. Visser, op. cit., p. 139.

[24] Piotrowski [17].

4.3 Public Choice Theory and Social Choice Theory Versus Islamic Finance

The public choice theory is yet another trend important from the viewpoint of convergence between conventional finance and Islamic finance in PPP. It is viewed to be part of institutional economics according to which the effectiveness and efficiency of public and economic spheres are determined by the quality of institutions. Therefore, the effectiveness and efficiency of public and economic spheres of a public-private partnership will depend upon the level of cooperation between private and public entities.[25] It is worth noting two trends in the new institutional economics, namely the choice theory and the science of contract. Institutionalists emphasised that economic choice referred not only to different goals and ways of utilising production resources but also to institutions that could facilitate or hinder their functioning. Ownership relations and types of contracts concluded between public and private partners would thus be significant from the point of view of a compromise between both types of investors. An obvious economic presumption that human needs are unlimited, but the resources available to satisfy those needs are limited would be an important reflection of this theory in PPP. This applies to the needs of any society, irrespective of religion, geographic location or level of prosperity. According to the idea of the functioning of public entities, societies will always need public services, whereas the resources that public entities have at their disposal to satisfy the needs of the community are increasingly changing.[26] This situation is one of the key reasons why PPP should be used in economic practice, and it will become particularly visible in those countries that are in greatest need of multifaceted development, such as the countries of sub-Saharan Africa. On the one hand, the needs of communities must be satisfied continuously; on the other hand, however, there are no sufficient funds to provide those societies with the required quantity or quality of public services. In conventional finance, the continuous obligation to provide public goods or services is imposed by constitutional laws and subsequent legislative acts specific to the various types of public entities or local authorities. In Islam, the basic law that imposes the obligation to provide public goods and ensure a broadly defined social welfare is the *Quran*. The delivery of any such goods or services is always based on a contractual relationship. For Islamic investors, the essence of the contract and the preservation of the contractual nature of cooperation are of key importance.[27] Thus, long-term SPV agreements will be widely accepted in the system of Islamic finance. In accordance with the original objectives of the public choice theory, both systems may be found to be convergent also in their attention to the quality of public institutions. The primary objective of public entities, both conventional and Islamic ones, is to ensure social welfare. In the conventional theory of public choice, the effectiveness of public institutions is evaluated through the quality and efficiency of provision of

---

[25] Wilkin [18].

[26] Kociemska [19].

[27] Tabash and Dhankar [20].

goods and services expected by the society. The institution of state or public entity can, therefore, be treated as a tool that facilitates the use or production of goods. For Islamic investors, the key element of public entity's evaluation is the reality of work performed in connection with the generation of specific assets that contribute to social welfare in accordance with the principles of *Quran*. Both types of objectives of conventional and Islamic public entities may be pursued by implementing PPP investment projects.

The public choice theory also includes a widespread acceptance of financial instruments that can be used to attain the goals of public and private investors. In the world of Islam, the aspect of choice of financial instruments should be interpreted through the prism of religious and social issues, and in this perspective, some similarities can be found with the social choice theory. Mutual functions of Islamic public entities and Muslim communities in the creation of economy which facilitates the maximisation of social welfare are based on the following obligations:

- The collective responsibility of Islamic community is to increase access to every branch of industry and knowledge.
- The collective responsibility of Islamic community is also to participate in the most important branches of industry and knowledge.
- The state should play a key role in the shaping of production and planning of public undertakings' operations.
- The state has the right to acquire and distribute resources to maximise the level of achievement of social objectives.
- The state enters the field of economic activity as the central planner and supervisor.[28]

Local community well-being is the principal value of public resource management in Islam. This stems both from the pillars of religion set forth in the *Quran* and from the *Shari'ah* law. According to those, the management of any resources provided by Allah[29] should meet the criteria of utility, servitude and accountability. In economic and religious terms, utility should be equated with transparent behaviour compliant with the pillars of religion, i.e. avoidance of prohibited business transactions, fulfilment of *zakah* obligations and activity in the area of social responsibility. The aforementioned axioms of the role of state and society in Islamic finance are fully consistent with the principles of PPP.

Public-private partnerships:

- are aimed at increasing access to public services (this is the purpose of PPPs).
- are present in key sectors of the economy for which public authorities or local governments are responsible.
- public entities can play a key role in their cooperation with private partners, especially in the area of ensuring both a specific access to and quality of public services offered.

---

[28] Adamek [21].

[29] Quran [22].

- by assumption, public partners are not profit-seeking: no founding acts of public entities or local authorities mention any need for them to maximise their profits; on the contrary, they refer to the maximisation of tasks performed in the public interest/utility function for the society.
- public entities may fulfil the planning role in PPPs, but they should always exercise supervision to ensure that the entity formed under the PPP provides the specific quantity and quality of public services.

The key PPP features from the point of view of the public partner are in keeping with the role of the state identified in Islamic economics.

It is worth noting here the social choice theory that is much more significant than just the state's or individual's social responsibility which can be achieved irrespective of the state's economic or religious systems. The social choice theory was formulated at the end of the eighteenth century in response to the need to improve collective decision-making methods. It developed intensively in the twentieth century, with the publication of Kenneth J. Arrow's *Social Choice and Individual Values* in 1951. Further significant contributions to its development were made by other Nobel Prize winners: James M. Buchanan (1986), John C. Harsanyi, John F. Nash, Reinhard Selten (1994), and first of all Amartya K. Sen. He was awarded the Nobel Prize in 1998 for his work on welfare economics, wherein he argued that famine did not result from food shortages but rather from poor distribution. He contributed to the development of the Social Progress Index.[30] According to the achievements of the aforementioned scientists, social decisions must always be taken using a clearly defined method. This is what sets them apart from subjective individual decisions. The selection of a decision-making method to be applied in a given situation oftentimes determines what social decision will be taken. In that regard, fierce disputes about which of the available methods (e.g. in electoral systems) should be applied are understandable, although it is commonly believed that social decisions should be taken democratically; that goods should be distributed fairly; and that individual autonomy and rights should be respected. Islamic public or financial institutions always operate in accordance with the *Shari'ah* law. The primary objective, as mentioned herein on multiple occasions, is to promote justice which is the natural moral goal. No Muslim who manages financial resources has to demand fair treatment because he believes that they are revealed and applicable in accordance with the rules of the *Quran* and the *Shari'ah* law and, as such, are indisputable. Islamic economies are thus driven by moral principles and religious standards that make up the Islamic Moral Economy (IME). The Islamic Moral Economy relies on the concept of *homo islamicus* whose standards of behaviour are compliant with the principles of Islam, irrespective of political or economic spheres. The non-dichotomous style of life and economic activity means that religious and lay or economic issues are not separated, owing to which individuals reach *falah* (salvation) and *akhirah* (afterlife).[31] The relationship between local communities or individuals and the state is different than in conventional economies. According to the *Shari'ah* law, the state is only a tool of social

---

[30] www.noblisci.pl/1998-amartya-sen/.

[31] M. Asutay, Yilmaz I., Istanbul 2015.

welfare in the hands of Allah. Therefore, the state's broader objective is to create a political framework for Muslim unity and cooperation. On a procedural level, the state must apply democratic principles, so that any choices relating to current issues can be based on agreement with communities or their representatives. The state must reflect individual decisions with respect to social choice as long as these choices are compliant with the *Shari'ah* law.[32] According to J. M. Buchanan (1974), the non-existence of Arrow's social welfare function does not need to indicate that the society will not act democratically. On the contrary, he believes that inconsistencies in majority voting are not only positive, but that they also have beneficial effects on the society.[33] Therefore, Arrow's law cannot be applied directly. Arrow identified axioms that, in his opinion, every social welfare function should satisfy, but at the same time, he proved that no such function existed. Arrow's social welfare function axioms are as follows:

- The social welfare function is identified for all profiles of individual expectations.
- Pareto principle: if all individuals unanimously prefer x to y, then the social welfare function should place x above y.
- The social ranking of x and y alternatives may only depend on individual preferences with respect to those alternatives; individual expectations regarding other alternatives are irrelevant here.
- Non-dictatorship condition: there is no such person or pair of x and y alternatives that if this person strongly prefers x to y, then the social ranking also places x above y, irrespective of individual preferences.[34]

It turns out, however, that there is no such social welfare function which would simultaneously satisfy the aforementioned axioms and exclude dictatorship. Since it is impossible for the Arrow's function to be satisfied in Islamic finance, either, one should focus on the very process of attaining social welfare rather than on the social choice function. According to Islam, this choice is given by Allah. There are, however, certain identified paths leading to social welfare. One of them is *zakah*. It is a basic instrument that enhances social welfare. *Zakah* means redistribution of wealth by transferring surplus income to those in need.[35] When a surplus of funds is generated above the value that is acceptable for the project, the so-called *nisaab*, then such funds are provided not only to the poor, but also to a broad group of eligible individuals in accordance with the principle of relative equality. Such individuals include tax collectors, people in need who support Islam, educators of Islam, debtors, etc.[36] Redistribution of those funds should include all groups of eligible beneficiaries. If, however, the receipts are too low, it is possible to allocate the funds to selected eligible groups only. This meets the rule of the highest possible utility of spare funds through maximisation of user benefits. If a small amount were to be allocated in equal shares

---

[32] El-Awa [23].

[33] Habib [24].

[34] Arrow [25].

[35] Usami and Qazi [26].

[36] Al Qardawi [27].

to all beneficiaries, then the utility of those funds would be significantly reduced.[37] *Zakah* is clearly an instrument of religious, social and financial nature. For private partners in project finance, the redistribution of income in excess of *nisaab* may be an innovative solution that has not yet been applied in conventional finance or directly in profit-generating undertakings. In conventional finance, income is redistributed by public entities or local authorities who first obtain those funds, among other things, from tax receipts. In PPP structures based on Islamic financial instruments, this role would partially be assumed by special purpose vehicles formed as part of PPP. From the point of view of social utility of business, it is a very desirable model for each type of investors. It is worth noting, however, that conventional public finance is devoid of any religious influence. Legal regulations governing the redistribution of public income are in no way connected with faith or religious social order. Thus, in business practice, private investors would have to attach considerable importance to understanding *zakah*. They would have to strive, among other things, to identify the groups of beneficiaries in as precise a manner as possible. As mentioned before, those who are eligible to receive funds include, among others, people who support Islam or those who promote Islam, including volunteer jihadists or soldiers defending Muslim countries.[38] It can thus be expected that conventional private investors will not accept such redistribution targets and that it is only through negotiations that they should identify beforehand the allocation of surplus funds generated by special purpose vehicles under PPPs.

The approach to cooperation under PPP projects should definitely take broad account of not just the rules of *Shari'ah* or be oriented towards the resolution of social problems, but also, from private investors' point of view, ensure profits that they expect. Private investors would, even before the commencement of their investment project, know the maximum level of available profit, above which any surplus must be socially redistributed to the identified group of eligible beneficiaries. Any surplus generated over and above the amount of *nisaab* stipulated in the agreement may be provided to the society for which, from the point of view of their financial situation, there is a limitation in access to public-private services under PPP. In business practice, the identified group of beneficiaries could enjoy public-private services free of charge. Thereby, the requirement of redistribution of financial surplus above the accepted level would be met, and at the same time, the pro-social purpose of the investment project itself would be achieved (Fig. 4.1).

Bearing in mind the aspect of universal social acceptance, one should also point out to another element of social choice theory, namely social acceptance of the state's activity by individuals. No social acceptance for projects that are non-compliant with the *Shari'ah* law would certainly prevent any planned investments. However, the idea underlying PPPs is that the purpose of such investments for public partners is to provide the society with the expected services or goods. Therefore, their activities must be subordinated to the primary objective , i.e. society's satisfaction stemming from

[37] Ethica Institute of Islamic Finance, Zakah Q&A Handbook, 2013, p. 6.

[38] National Zakat Foundation, www.nzf.org.uk/Content/PDF/NZF_Zakat_Guide.pdf.

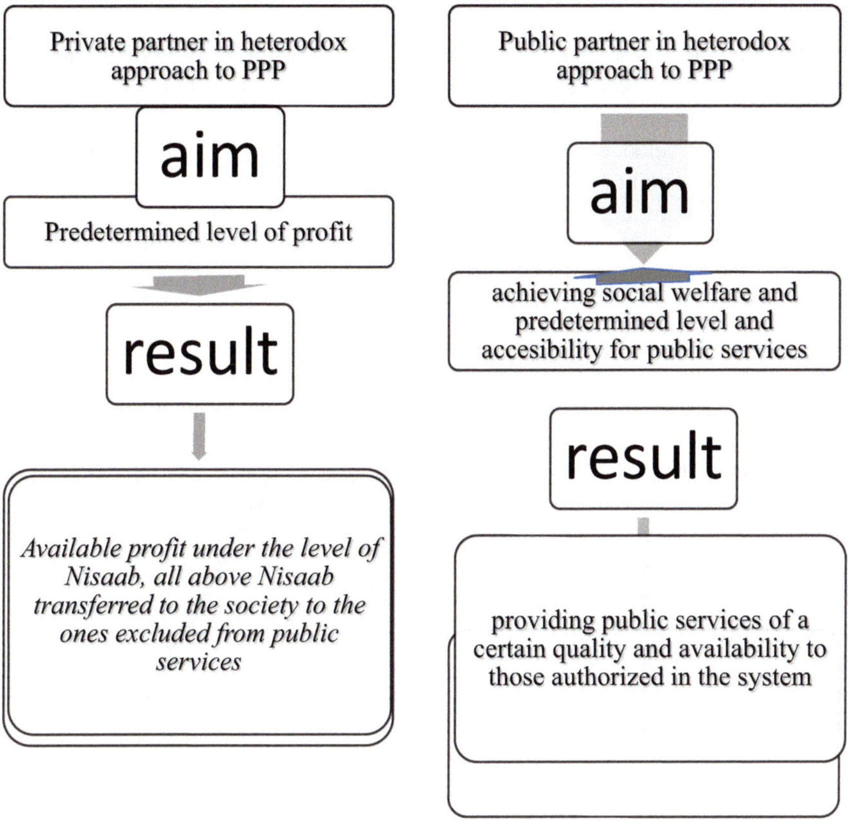

Fig. 4.1 Public and private investors in PPP from a heterodox point of view. *Source* author's own study

access to the specific quantity of services and their adequate quality. Such interpretation of the social choice theory would find acceptance among Islamic communities and PPP investors.

Summing up, it should be stated that the aforementioned social choice theory is analogous to the Islamic world's principle of universal acceptance of public choice, including the directions and methods of investing. It provides theoretical foundations for each type of investors to limit the key risk, i.e. the lack of social acceptance for their infrastructural project, and it may be fully accepted and implemented by conventional partners. The public choice process itself is limited to the fulfilment of the rules of *Quran* and *Shari'ah* law, where the role of the state and, consequently, of the public-private special purpose vehicle (SPV) is only to follow those rules. The maximisation of profits desired by conventional investors is limited to a specific level. One should, therefore, assume a certain social fairness, which is far removed from the assumptions underlying conventional financial markets, under which portions of financial surplus over and above the agreed level of *nisaab* are appropriated for broadly defined social purposes rather than given to the owners. The very determination of the *nisaab* level may be enough to raise controversies among conventional investors because such an action has never been taken by them before. Those investors must answer the question of what profit value is sufficient for them and, irrespective of any sums in excess of that value, accept the idea of providing funds to the identified eligible groups. From the point of view of conventional finance theory, this may lead to the principal-agent conflict, as described hereinabove, and to moral hazard. However, it is not the principal who imposes the limitation on profits but the indisputable religious and social system which translates the maximisation of individual's profits to the pro-social nature of economic operations of businesses. Conventional and Islamic investment projects under the PPP mechanism should have as their primary objective the consensus of two goals: maximum profit and maximum social welfare. It is, however, worth quoting T. Kuran[39] here who said that religious norms are not able to fully override individual's aspirations to maximise their individual profit. The structures of conventional and Islamic transactions will thus first be subject to conventional objectives of profitability and then to the objectives of following religious laws. Thereby, Islamic investors should be expected to redefine the notion of maximisation of the social objective, while conventional investors should be expected to redefine the notion of maximisation of profits. Such an approach should lead to a compromise between "corrupt behaviour" which, for one partner, is profitable but unethical and the generous behaviour of the other partner which is ethical but unprofitable. The selection of the form of such cooperation will always be relative to the values professed by the partners and their financial expectations.[40]

4.4 Islamic Moral Economy (IME) Versus Social Responsibility in Conventional Business

Having analysed the achievements of selected public finance theories, it is worthwhile to re-examine more broadly the achievements of Islamic theoreticians and try, under those conditions, to find possibilities for conventional entities to operate in accordance with the principles of social responsibility of business. In the Islamic Moral Economy, attention is drawn to the clear conceptualisation of social welfare function. Social responsibility of business in Islam is also one of the major canons of conducting business. As mentioned hereinabove, the idea of social responsibility and maximisation of social welfare are the most important objectives of economic activity in the Islamic Moral Economy, unlike in classical economics where the primary objective of economic activity is to earn profit. For conventional investors, social responsibility in economic activity is an element of marginal importance. More often than not, however, this is related to the lack of any tax advantages. If neither religion nor ethics affect investment activities, the social welfare factor is not that

[39] Kuran [28].

[40] Le Menestrel [29].

important in the absence of any ethical or religious imperatives in that field. The code of ethics becomes a complementary tool of management that is often mainly applied in international and multicultural corporations. In Islam, it is quite the opposite: the aspect of social acceptance and the real positive influence of economic undertakings on Muslim communities is an essential condition of economic activity. The assumptions underlying the concept of social welfare in Islamic markets are as follows:

- to develop an *ihsani social capital* (society's optimality) through *falah* process (individual optimality);
- to achieve distributive justice for harmonious growth (*tazkiyah*) by recognising and enabling individual and society nature of IME for sustainability.[41]

The aspect of social responsibility of economic activity is, however, of particular significance to the proposed heterodox approach to public finance. On the one hand, the satisfaction of communities using PPP services is crucial for the success of the investment project, on the other hand, however, the cultural, religious, social and economic diversity existing, for instance, in sub-Saharan Africa, makes it more difficult to find the social welfare function which is indispensable in the trend described. As mentioned before, the level of access to basic public goods and services in the aforementioned region is often minimal. The development of a process to ensure long-term social welfare can start with the basics, taking account of conventional and Islamic finance trends in PPP structures. There are multiple social welfare ratios and measures. Their authors' objective is to show the degree of satisfaction of human needs. The various measures differ from one another in their selection of variables or aggregation methods. The most popular, albeit non-traditional measures of social welfare include the following: J. Drewnowski's Geneva method; A. Sen's welfare measure; Index of Sustainable Economic Welfare or Genuine Progress Indicator.[42] From the point of view of PPP investments, this author's attention is focused on one of them, i.e. the welfare measure by A. Sen. According to him, utility in the sense of representation of consumer choices does not need to properly reflect their welfare because individuals, while making their choices, also follow motivations other than their own welfare. In Sen's opinion, income or consumption are not good measures of welfare, either. Specific income may correspond to significantly different levels of welfare, if one takes into account the existing differences in private or social characteristics of individuals (e.g. rate of metabolism, health, age, social position and customs or habits in a given community). Happiness or fulfilment of desires, in turn, are inadequate measures of welfare because they are totally subjective, "The battered slave, the broken unemployed, the hopeless destitute, the tamed housewife, may have the courage to desire little, but the fulfilment of those disciplined desires is not a sign of great success and cannot be treated in the same way as the fulfilment of the confident and demanding desires of the better placed".[43] According to Sen, "capability to function" is the best metric for welfare, with functioning understood

[41] Asutay and Yilmaz [30].

[42] Kubiczek [31].

[43] A. Sen 1987, p. 11.

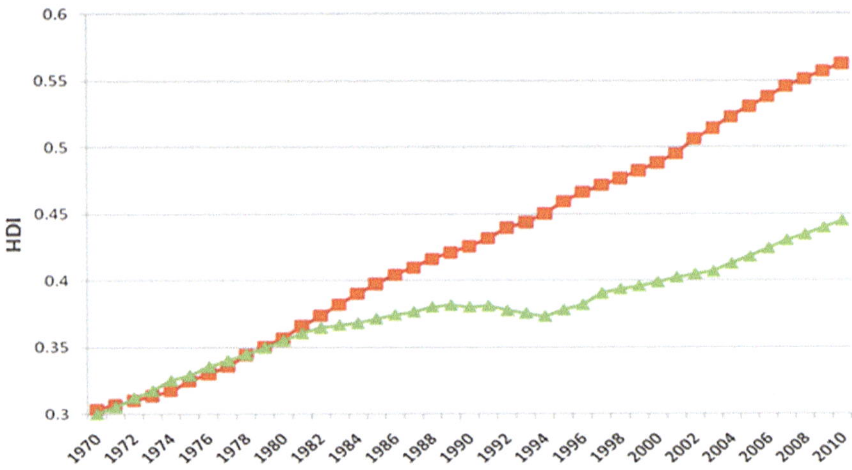

Fig. 4.2 HDI in the years 1970–2010. Legend: red—non-African countries, green—sub-Saharan Africa. *Source* www.nyudri.org/what-the-new-hdi-tells-us-about-africa/

as being and doing: being adequately nourished, being in good health, avoiding premature mortality, being happy, not suffering from lack of self-respect, taking active part in the life of the community, etc. Thus, such definition of welfare is much better adjusted both to the achievements of numerous communities in the region and to their expectations for development. This index for selected countries, including those of sub-Saharan Africa, is presented in Fig. 4.2.

It can, therefore, be hypothesised that the implementation of the social welfare function under joint conventional and Islamic PPP projects, especially in sub-Saharan African countries, will be much easier to be achieved. The specific features of those countries vis-à-vis PPP assumptions are as follows:

- The needs of the population are basic; therefore, the technology to fulfil/create them has been known to external investors, both conventional and Islamic ones, for years and does not require any innovative or expensive solutions.
- The progressive Islamisation contributes to the promotion of *nisaab*, i.e. the direct distribution of financial surplus above certain level to local communities/users of infrastructure, which makes it possible to bypass public entities' red tape and avoid the problem of corruption.
- The community's satisfaction manifesting itself through the features of A. Sen's measure can easily be achieved because even the simplest investments in water supply systems, roads or health will lead to a rapid increase in the welfare measure understood in accordance with Sen's theory. PPP investors will thus clearly fulfil one of the key objectives of international Islamic and conventional cooperation.

Unfortunately, such conclusions bring with them a contradictory reflection on a high-welfare situation where investors may find it more difficult to fulfil the social function of business towards the community whose needs are not that obvious. Nevertheless, the aspect of Islamic social responsibility of business should be implemented at all times, also in profit-generating undertakings. Irrespective of the wealth of Muslim nations, the principle of redistribution of funds over and above *nisaab* is a religious rule that is binding upon every entrepreneur. It may also be the reason why in some countries, e.g. in the United Arab Emirates, the quality of public services, e.g. public transport, education, health care, significantly exceeds European levels of quality for such services.[44] Public partners aim at maximising their objectives, i.e. the quality of their services and the highest level of welfare, irrespective of having achieved the socially acceptable level of public services. Combining social responsibility of business, acceptance of predefined lower level of profit and redistribution of specific financial surplus to those in need in order to fulfil the key principles of Islamic economy becomes a priority task in the area of sub-Saharan countries described herein in view of low level of quality or availability of the majority of public goods and services. Linking the theological norms of Islam with the principles of economic activity of conventional partners in the area of satisfaction of social welfare needs will be a transparent and feasible process to be implemented by a special purpose vehicle under PPP, based on a heterodox approach to public finance, presented below.

4.5 Heterodox Approach to the Pillars of Public-Private Partnership

When it comes to neoclassical economics, an important scientific contribution was made by Alfred Marshall. He is believed to be one of the founders of that school of thought, along with Leon Walras. He claimed that the main objective of economics was to improve social welfare. His significant achievements include the theory of consumer surplus whose increase, being a measure of consumer satisfaction, is supposed to be an indication of social welfare. Surplus increase for high-income individuals is lower than that for lower-income individuals. Thus, Marshall called for progressive taxation of communities' income and for support to be provided to the poorest through a more equitable distribution of national income.

Social welfare has become a key subject of many schools of scientific thought, but also a priority objective of government policies in the majority of countries with both conventional and Islamic economies, especially today, i.e. in times of increased migration of population from that region. Therefore, it is a phenomenon that is also important to sub-Saharan African populations analysed herein. As mentioned before, there is no question of social welfare with respect to the majority of countries in sub-Saharan Africa. Hence, methods are being sought to create stable economic conditions to facilitate the dynamic growth of those countries, and to establish optimum investment conditions for Islamic and conventional partners. However, the more

[44] www.kwinta.be/sites/default/files/bijlage/artikel/achieving-excellence-in-govt-service-adopting-efqm.pdf.

diverse in financial, demographic or religious terms the society of the region is, the more difficult this process becomes. The analysis of various macroeconomic ratios reveals a significant economic and social diversity of those countries; no political stability; and progressive Islamisation of life. At the same time, the needs of sub-Saharan Africa and its inhabitants are incommensurably greater than the needs of the majority of societies living on other continents. Therefore, what is being sought are any opportunities to improve the situation in the region concerned. The development of a new approach in the public finance theory that will combine conventional and Islamic finance principles to implement joint infrastructural projects under the PPP mechanism may be useful, among other things, specifically in sub-Saharan Africa. This approach will, however, present a theoretical concept for many developing world economies, as well as conventional and Islamic investors who aim at improving social welfare. While proposing a heterodox approach to PPP, one should take note of current scientific achievements in that field other than those of Marshall or Walras. These, however, refer mostly to economics. The development of neoclassical economics led to the emergence of some innovative trends in science, such as the historical school or Austrian school of economics.[45] Those two schools share a criticism of classical, and then also of neoclassical, economics. The scientists claimed that the laws governing the economy were never universal, and that they should be discovered along with the changes taking place in the development of societies. Therefore, the proposed heterodox approach to PPP is a significant contribution to the development of finance in economic sciences as it refines the heterodox approach in economics with respect to strictly financial phenomena, such as public finance, public-private partnership or risk management in investments. The heterodox economics is based on the theoretical criticism of neoclassical theory of economics, while at same time laying foundations for an alternative school of thought. It is a combination of various economists' approaches, including one of the first authors to contest the achievements of orthodox economics, namely J. Dorfman (in the late 1960s). He used the term of heterodox economics to describe not only his own achievements, but also those of other authors, including, among others, J. A. Hobson, T. Veblen or J. R. Commons. Those authors rejected the orthodox, neoclassical trend in economics, although not necessarily the neoclassical theory as a whole. T. Veblen underlined that economics should treat institutions as certain thinking habits that require research and evolutionary approach. He argued that culture strongly affected economic policy. J.A. Hobson, in turn, criticised laissez-faire and called for strong public scrutiny with respect to economy. He rejected profit orientation considered to be a priority in modern economies. Similarly, J.R. Common pointed to the importance of interference of state and society in the functioning of the economy for the achievement of social justice.[46] Similar research was conducted by A. Grunchy who, in 1987, applied the

[45] de Soto [32].

[46] A. Horodecka, *Instytucjonalizm i podejście instytucjonalne do polityki gospodarczej*, www.instytut.info, p. 125.

notion of heterodoxy in the context of institutional and Post-Keynesian economics as those in opposition to the then mainstream economics.[47]

Both Grunchy and other institutionalists were alone in their views that had, until 1990, often been regarded as blasphemous by Keynesists, Marxists and other radical economists. After that period, numerous schools of thought came into being that stood, to a certain degree, in contrast to the neoclassical theory, including, among others, Austrian economics, mentioned before, as well as feminist economics, institutional-evolutionary economics, Post-Keynesian and Sraffian economics (after Pierro Sraffa), social and ecological economics. Such non-traditional and non-neoclassical trends came to be termed "heterodox". The heterodox approach in economic sciences was also promoted by a circle of scientists grouped together in one of the societies, i.e. in the Society of Heterodox Economists that was formed in 1999 at the University of Glasgow in Scotland, UK. It is committed to pluralistic analyses of contemporary world, including, among other things, globalisation and geographical inequality, influence of religion and social norms on economic phenomena, ethical bases for competing economic systems, fundamental uncertainty, value and debt.[48] In addition to the aforementioned Society, there are 20 other similar scientific organisations in place that bring together theoreticians of the new school of thought in economics, partially contesting its neoclassical foundations.[49] They try to find a common ground between the achievements of:

- social economics, focusing on ethics, morality, social justice in the institutional environment;
- pragmatic approach of institutionalists as shown in the normative theory of progress;
- Marxists in the area of class theory and economic surplus;
- feminist economics, taking account of gender, class and ethnic origin relations in the context of differences in social development;
- Post-Keynesianism, with respect to real-time institution analysis and its influence on the effectiveness of demand, uncertainty and monetary policy.

The heterodox approach in economics should also be mentioned in the context of Islamic Moral Economy (IME). M. A. Choudhury is a key author in this area, developing Islamic, heterodox, epistemological theory of social ethics and pointing to the development of this field and its broad application opportunities.[50]

In his opinion, the limited scope of current schools of economics is devoid of any broader analysis or reflection in the area of morality and ethics. He emphasises a potential contribution of the monotheistic religion of Islam to the development of new trends in economics. In Chap. 5 of his book, he states that it is even harder for economics to be heterodox under the outdated rules of *Shari'ah* law or under

[47] www.heterodoxnews.com/directory/intro.htm z dnia 01.08.2016.

[48] www.hetecon.net.

[49] www.hetecon.net/?page=about&side=heterodox_economics.

[50] Choudhury [33].

the rules of Islamic finance that are often subject to commercialisation.[51] A more widespread application of the philanthropist rules of Islamic Moral Economy turned out to be impossible and has not as yet been followed as a development direction. The main message of the post-orthodox trend in economics would be for economics to be more deeply rooted in the moral, ethical and social aspects of economies. Quoting H. Henderson,[52] Choudhury states that economics inexorably moves towards departing from the constant dimension of economic development measured with GDP towards services and provision of real goods that affect the standards of living of societies. Their welfare and living standards should be described by a new key economic metric in the evaluation of economies. The trend proposed herein significantly refines Choudhury's findings, especially in the narrower area, i.e. in the discipline of finance. In that field, considerably less new trends have emerged so far that could be viewed as heterodox in financial sciences. They refer mainly to financial crisis theories and heterodox scientific approach to combating them.[53] An in-depth analysis of causes and consequences of financial crises including the identification of similarities and differences in solutions proposed by economists to resolve post-crisis market problems is presented by J. Munoz in his article entitled *Orthodox versus heterodox (Minskyan) perspectives of financial crisis: explosion in the 1990s versus implosion in the 2000s.*[54] Analysing the comparison between the Keynesian achievements and the findings that further expand them, e.g. those of H. P. Minsky, in the aspect of the state's role in the face of financial crises, he underlines that the discretionary intervention of both the government (creating budget deficit) and the central bank (as a lender of the highest instance) limits market instability by setting upper and lower limits of financial system dynamics. He calls for the socialisation of investments and restructuring of government activities. Governments may generate deficits in order to fulfil their stabilising role and implement discretionary policy which is aimed at economic recovery rather than alleviation of economic ills.[55] Within such meaning, one may see an intention to depart from debt finance and move towards equity finance as a permanent method to mitigate risks stemming from interest rate increases.[56] It is, however, both an institutional problem and a problem of financial system's underdevelopment. For innovative financiers, financial crises are an intrinsic element of both emerging and developed economies. According to orthodox scientists in that field, financial crises will not happen if economies are based on strong assets,[57] are not excessively indebted[58] and are internally independent.[59]

[51]Choudhury and Bhatti [34].

[52]Choudhury [35].

[53]Ryner [36].

[54]Levy Economics Institute, 2011.

[55]Munoz [37].

[56]Muñoz and Snowden [38], World Development 6(40), p. 1109 (pp. 1109–1121).

[57]Caballero [39].

[58]McKinnon and Pill [40].

[59]Dornbusch [41].

This study proposes a heterodox approach to PPP which is, similarly to the critics of neoclassical theory of finance, based on induction rather than deduction. It proves the hypothesis that it is possible to achieve convergence between mainstream trends in the science of public finance and Islamic finance. Public-private partnership is a key method of achieving convergence because it proves that a long-term cooperation between partners who follow different canons of financial sciences is indeed possible. The heterodox approach to PPP should:

- reject Pareto-optimal choice;
- transform Arrow's utility function into a developed concept of social utility of business;
- introduce real corporate social responsibility not only for public but also for private entities;
- avoid the agent-principal conflict by adopting predetermined objectives and predetermined financial results.

The application of heterodox approach to public-private partnerships between conventional and Islamic investors must mean that:

- The purpose of the company to be formed under PPP is to provide the society with a specific quantity and quality of public goods in exchange for a satisfactory profit to owners.
- Investment projects are implemented in accordance with corporate social responsibility principles.
- Articles of association of the company to be formed under PPP are to be drafted in such a way that the predetermined portion of financial surplus is always provided to the identified eligible entities while, at the same time, ensuring profits for investors and a sufficient quantity and quality of public goods for the society.
- Private investors do not maximise their desire to make a profit but rather accept a feasible and predetermined value of profits.

The first prerequisite for PPP to be implemented on the basis of the heterodox approach proposed herein provides for the fulfilment of the key public purpose of PPP, i.e. the public-private entity's long-term provision of public goods/services for a predetermined price and in accordance with the availability and quality of such goods/services for local communities as imposed in the PPP agreement. Pareto-optimal choice is thus rejected. This would mean a situation where it would be impossible to improve one person's situation without adversely affecting that of another person. Here, however, the aim is to reach consensus between profit expectations on the part of private investors and the fulfilment of welfare function by public entities. To attain one goal must not mean that the other key objective of PPP is to be abandoned (Fig. 4.3).

The second prerequisite of the approach concerned is the obligation to apply corporate social responsibility, as existing under conventional conditions. It is not, however, a universal trend or a trend that would be required under conventional conditions by specific legal norms. It should be assumed that from the point of view of an Islamic investor, the obligation to ensure social welfare is an obvious

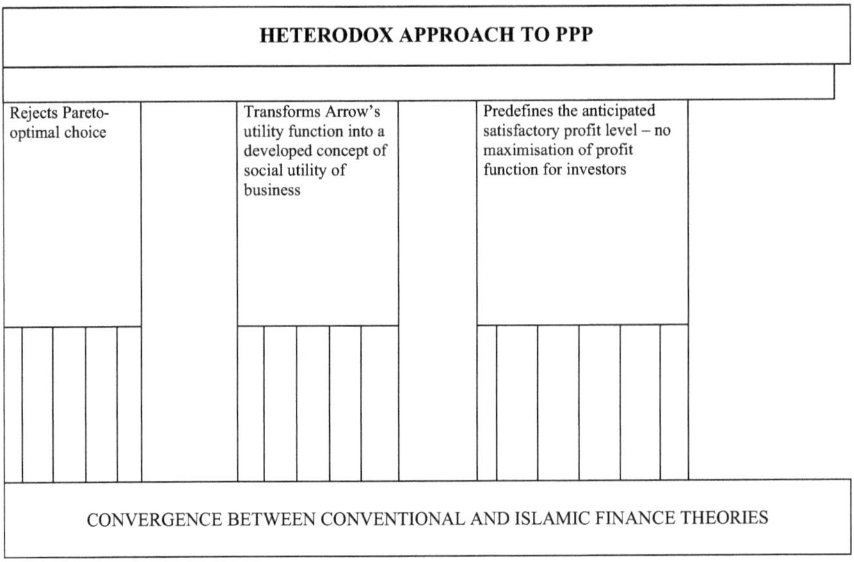

Fig. 4.3 Graphical overview of the key pillars of heterodox approach to PPP. *Source* author's own study

transposition of *Quran's* principles and the basic objective of economic activity in Islam. This principle, as mentioned hereinabove, is of religious nature and it is indisputable. It does, however, constitute a precondition for Islamic investors to conduct business. For conventional private investors, it will be a new tool. The level of sums to be provided over and above *nisaab* will always be subject to negotiations between partners, although, if predetermined, it will protect the investor against moral hazard or searching for other possibilities to maximise the profit function. Forcing conventional investors to support social welfare of those who will use the infrastructure built and managed under the PPP may be a win–win situation. On the one hand, the final beneficiary (representative of the community) will gain access to the desired public service, whereas, on the other hand, the private entity will earn the predetermined profit by ensuring that there are regular users of the infrastructure in question.

The third prerequisite fully implements the PPP function, as well. For instance, if we rely on the principles of operation of a publicly funded healthcare institution, the logical reasoning would be as follows:

- If the costs of a medical procedure are fixed (there is a fixed set of procedures, technologies, tools and costs of labour related to each medical procedure), then with the fixed value of revenues for the procedure (public or private payer will pay the healthcare institution a predetermined sum for a specific procedure), the public-private investor (healthcare institution) should agree to and accept the predetermined value of profit.

- It may then also agree to the predetermined value of financial transfers over and above *nisaab*. Why wouldn't it maximise its profit function by accepting financial transfers above *nisaab*? Because in the face of a fixed level of funding from the public payer it does not have too many opportunities to save costs without compromising the quality of services or causing, e.g. an increased number of deaths or complications. Therefore, the public payer ensures not only the provision of public services to the community via the special purpose vehicle, but also the redistribution of financial surplus over and above *nisaab* at the place where it has actually been generated (which is more effective and procedurally less expensive from the society's point of view). It is, therefore, on the one hand, compliant with the theory of Islam and, on the other hand, provides a real chance to achieve compromise between the two investors coming from different economic systems.

Such a structure of financial transfers is, however, possible only in the case of PPP, because otherwise a private healthcare institution operating under purely conventional conditions would each time maximise its profit without fulfilling the corporate social function. It would thus fail to fulfil the fourth condition of heterodox approach to PPP presented herein. Under conventional conditions, the private investor not only wants to, but is indeed bound by law to generate profits. A negative financial result maintained over a long period of time might mean that a bankruptcy petition will be filed against such an entrepreneur, irrespective of their future plans. It is also true that each private investor undertakes economic activity under conventional conditions to make a profit. In the case of heterodox approach, it is assumed that the convergence of Islamic and conventional finance prompts investors to establish a specific point—the value of anticipated profit that would guarantee business satisfaction. Any financial flows generated over and above the identified level will be used to fulfil the aforementioned social function of economic activity. This argument of heterodox approach can be applied even under the currently applicable principles of conventional corporate accounting both in Poland and worldwide, irrespective, however, of the impact that such financial transfers may have on tax optimisation of those companies.

It is further worth noting that the heterodox approach to PPP, as proposed herein, may also form an application solution to the problem of provision and financing of public services which, in their essence, will never generate profits. These include, among other things, such public goods as defence, road or administrative infrastructure. By adopting the principles of the theoretical heterodox approach to PPP proposed herein, partners will be obligated to seek sources of profit. Otherwise, no long-term cooperation would be possible, but also, in view of public finance crisis, it might mean in specific situations that the state would fail to fulfil its function. The convergence of public and private partners' objectives, with the use of specific principles derived from the theory of Islamic finance, would therefore become a key element in the process of fulfilment of the public finance function. In view of the anticipated financial involvement of the public entity in the special purpose vehicle formed under the PPP, an in-kind contribution to such SPV may include, e.g. assets that are not the subject of the public service provided. Thus, the SPV would have a chance to generate profits and have some of its liabilities secured by its assets which are often much more liquid than the assets being the subject of public investment or used for the provision of public services. The most striking example of the use of public assets to generate quantifiable profits is gambling in Monaco. Gambling, as an activity not easily associated with broadly defined public services, may also be the source of positive financial results for public companies. Therefore, it may be assumed that the public-private entity will provide an unprofitable public service consisting, e.g. in the maintenance of bridges, parks and cycling paths. It could then make profits on another, auxiliary activity, with respect to which it has contributed specific tangible assets to the same SPV formed as part of the PPP. Such activity could relate to any areas permitted under both conventional legislation regarding public finance and the *Shari'ah* law. Once the objectives of each of the partners are satisfied, any surplus profits in excess of a predetermined value would be redistributed back to local communities using the infrastructure built. It may even be argued that such an organisational model would be more fair from the viewpoint of local communities with respect to the implementation of public entities' policies. Public investment projects implemented currently, e.g. in Poland, with respect to the construction of water parks are a good example of searching for profitable activities by public entities. However, one criticism here is that access to such public services is limited by the application of high prices for the use thereof by the community. This type of project is thus prevented from being a manifestation of the fulfilment of the state's function or local authorities. If, however, a special purpose vehicle were to be formed to maintain public infrastructure, and if it were to additionally generate profits from "commercial" activities, then, as part of the trend concerned, and following satisfaction of owners' expectations and achievement of the maximum level of profit anticipated for them, any remaining financial surplus should be used, e.g. to fund free sporting activities for local students at the water park concerned. It would be a manifestation of social justice, while at the same time offering an opportunity to perform the basic public service, i.e. maintain road infrastructure that would be funded using means from commercial activities. However, in order to ensure balance between the interests of public-private company's owners and those of the local community, a portion of the financial surplus would be used to fund access to commercial services for eligible individuals, in this case public school students (Fig. 4.4).

The vision of public finance development presented herein is based on the use of possibilities offered by the existing schools of economic thought, neoclassical theories that are critical towards them, as well as the religious and social trend of the Islamic Moral Economy. The selected public finance theories may, in their component elements, be compatible with the principles of Islam. The proposed heterodox approach to public finance theory, although referring herein specifically to PPP, lays foundations for the development of long-term forms of international cooperation under PPPs. The successful convergence and co-existence of conventional and Islamic trends may depend on the proper interpretation of Muslim religious rules and current achievements of financial sciences. Another determining factor for the symbiosis between both systems is to achieve a compromise between the basic objectives of economic activity, such as profit and social welfare. The proposed heterodox approach to PPP is consistent with and reflects those expectations, preliminary find-

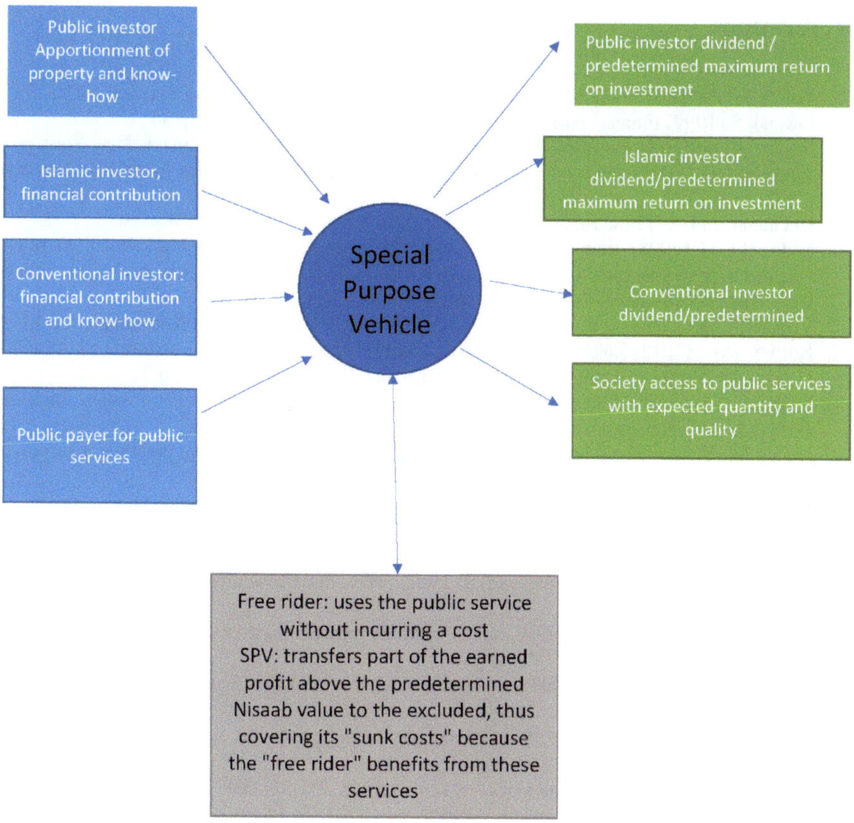

Fig. 4.4 PPP for unprofitable public services. *Source* author's own study

ings and deliberations of the above-named economists in the area of new trends in economics, although to a much narrower extent, as it applies the proposed principles to financial instruments and solutions with respect to risk management in investment projects. What is more, the developed principles broadly reflect the ethics, morality and fairness to the society in the area in which the investment project is being implemented. The convergence between investor expectations and the needs and expectations of local communities may happen in reality with the application of combined conventional and Islamic finance principles, determination of *nisaab* and financial transfers in excess of a predefined profit level to the society, while simultaneously ensuring partners' satisfaction with the level of return on investment in the long term. It is a solution adequate to every model of economy, with particular emphasis on developing countries, and one that offers opportunities for both conventional and Islamic investors, including the public ones, to expand into new markets.

References

1. Loughlin M (2012) Foundations of public law. Oxford University Press, Oxford, p 420
2. Owsiak S (1999) Finanse publiczne. Teoria i praktyka, PWN, Warsaw, p 34
3. Stiglitz JE (1999) Economics of the public sector. W.W. Norton & Company, New York, p 6
4. Eatwell J (eds) (1899) Palgrave's dictionary of political economy. Palgrave Macmillan, London, p 357
5. Buchanan J (1997) Finanse publiczne w warunkach demokracji. PWN, Warsaw
6. Sadowski M (2008) Elementy prawa cywilnego, ze szczególnym uwzględnieniem prawa własności, w świetle prawa islamskiego, In Kozerska E, Sadowski P, Szymański A (eds) Problemy własności w ujęciu historyczno-prawnym, pp 47–56
7. Visser H (2009) Islamic finance principles and practice. Edward Elgar, Northampton, p 11
8. Karwowski J (2012) Zakazy i nakazy w finansach islamskich, Studia Ekonomiczne, Science Notebooks, Wrocław University of Economics, no. 106, Yearbook 2012, p 91
9. Erdem E (2010) The functions of state in determining economic policies in islam tradition. Erciyes Univ J Econ Adm Sci 21–24
10. Nejatullah Siddiqi M (2006) Islamic banking and finance in theory and practice: a survey of state of the art. Islamic Econ Stud 13(2):4–6
11. Khoutem BJ, Hichem H (2014) Profit and losses sharing paradigm in Islamic banks: constraints or solutions for liquidity management? J Islamic Econ Banking Finan 10(3):30
12. Karwowski J (2011) Sukuk: islamskie certyfikaty inwestycyjne, In Finanse: nowe wyzwania teorii i praktyki. Rynki finansowe. red. K. Jajuga, Wrocław University of Economics, Wrocław, p 234
13. Alexander AJ (2011) Shifting title and risk: Islamic project finance with western partners. Mich J Int L 32:575
14. Kabir H, Lewis MK (eds) (2007) Handbook of islamic banking. Edward Elgar, Northampton, p 39
15. Eisenhardt KM (1989) Agency theory: an assessment and review. Acad Manag Rev 14(1):58 (57–74)
16. Salanie B (2005) The economics of contract: a prime, 2nd edn. MIT Press, Cambridge, p 119
17. Piotrowski D (2014) Zastosowanie podstawowej zasady finansów islamskich PLS celem ograniczenia zjawiska moralnego hazardu na rynku usług finansowych. Acta Universitatis Nicolai Copernici Pedagogica, Toruń, p 107
18. Wilkin J (2012) Teoria wyboru publicznego: Główne nurty i zastosowania. Scientific Publisher Scholar, Warsaw, p 11
19. Kociemska H (2015) Ryzyko w partnerstwie publiczno-prywatnym w teorii finansów publicznych i w praktyce. Scientific works of the Wrocław University of Economics, no. 404, Finanse samorządu terytorialnego, eds. L. Patrzałek, H. Kociemska, UE, Wrocław 2015, p 161
20. Tabash IM, Dhankar RS (2014) The relevance of Islamic finance principles in economic growth. Int J Emerging Res Manag Technol 3(2):52
21. Adamek J (2014) Mikrofinanse islamskie: założenia, produkty, praktyka. CeDeWu, Warsaw, p 53
22. Quran (2009) Sura II, verse 284, p 150
23. El-Awa MD (1980) On the political system of the Islamic State. American Trust Publications, Indiana
24. Habib A (2002) Incentive—compatible profit sharing contracts: a theoretical treatment. In: Iqbal M, Llewellyn M (eds) Islamic banking and finance: new perspectives on profit sharing and risk. Edward Elgar Publishing, pp 101–123
25. Arrow JK (1951) Social choice and individual values. Wiley, New York
26. Usami M, Qazi B (2010) Guide do zakah understanding & calculation. Product Development & Shariah Compilance, Maktaba Ma'ariful Qur'an, p 5
27. Al Qardawi (2015) Y Fiqh Al Zakah (Volume I) A Comparative Study of Zakah, Regulations and Philosophy in the Light of Qur'an and Sunnah, Scientific Publishing Centre King Abdulaziz University Jeddah, Saudi Arabia, pp 5–82. http://islamfuture.les.wordpress.com/2010/07/qh-az-zakat-a-comparative-study-volume-i.pdf. Accessed 01 Sept 2015

28. Kuran T (1995) Further reflection on the behavioral norms of Islamic economics. J Econ Behav Organ 27(1):159–163
29. Le Menestrel M (2002) Economic rationality and ethical behavior: ethical business between vanity and sacrifice. Bus Ethics A Eur Rev, pp 11–12
30. Asutay M, Yilmaz I (2015) Constituting islamic social welfare function: an exploration in islamic moral economy, pp 8–9. Istanbul, http://pubdocs.worldbank.org/en/777314466550991 71/pdf/P2-Isa-Yilmaz.pdf
31. Kubiczek A (2014) Jak mierzyć dziś rozwój społeczno-gospodarczy krajów? Nierówności społeczne a wzrost gospodarczy 38(2):44
32. de Soto JH (2010) Szkoła austriacka. Ład rynkowy, wolna wymiana I przedsiębiorczość. Fijorr Publishing, Warsaw, pp 45–68
33. Choudhury MA (1996) The nature of globalization and the muslim world. Spec Issue Manag Finance Struct Change 22(5/6):34
34. Choudhury MA, Bhatti I (2017) Heterodox islamic economics: the emergence of an ethico-economic theory. Routledge, London (Chap. 5)
35. Choudhury MA (1999) Global megatrends and the community. World Futures 53(3):56
36. Ryner M (2012) Heterodox analysis of financial crisis, orthodoxy and heterodoxy in the production of knowledge about the EU. Milenium J Internationa Stud 40(3):647–673
37. Munoz J (2011) Ortodox versus heterodox (Minskyan) perspectives of financial crisis: explosion in the 1990s versus implosion in the 2000s. Levy Economics Institute, working paper no. 695, listopad, p 20
38. Muñoz J, Snowden N (2012) Building a bric? Stock market opening and investment finance in India since liberalization. World Dev 6(40):1109 (pp 1109–1121)
39. Caballero RJ (2006) On the macroeconomics of asset shortages. The National Bureau of Economic Research, working paper no. 12753, pp 3–4
40. McKinnon RI, Pill H (1996) Credible liberalizations and international capital flows: the overborrowing syndrome. In: Financial deregulation and integration in East Asia, vol 5. University of Chicago Press, Chicago, pp 10–15
41. Dornbusch R (2001) The National Bureau of Economic Research. Cambridge, working paper no. 8326, pp 1–2
42. El-Gamal MA (2006) Islamic finance: law economics and practice. Cambridge University Press, New York
43. Rehman AA (2010) Gulf capital and islamic finance. The rise of the new global players. McGraw-Hill, New York, p 4

Chapter 5
Determinants of the Attractiveness of a Public-Private Partnership in a Heterodox Perspective

5.1 Determinants of the Attractiveness of Public-Private Partnerships from the Point of View of a Conventional Investor

In the broadly understood field of finance, motives and objectives of investment are one of the frequent areas of research. The attractiveness of the subject of the transaction often justifies making an investment decision. When proposing a new heterodox approach to PPPs, it is important to emphasise the role that investors can play and to define new objectives that they can achieve in the implementation of PPP investments based on the proposed new theoretical trend in public finance. The growing criticism of classical finance and the growing interest in behavioural finance suggests that the trends being created do not reflect the reality, nor do they provide a solution to the problem of global economies, emerging as a result of the financial crises.[1] The features of the current conventional financial market are as follows:

- Implementation of the classic investment paradigm, which places the profit of the individual as an emanation of *homo oeconomicus*.
- Basing national economies and corporate funds on debt. The creation of debt is disproportionately higher than the accumulation of assets or the production of goods.
- Financial decisions are being taken more and more quickly thanks to strong technological progress. Thus, these decisions are burdened with higher and higher risks through the promotion of derivatives and speculative instruments with an increasingly shorter duration.
- Social objectives of management are always pushed into the remote background, also due to the lack of real incentives to use socially responsible forms of management.

[1] K. Jajuga, *Nauka o finansach: nowe wyzwania metodyczne*, 9th Congress of the Polish Economic Society, www.pte.pl.

H. Kociemska, *Public-Private Partnership for Sub-Saharan Africa*, Advances in African Economic, Social and Political Development, https://doi.org/10.1007/978-3-030-14753-2_5

- The financial crisis has led to a shrinkage of investment resources for conventional investors, which may lead to economic stagnation, especially on the European market.
- Conventional investors are at a competitive disadvantage compared to Islamic investors given smaller financial resources. This limits their ability to expand. The large financial base of Islamic investors, in turn, enables them to easily take over low-capital enterprises in classical economies.

The proposed heterodox approach will be optimal for conventional investors under the following conditions. It is difficult to find financial theories that always and fully meet the expectations of each type of investor. The heterodox approach to PPP can help fulfil the expectations of conventional investors in the conditions of an investment using this method by using safer Islamic financial instruments and by constantly ensuring the implementation of the social function of business.

The first principle of the heterodox approach, which is important for a conventional investor, is to make a profit. This is not about the maximisation of the usefulness of an investment in the understanding of the rational investor model. There is no optimisation in the sense of Pareto. However, the attractiveness of heterodox approach is supported by the fact that profit is indicated as the objective and condition for the performance of the PPP contract. The private partner should co-manage with the public partner in such a way as to achieve the level of profit specified in the PPP agreement for the price of reducing uncertainty as to the result of undertaken actions. According to this theory, the parties to the contract agree on the level of expected profit before it is implemented. They also undertake to cooperate with each other on a long-term basis in order to reach this level. A party to the agreement is also often a public payer, whose financial transfers for public services provided in PPP guarantee the expected return on investment for the owners. It should be assumed, however, that due to different objectives of the cooperating partners—public and private—and the specific subject of management, i.e. public service, the level of expected profit will be lower than in the case of fully commercial investments, but often much longer-lasting. However, it is not possible to achieve high profitability of the sale of public goods in the short term. If this were the case in the economy, that the provision of all public services brings the expected profitability and a quick return on investment, then we would not be faced with public finance crisis or with the need for the state to function at all.

The inability to privatise all public services is emphasised by both economic theoreticians and business practice. The functions of the state were presented by successive doctrines. The seventeenth century brought mercantilism and a strong tendency to raise the significance of the role of the state, protect public ownership of part of the economy and accumulate capital from tax revenues, while taxes were higher for the poorest groups and lower for the groups of potential investors, i.e. the most affluent citizens. The end of the next century was the era of Smith's achievements and economic liberalism, in which the role of the state should be limited to the minimum, to the function of the so-called night watchman of the economy, where public expenses are spent mainly on ensuring the security of countries and foreign policy, and the tax burden should be as low as possible. The development of liberal theory is due to an orthodox theory from the early twentieth century, based on the concept of a small budget, but constantly balanced, and equally limited role of the state. The doctrine of state interventionism popular at the turn of the nineteenth and twentieth centuries, created by the German economist Adolf Wagner, proposed stronger interference of the state in the market. For the first time, the idea of the role of the state arose not only in the sphere of income distribution but also in the sphere of production, the so-called generation of revenue. He also stressed the role of the state in shaping social policy and social security. Wagner's law assumed that real public spending would always increase with increasing public needs, with public needs growing faster than individual needs. In the twentieth century, according to the Keynesian doctrine, the state must stabilise the development of national economies by stimulating demand and at the same time the development of the income side of the state budget to stabilise its expenditure side. After World War II, many subsequent trends were formed, some of which were already described in this monograph. For example, Lerner, an American economist, proposed a role for the state limited to regulating expenditure, especially in combating inflation and unemployment. James M. Buchanan, on the other hand, created the aforementioned *social welfare function,* where the role of the state is to maximise the function of social utility. At the end of the twentieth century, the need to limit the role of the state in the economy was demonstrated by the creators of neoliberalism, such as Milton Friedman.

Further theories of public choice, social choice (discussed earlier) or *New Public Management* (NPM) emerged. None of these doctrines was about a complete departure from certain functions of the state in the economy, but about a different degree of interference of the public authorities in the market. In each of the proposed systems, investors found opportunities for their own development and were able to adjust their goals to the adopted rules of the economies of these countries. Each of the doctrines also assumed a kind of correlation between public and private actors. The proposed heterodox approach calls for a certain balance between the interests of the parties, a consensus between the potential expectations of private investors and the function that should be performed by the public entity in cooperation with the private one. This creates the possibility of convergence between the pillars of conventional public finances and Islamic finances, while at the same time ensuring that the function of social welfare is performed by a public-private entity.

It can be assumed, however, that the lower level of profit specified in the agreement will not decrease the attractiveness of the investment/project in the heterodox approach for private investors. In principle, contractual cooperation in PPP lasts several dozen years. Typical periods for which PPP agreements are concluded are 20 and 25 years, regardless of the market in which they are concluded. This, therefore, completely alters the optics of the conventional investor. In the most extreme conditions, it might mean the transition from investing in *high frequency trading* (a short period of holding a position on the stock exchange, measured in milliseconds) to a contract with a duration of several dozen or so years for cooperation and asset management, with predetermined profitability of sales in the long term. This is certainly a key factor determining the potential attractiveness of the heterodox approach for conventional investors in PPPs.

Another area of attractiveness for the heterodox approach to the interests of a conventional investor is relying on Islamic instruments and applying economic practices so that the transactions undertaken are accompanied as much as possible by the production of real goods and services and the accumulation of assets. Thanks to this way of working, the business venture becomes much more resistant to the impact of financial crises. These are most often the result of speculative stock market bets by entrepreneurs, bankers and governments. From the point of view of a private investor, this guarantees business stability, which is difficult to achieve in a constantly changing economic environment. Stability and resistance to crisis are also a result of the specific nature of the service or public good. According to the definitions of J. M. Buchanan[2] or J. G. Head,[3] the public good is characterised by two features:

- is a *non-rivalry* good, which means that once it is created and available on the market it can be consumed by another person at no extra cost to them; and
- is *non-excludable*; therefore, potential consumers of the public good thus produced cannot be excluded from its consumption.[4]

Public goods in public finance are divided into pure public goods, which theoretically cannot be outsourced to a private entity, and mixed public goods (universal), for which it is already possible to outsource their production to a public entity.[5] Regardless of the type of public good in question, demand for them remains constant and depends only on the number and characteristics of the local community, such as demography, epidemiology, wealth and technological accessibility. The local community always needs access to water, waste management, roads, bridges, motorways, schools, kindergartens, clinics and hospitals, prisons and courts, police and army.[6] These are tasks (mixed goods), the majority of which can be entrusted to public-private investors as part of the PPP concept. There have been many contradictory trends in the history of economic thought regarding this subject. In general, liberals traditionally claimed that the theory of public goods supports the model of the state, but at the same time indirectly pointed to the most important functions of the state, i.e. defence and security. In this area, they assumed the exclusivity of state production of goods. In his research on the usefulness of public goods for consumers and social usefulness, Samuelson concludes that as a result of the common consumption of goods and inefficiencies in charging for a product that has a zero marginal cost of production (public goods), it is not possible to provide these goods on the basis of a decentralised market.[7] He also identifies ineffectiveness of private

---

[2]Buchanan [1].

[3]Fijor [2].

[4]Buchanan [3].

[5]Kleer [4].

[6]Cf. Owsiak [5].

[7]Kwiatkowski [6].

solutions in maximising usefulness. The founders of the Austrian school partly agree with Samuelson, approving of his definition of public good. However, they argue that the definition of public goods does not pose particular problems for the provision of public goods at market conditions. The very nature of public goods in the "mainstream" understanding does not make it necessary for the state to provide them.[8] According to the proposed heterodox approach in public finances, the conventional partner, seeing such a possibility of production/provision of public services, gains a stable number of consumers in its undertaking, and at the same time, according to the assumptions of Islamic finances, it deals with real production of goods and services, without a significant risk of demand or stock market speculation in terms of prices. This is an extremely rare situation on the market regarding private goods. Therefore, the attractiveness of such a situation for the private partner, who prefers to choose a presence on the market with limited competitiveness and profitability imposed in advance of their activity, instead of a strong competitive struggle on the market of private goods and uncertainty as to the financial result.

The third element of this approach, which may satisfy private investors, is the implementation of corporate social responsibility, but not according to Arrow's social function of business. The social objective of management will always be of secondary importance for a private investor, as it may mean bypassing the performance of business functions and maximising profit in its entirety. Meanwhile, a heterodox approach in PPP assumes the implementation of corporate social responsibility and—simultaneously—making profits, while both objectives are made credible thanks to two tasks:

- the very implementation of the PPP itself, the aim of which is to provide a specific public service and not a typical commercial one;
- transfer of funds above the fixed value of *Niṣāb* to the group of entitled persons specified in the agreement. Often, these transfers may take the form of a guarantee by a PPP company that a certain number of final beneficiaries will have free access to public services. This is a multiplication of potential benefits, resulting not only in the implementation of infrastructure investments needed by the society but also from the creation of direct financial transfers to the indicated social group.

Realising this basis for a heterodox approach in PPPs gives conventional investors the opportunity to develop long-term programmes to support society. The long-term nature of these activities is strictly or even inextricably linked to the long-term nature of PPP projects (a key characteristic of PPP structures). Ad hoc transferring of financial resources to selected organisations often raises doubts not only of the owners but also of tax authorities as a tool for broadly understood tax optimisation. However, the allocation of predetermined amounts in the long term, in accordance with the long-term policy of supporting the local community, may make a real contribution to the improvement of the situation of the final beneficiaries. From the point of view of a private investor, this may translate into an increase in the population using the services provided so far. Therefore, the scale of their business activity may increase

[8] Ibid.

(the condition is, of course, an increase in the sources of financing from the payer along with an increase in the number of persons entitled to use the public service provided by the PPP company).

The presented attractiveness factors stem directly from the previously presented pillars of the heterodox approach in PPP. It is worth mentioning other advantages to be taken into account in the context of a broader activity of a conventional investor. Implementation of PPP investments on the basis of achievements of a heterodox economy may be connected with wider access to new markets for a private investor. Independent expansion might not be possible due to limited financial resources. Meanwhile, thanks to the acquisition of an Islamic investor, many markets become accessible due to the capital held by the PPP company. This means the possibility of expansion into new markets and new areas of the industry. The presented data show the value of Islamic investment as well as the target markets in the future. These are often areas where the individual presence of a conventional investor would be significantly hampered, for example, for religious or cultural reasons, but also for historical reasons (colonialism, armed conflicts, etc.) (Fig. 5.1).

The risk of such expansion is again significantly reduced in comparison to conventional export activities, for example, by avoiding risk manipulation, searching for virtual securities and the necessary acceptance of other sociocultural market conditions. A different risk management methodology according to the proposed approach is that the risk is assumed by the entity generating the risk. The new risk management methods will be a kind of added value to the investment, which can already be successfully used in purely conventional financial transactions.

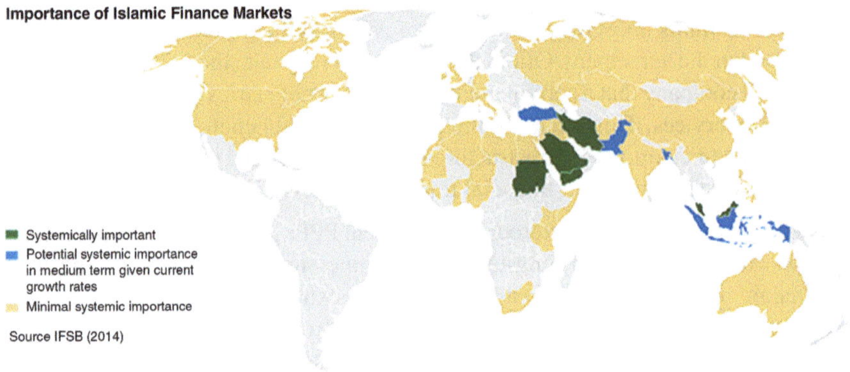

Fig. 5.1 Importance of Islamic financial markets in 2014. *Legend* green—systemically important, blue—potential systemic importance, beige—minimal systemic importance. *Source* International Monetary Fund, http://www.imf.org/external/pubs/ft/fandd/2015/09/prasad.htm

5.2 Determinants of the Attractiveness of Public-Private Partnerships from an Islamic Investor's Point of View

The proposed heterodox approach to public finance provides an opportunity for an Islamic investor to make an investment and manage the long-term assets of a PPP company with a predetermined return. This means that they can balance the goals of the project in terms of profitability and to fulfil their social welfare functions, in line with the *Islamic Moral Economy*. Since cooperation in PPP is always based on an agreement, the provisions of the agreement worked out with a conventional or public partner, in accordance with a heterodox approach, will enable the implementation of cooperation on principles acceptable to religious and social interpretations of the *Quran* and the *Shari'ah* law. A predetermined level of profit is a realistic opportunity to further utilise the long-run surpluses in other markets or in other investment projects, including PPPs, also outside Islamic areas. An important feature of the proposed theoretical solution for Islamic (but also conventional) investors is that the assumed profit level is based on the actual production of public goods or the provision of real public services; this type of financing and long-term management is based on the accumulation of assets and the financing of owners' expectations from the real income generated by the project. The underlying assumptions of the heterodox approach should induce investors to raise capital rather than debt with no coverage in assets. This trend would not only protect the investment project from the effects of financial crises but would also be fully in line with the principles of financial management in Islam. The move away from generating profits from actual production or providing services, the constant financing of these activities using debt with no coverage in assets, all contributed to a decline in the ability to create new products. In return, achieving profitability through speculation on increasingly sophisticated financial instruments was limited to creating opportunities to generate profits for a certain group of investors, owners of banks, brokerage houses and stock exchanges. Profits are often transferred to markets other than those in which they were generated. The economies of the countries also focused on debt transactions and not on creating permanent sources of income in the future. Hence, the assumption of the heterodox approach to PPP on the application of a strong correlation between generating profit and assets in cooperation in a PPP company should encourage Islamic investors to engage in this type of projects, including those with a global reach. This is consistent with the Islamic understanding of the principle of risk-free management, which is always based on the principle of covering financial transfers with the real flow of goods or services. This would, therefore, open up broad access to new investment areas for Islamic investors. So far, investment projects based fully on the classical approaches to financial theory have not allowed Islamic investors to become involved. Hence, the market for the projects carried out was often limited to the territory of the Gulf countries, Asia and selected African countries. Meanwhile, applying fully the assumptions of the heterodox approach to PPPs, consisting in *equity-based* economic transactions (based on assets, real values), may contribute to a greater willingness of Islamic investors to cooperate with conventional investors.

Another source of the attractiveness of heterodox PPPs for Islamic investors is the transfer of *know-how*, technology and human capital in the framework of a PPP. Despite their wealth, these countries have a serious problem in attracting educated and experienced staff. They are highly dependent on the transfer of knowledge and experience with the influx of workers from outside the Gulf States. The highest human resources deficits are recorded in the technical, industrial and IT sectors, health care and education. The educational system which is not adjusted to the needs of the labour market further complicates the situation on the labour market (Table 5.1).

As a result, in a heterodox PPP project, an Islamic investor will have access to resources that they did not have before, including qualified workers and state-of-the-art technology, scientific achievements and the opportunity to use research results for economic purposes. These advantages are often the backbone of conventional markets due to the long tradition of scientific centres and many years of investment in the development of human capital in Europe. Cooperation in PPP, based on heterodox assumptions, enables an Islamic investor to construct such a contractual character of cooperation, in which their involvement is based on ensuring financing, and the conventional partner—material contributions in the form of *know-how*, technology, and the results of research work. The effect of such cooperation is all the more important for an Islamic investor, as the cooperation with a conventional investor is not of a temporary, but long-term nature. The process of "learning" in the organisation discovering new technologies and scientific achievements will thus imply, according to the proposed heterodox approach to PPP, a lasting, stable, long-term effect for both the company itself and the Islamic investor.

It is also worth appreciating another positive result of the existence of a heterodox approach to PPP binding the interests of conventional and Islamic investors, manifested in the more widespread acceptance of *Islamic Moral Economy* in the world of classical finance. A conventional investor cooperating with an Islamic investor in the long term may act as a promoter of such a partnership on the conventional financial markets. This may contribute to the blurring of well-established views on Islam and disappearance of aversion to cooperation in unconventional conditions. The transparency of the proposed approach argues in favour of a high chance of

Table 5.1 Need for human capital in selected Islamic economies by 2020

Growth rates of global Islamic economies	
Assets exceeded USD 1.8 billion (2013F); CAGR 15.2% (1995–2013)	The assets are estimated to reach USD 6.5 million by 2020
Strong lack of highly qualified human capital	
It is estimated that one million experts will be needed in the area of the application of Islamic finance by 2020	Malaysia alone needs additional 56,000 (Islamic and conventional) financial specialists by 2020

Source Own elaboration based on the following documents: *Human capital development. sustaining the growth of Islamic finance*, Malaysia's Islamic Finance Marketplace, 15th Nov. 2013., Malaysia International Islamic Financial Center, p. 1

acceptance of quite obvious solutions by investors, which do not contradict their basic foundations of conventional management. Moreover, the history of this type of long-term cooperation, which is being built within the framework of PPP, speaks for itself in a convincing way.

5.3 Determinants of the Attractiveness of Public-Private Partnerships for the Public Partner

According to public law, including constitutional law, in many countries, the public partner has a statutory obligation to provide public goods and manage financial resources. The provision of public services or their production need not be profit-driven. The economic viability of a public service is not an indicator of the scale or quality of that activity. However, the heterodox approach to PPP allows for effective implementation of public tasks, linked to the profitability of sales expected by the partners. This gives the public entity a chance to optimise between the scale of provided services, their quality, accessibility for the community, but most importantly—to ensure an acceptable level of profit at the same time. This may force public entities to constantly search for the level of optimisation of public service provision in various other areas of the state or regional budget management. Thus, a managerial approach to managing financial resources provides an opportunity for more stable development and improvement of the financial situation of public and local government entities. This is not a new objective in the theory of public finance. For the first time, the term *New Public Management* (NPM) was introduced by Ch. Hood in *A Public Management for All Seasons*?[9] The key values of NPM indicated by F. Naschold and C. von Otter are:

- separating the role of producer from that of supplier or service contractor;
- development of contractual agreements;
- accountability for results;
- making pay and working conditions more flexible;
- separating political action from management processes;
- introduction of market or *quasi-market* elements;
- the application of the principle of *society as a customer*;
- regulation of the processes of providing public services.

Further details on the *New Public Management* model can be found in the theses from *The New Public Management in Action* paper presented in Tables 5.2 and 5.3.

However, the achievements of this theory differ from the proposed heterodox approach to PPPs. The common elements of the NPM and the heterodox approach to PPPs are:

---

[9]Hood [7].

Table 5.2 Characteristics of the NPM model—public service orientation

Detailed characteristics
Implementation of quality promotion programmes in services Implementation of management by quality in public organisations Formulating missions striving towards excellence in the delivery of public services
Analysing the opinions of recipients of services and taking those opinions into account in the management processes
Emphasising the need to empower elected authorities at the expense of the appointed authorities Sceptical assessment of the role of the market in the system of providing public services
Paying attention to the development of knowledge about public services among citizens (e.g. by organising community work, carrying out assessments of social needs)
Provision of services in cooperation with other public administration entities Establishing positions that are accountable for the services provided Introduction of mechanisms of public participation in service management

Source Ferlie et al. [8, p. 15]

- emphasis on improving management skills in public administration;
- promoting contractual forms of cooperation;
- focus on the efficiency of the public service process.

The differences in the basic objectives of public finance sector management according to the proposed heterodox approach to PPP in relation to NPM consist in the assumption in the proposed approach:

- positive assessment of the role of the market in the system of providing public services;
- emphasis on profitability of providing public services, but closely connected with real financial transfers to the community in order to emphasise real corporate social responsibility;
- strict connection of the quality and availability of provided services with the value of financial result obtained in the process of their provision; every investment project should be "self-financed"—the idea of *ring-fenced* in *project finance*, which assumes the lack of guarantees from other public entities for the planned infrastructure project;
- a clear definition of the structure of the public service entity as a public-private entity, whose activities are based on a long-term contract resulting from the convergence of classical financial instruments with those of Islam;
- departure from the assessment of public employees in the light of the financial results obtained from public or investment activities. This is all the more important since the heterodox approach assumes long-term cooperation for the implementation of investments and the management of the public service process for as many as 25 years. It would then be impossible to make the decision to assess the quality of public employees' work dependent on the results of such a long-term cooperation. On the contrary, it could discourage public representatives from undertaking

Table 5.3 NPM model characteristics—orientation on performance

Detailed characteristics
The growing role of financial control Paying attention to the value obtained in exchange for certain funds Maximising results while reducing costs Improving the level of detail of the financial analyses to be carried out Development of information systems used for financial control
Greater importance of managerial leadership Command and control management style Formulating clear objectives for activities and monitoring their fulfilment Empowering senior management in the organisation
Development of financial and substantive audit Implementation of more transparent methods of business analysis Popularisation of the use of standards and benchmarking techniques Promoting the use of questionnaires as a tool to assess performance
Emphasising the responsibility of providers towards service recipients Enhancing the role of the private and non-governmental sectors in the provision of services Increasing market and customer orientation Conducting market experiments with the aim of turning a profit
Deregulation of the labour market Moving away from negotiating working conditions and wages and signing collective agreements at central government level Introduction of high and individually negotiated bonuses for senior managers in connection with shorter periods of employment Increasing turnover of senior management staff
Limiting the possibilities of shaping professional regulations by professional associations Increasing the role of managers at the expense of the influence of professional associations Involvement of freelance professionals (organised in professional associations) in management processes Introducing more transparent rules for access to and activities in the liberal professions, regulated by professional associations
Increasing the empowerment of business managers while ensuring that they are held accountable for their performance
Introduction of new standards in *corporate governance* Limiting the role and influence of representative bodies Growing importance of the governance model for organisations based on boards of directors Moving the centre of power towards strategic decision-making units

Source Ferlie et al. [8, p. 11]

conventional–Islamic PPP initiatives due to the lack of quick and tangible positive financial results of such cooperation. It is also worth criticising the fact that public decisions are short-sighted in NPM or in conventional systems if the reason for making certain decisions is the subsequent evaluation of the quality of public administration, based on short-term financial results of the project. Often, such a system of evaluating the effectiveness of public administration is subject to periods consistent with the term of office of political authorities, where a positive short-term evaluation gives a chance of stable employment to representatives of public administration. The lack of measurable short-term positive results of a PPP project (especially at the investment stage or at the stage of achieving optimum revenues from the payer) in a heterodox approach would mean a negative assessment of the administration or a reluctance to make such investments and related decisions. The implementation of the heterodox approach, therefore, rejects the managerial aspect of assessing the quality of administration, especially on the basis of measurable short-term financial results.

However, the aspect of public administration assessment based on a heterodox approach to PPP is not overlooked by the proposed new theoretical solution. Certainly, the basic instrument used to assess the effectiveness of a public entity's activity in Islam is the *Zakah* instrument described above. PPP projects based on the convergence of Islamic and conventional finance, a number of factors, will hàve a significant impact on the assessment of the public entity:

- the presented knowledge of representatives of the public entity and experience in providing public services used directly for the implementation of the investment process and co-management of the infrastructure created in the long run (knowledge and technology may constitute a contribution-in-kind to the PPP company);
- involvement in the right choice of beneficiaries, counselling on the identification of a group of eligible final beneficiaries, who will receive financial transfers from the company above the value of *Niṣāb*—appropriate pro-social policy;
- effective monitoring of the current activity of the company in order to achieve the expected level of profit, but also of the quality of the public service provided together with commercial partners and additionally monitoring the availability of the service provided to the public.

In principle, a public entity is assessed by the society. The clearly pro-social nature of the investment, based on the creation of long-term prosperity in the region, may contribute to the high approval of the activity. In conclusion, it can be argued that in some areas the heterodox approach to PPP will be identical with the idea of *New Public Management.* In many of the other cases presented above, it constitutes an innovative proposal for the creation of public-private relations in the process of providing public services.

The main attribute of the heterodox approach to PPPs for the public entity is access to a wide range of potential investors, including financing entities, conventional investors and Islamic investors. The need for financing public expenditure is increasing in view of the often-shrinking sources of revenue. The problem of the budget crisis of states or local governments is significant for the countries of Europe, America and, most certainly, sub-Saharan Africa. Additionally, in African countries, the problem is exacerbated by the extensive administration and military structures, which absorb most of the budget revenue. Major external financing needs, therefore, persist, not only in Africa but also in other continents. This financing is necessary not only to implement the required investments, in many countries the indicators of public or local government debt indicate the loss of liquidity, as well as financial difficulties in fulfilling basic public tasks. The financial background of conventional investors, especially Islamic ones, is a key factor in determining the attractiveness of the heterodox model.

Another factor in the positive assessment of the heterodox approach to PPP from the point of view of a public entity is the security of rules of financing investments in the framework of PPP using certain instruments typical for Islamic finance. Basing financial transactions on the transfer of capital and assets helps to prevent speculation. The investment is intended to be self-financing and to produce real services/good goods as a *project finance* initiative. Profit results from direct business activity. It is therefore proposed that this is a fair, transparent way of obtaining a return on invested funds, which should be particularly important for the management of public funds.

Another area which proves the attractiveness of the heterodox approach to PPP is the internationalisation of public-private investments. This may lead to the internationalisation of the economies of the countries undertaking such investments and acting on the basis of the proposed approach. This may be called a synergy effect, where combined public and private forces, as well as conventional and Islamic systems, may contribute to a wider globalisation of the solutions adopted, as well as to the rapid spread of implemented public service paths to other markets. It will not only result in the promotion of the region or the state, but also in the growth potential of a given country for other investors in future investments.

A further benefit of this approach to PPPs from a point of view of a public entity is a greater independence from international aid. Attracting private investors for projects and their implementation in the proposed form of PPP will contribute to increasing the welfare of the society. This will reduce the funding for public needs through international assistance. It is often postulated that the flow of aid capital does not fully contribute to the development of the economies of the countries to which such aid is granted. This is particularly evident in countries of sub-Saharan Africa, where the high inertia of public authorities, on the one hand, and the lack of knowledge and technology to develop public infrastructure, on the other, result in a waste of resources or at least a low level of efficiency. In some cases, non-repayable aid in the form of subsidies to other economic areas distorts the market by artificially inflating the prices of services provided to public entities. It also causes a kind of stagnation among local investors in view of their willingness to acquire individual sources of financing for their own development.

The final advantage of the heterodox approach to PPPs for the public entity is the direct realisation of the social welfare function. The directness of the implementation of the pro-social policy consists in transferring the funds exceeding the *Niṣāb* level accumulated by the company for the benefit of the entitled groups or even entire societies. These transfers are made directly by a public-private entity, while at the same time often bypassing the often-extensive public administration functioning on the basis on other principles. This contributes to higher values of such transfers, thanks to avoiding administrative costs. Social acceptance of a business venture will increase if the populace is not only a direct recipient of public services but also the monetary transfer above the *Niṣāb* level. Thanks to these transfers, additional access to public services is guaranteed for the general public, especially for people who have been excluded from such access for various reasons, e.g. those who do not have health insurance.

5.4 Heterodox Approach to Public-Private Partnership and the Resilience of Infrastructure Investment to Global Financial Crises

The global financial crises of the last several decades have had a strong negative impact on the economies of many countries, including the economic system of Sub-Saharan Africa that serves as an example for the purpose of this monograph. There has been a slowdown in stable development, and in many of its countries, the food, energy and climate crisis (agriculture) have become even more destructive. As a result of the decrease in foreign trade after 2009, trade turnover decreased significantly, in view of the growing aversion of conventional investors to economic and political risk. Sub-Saharan Africa's share in global trade has consistently fallen from 4% in 1970 to 2% in 2007 and remained at a similar level in subsequent years. Intra-continental trade is characterised by the same low values.[10] Monoculturalism is another characteristic feature of these countries, with more and more often the dominant Islamic approach to management. The main factors of economic errors are: low level of labour productivity, incorrect choice of technology or complete lack thereof, bureaucratisation of the public sector and corruption, unfavourable long-term trends in the prices of natural resources, lack of efficient communication system, including difficult access to the sea, lack of interest on the part of foreign investors, social unrest and political instability. This means that these countries will continue to be embroiled in a deepening structural crisis. Before 2010, the region was not particularly attractive as an investment area.[11] However, conventional investors have suffered significant financial losses as a result of successive crises in Europe and the USA. Thus, they have started to notice many other territorial investment opportunities in the future, including in sub-Saharan Africa. With the instability of world markets caused by the global crisis, opportunities for foreign investment in other areas emerged. These include new markets for conventional investors such as Saudi Arabia, the United Arab Emirates, Qatar, Kuwait, Oman and Lebanon. The growth of foreign investment in these countries in recent years has remained stable, despite the so-called Arab Spring.[12] It was noted that these countries experienced the effects of the deteriorating global market situation to a much lesser extent. Basing their economies on safe financial instruments linked to assets has protected investors from speculative

---

[10]Zajączkowski [9].

[11]Cf. K. Ćwikliński, *Specyfika zadłużenia publicznego krajów Afryki Subsaharyjskiej*, p. 282.

[12]Region Bliskiego Wschodu i Afryki Północnej: postęp po arabskiej wiośnie, http://www.coface.pl/layout/set/print/AKTUALNOSCI-I-MEDIA/Biuro-prasowe/Region-Bliskiego-Wschodu-i-Afryki-Polnocnej-postep-po-Arabskiej-Wiosnie.

risks and high financial losses due to currency fluctuations. At the same time, this meant that the financial rules of Islam were becoming increasingly understandable and acceptable to conventional investors, thanks to the fact that they guaranteed much less risk. Unfortunately, sub-Saharan Africa has not yet become an attractive region for conventional foreign investors who do not use Islamic instruments. Therefore, both politicians and economists are still looking for optimal ways out of the difficult economic and social situation of the region in question. Among other things, they assume that it is possible that a part of the foreign currency debts of the countries of Sub-Saharan Africa can be written off. Moreover, the drainage of natural resources should be stopped by promoting investments inside the continent and preventing the mechanism of exploitation of the poor countries by the rich ones.[13]

In conclusion, the implementation of the assumptions of the heterodox approach to PPP could lead to a slow recovery of selected countries from the crisis by strengthening the role of these economies in the international arena and seeking paths of exit in cooperation with conventional and Islamic investors. Attention to the economic potential of sub-Saharan Africa and the possibility of implementing safe Islamic financial instruments could increase interest among investors in this area. This will ensure, on the one hand, the required inflow of capital to public-private investments in the framework of PPPs and, on the other hand, a much safer but often predetermined rate of return for conventional investors.

An investment using the PPP model on Islamic–conventional terms avoids part of the risk and makes it impossible to use speculative instruments (derivatives). Linking every financial transaction with the transfer of assets and a fixed credit price makes the economic processes more realistic. This may become a real tool to mitigate the international exchange rate risk. The use of Islamic financial instruments would also limit fluctuations in the price of natural resources, which have often been a form of repayment of debts to other countries. What is more, *sukuk*, could turn out to be one of the more important instruments in international exchange. The structure of *sukuk* stems from the traditional idea of securitisation, according to which a special purpose vehicle (like in PPP) is created, which acquires assets and issues ownership titles to shares and rights in these assets. Such investment certificates—*quasi-bonds*—confirm the ownership of a portion of the assets and benefits derived therefrom for a specified period of time. The risk and rate of return related to the cash flows generated by the assets in the SPV portfolio are transferred to the investors.[14] Both the primary and secondary markets for the trading of these certificates are free from speculation. The safety of a *sukuk* instrument is based on its fixed rate of return on investment. *Sukuk* characterised by a variable rate of return constitutes only a small part of the overall market. Fluctuations in the market interest rate have the greatest impact on the valuation and profitability of investments in *murabah sukuk*. In the case of this category of *sukuk*, the rate of return on purchase

---

[13]Report: "Overcoming Fragility in Africa: Forging a New European Approach." European Cooperation Report 2009, Robert Schuman Centre for Advanced Studies, European University Institute, San Domenico di Fiesole.

[14]Cf. Mannan [10].

and sale of assets is fixed and unchanged, and it results from the risk of holding the acquired assets. The source of this risk may be a deterioration in the quality or a decrease in the market value of assets. On the other hand, the impact of interest rate changes on the valuation of *musharakah sukuk* is negligible.[15] The majority of the types of *sukuk* instruments meets the postulated idea of *profit and loss sharing* in a PPP SPV. The problem of agent-principal relationship is eliminated by setting a predetermined expected rate of return. Other *sukuk* instruments used in practice are presented in Table 5.4.

The use of safe Islamic financial instruments, including *sukuk* certificates, will contribute, on the one hand, to strengthening the internal market through a permanent link between the economic exchange and the assets being traded. On the other hand, it will make it possible to attract conventional and Islamic investors, creating new standards of international exchange. This type of trade will not lead to a further reduction in the raw material base of the countries concerned by manipulating the exchange rates in the settlements of international sales or purchase transactions, as well as credit.

The implementation of further principles of the heterodox approach to PPP, focusing on increasing the social utility of business, should also prove to be an effective tool to counteract the crisis, in this case the outflow of all cash or cash transactional profits or tangible assets abroad. Introducing the requirement to transfer the previously indicated amounts of money above *Niṣāb* to the religiously entitled would counteract the exploitation of local communities by the SPVs. It could also induce an investor in PPP to engage the local residents in cooperation with a special purpose vehicle and to transfer *know-how* to local communities, public authorities or investors in the scope of the organisation of economic processes. The structure of PPP and its primary objective for the public partner, which is to provide access to public services, such as medical care, is a major contribution to increasing social welfare in the region. Therefore, it is an example of the implementation of the assumptions of the proposed heterodox approach to PPP. Increased levels of social welfare may contribute to better management skills in these countries and, consequently, to greater resilience to the consequences of financial crises in the future. The greater independence of these economies and the mobilisation of their own human and production resources are important factors in shaping local prosperity. However, it should be remembered that the implementation of the heterodox approach to PPP is based on the connection of public and private capital and thus on finding a compromise between the expected maximisation of profit of private investors and the achievement of the social goal of a public or Islamic entity. A private investor must identify certain attributes in order to be able to operate in a manner consistent with the proposed heterodox approach. From the point of view of a conventional private investor, these positive arguments could be:

- the reduction of speculative risk by using secure financial instruments with a fixed rate of return or a specific level of profit;

[15] Akkizidis and Khandelwal [11].

Table 5.4 *Sukuk* certificates built on the basis of a homogeneous group of assets

Type of *sukuk*	Description of an instrument
Sukuk al-ijarah	Securitisation of existing leased tangible assets. The certificates confirm the ownership of clearly defined, existing assets, which are linked with the *ijarah* contract
Sukuk al-murabaha	Raising funds for the purchase of goods to be sold according to *murabaha* rules
Sukuk al-musharaka	Sale of shares in a company. The owner of the company may look for new shareholders by issuing *sukuk*. Holders of the *sukuk* certificates bear the risk connected with the company's activities and participate in potential profits
Sukuk al-mudarabah	Mobilisation of financial resources from capital providers. An entrepreneur who has an idea for a business but does not have sufficient financial resources can obtain funds from capital providers in this way. Holders of the *sukuk* certificates bear the risk of business activity and participate in the profits from *mudarabah*
Sukuk al-salam	Advance sale of goods and merchandise which will be delivered on a specified date in the future
Sukuk al-istisn'a	Raising funds for the construction or production of specific assets
Sukuk al-wakala	Acquisition of certain assets, which are subsequently entrusted to a specialist managing them on behalf of their owners. Holders of the *sukuk* certificates bear the risk connected with the base assets and are entitled to receive profits generated by the assets
Sukuk ijarah mowsufa Bi-thima	Acquisition of funds for the purchase of tangible assets, which will be subsequently leased
Sukuk manafaa ijarah	Securitisation of revenues from existing leased assets
Sukuk manafaa ijarah mowsufa bi-thima	Securitisation of revenues from assets to be acquired and leased
Sukuk al-muzra'a	Raising funds to finance the cultivation of agricultural land. Holders of such *sukuk* certificates are entitled to a part of the profits from the sale of the crops, in line with the terms of the concluded contract
Sukuk al-musaqa	Acquisition of financing for fruit tree irrigation systems and maintenance costs
Sukuk al-muqarasa	Obtaining funds for planting trees and covering their maintenance costs. Certificate holders are entitled to profits from tree plantations

Source Brugnoni [12]

- opening up the potential of new Islamic markets, which so far have given purely conventional partners the opportunity to make very limited international investments, both in terms of their values and in terms of their industries;
- with gradually falling interest rates and profitability of capital investments on conventional global markets, a conventional investor would have a chance to achieve not returns on investment that would not be necessarily higher, but certainly more realistic, especially in the case of PPP projects with guaranteed monetary transfers from the public payer for services provided by the company;
- clear capital separation of the special purpose vehicle in PPP, including in Islamic–conventional conditions, allows the investor to avoid the domino effect, i.e. the loss of liquidity due to bankruptcy of entities related to a special purpose vehicle, or insolvency of a public entity (management based on the principle of *profit and loss sharing* concerns only special purpose vehicles, in which guarantees are eliminated both in *project finance* and the Islamic financial rules).

In conclusion, the proposed assumptions of the heterodox approach to PPP translate into greater resilience of investment undertakings using this model to the financial crisis, because:

- wide introduction of *sukuk* certificates with a fixed rate of return eliminates the problem of maximising uncertain profit and unlimited speculation;
- leaving a part of the profit earned in the countries where the investment was carried out, i.e. the place where the PPP special purpose vehicle operates, limits the outflow of all capital to other markets;
- transferring some part of the generated profit exceeding the *Niṣāb* level to local communities constitutes management based on the idea of increasing social welfare and business responsibility, thus providing access to financing from the Islamic investors, who consider this goal a priority;
- involving local public authorities, national authorities, entrepreneurs and the public in the functioning of PPP companies in order to enable the transfer of knowledge and skills; increasing the level of knowledge and improving the qualifications of management gives a better chance of finding adequate tools for crisis prevention in the future, both locally and globally.

The implementation of the heterodox approach in these countries is threatened by the lack of stable public authority and, therefore, by social and political turmoil. This factor disturbs the principles of this approach, especially in the area of expectations of achieving a predetermined level of profit by conventional partners. The impact of unstable public authorities may translate into changes of representatives in the PPP SPV. As a result, cooperation based on the giving up some of the powers and privileges by investors—both Islamic and conventional—may become increasingly difficult. However, due to the important objective of transferring surplus financial resources to the eligible entities, but only after the target profit has been reached, the wasteful behaviour of public partners in the special purpose vehicle may be limited. This will limit the impact of unfavourable political changes on the loss of resilience of Islamic–conventional structures in the face of a crisis. The objective of the public body is to ensure social welfare, and the financial transfers to the needy will only occur once the level of *Niṣāb* has been reached. Each of the partners in such a joint venture is interested in fulfilment of contractual assumptions, and the level of achievement of particular interests of each of the parties is conditioned by a consistent, contractual Islamic–conventional cooperation.

References

1. Buchanan JM (1968) The collected works of J.M. Buchanan, vol 5. The Demand and Supply of Public Goods. Liberty Fund Inc. http://oll.libertyfund.org/titles/buchanan-the-collected-works-of-james-m-buchanan-vol-5-the-demand-and-supply-of-public-goods
2. Fijor JM (2011) Czy dobra publiczne są naprawdę publiczne. Stud Ekon 1:88 (Fijorr Publishing)
3. Buchanan JM (1997) Finanse publiczne w warunkach demokracji. Wydawnictwo Naukowe PWN, Warsaw, p 29
4. Kleer J (2006) Sektor publiczny w Polsce i na świecie. Wydawnictwo CeDeWu, pp 274–275
5. Owsiak S (2005) Finanse publiczne. Teoria i praktyka. Wydawnictwo Naukowe PWN, Warsaw, pp 25–26
6. Kwiatkowski S (2014) Teoria dóbr publicznych i rynkowe mechanizmy ich produkcji. In: Pod prąd głównego nurtu ekonomii. Instytut Misesa
7. Hood Ch (1991) A public management for all seasons? Public Adm 69(Spring):3–19
8. Ferlie E, Ashburner L, Fitzgerald L, Pettigrew A (1996) The new public management in action. Oxford University Press, Oxford
9. Zajączkowski K (2010) Przestrzeń i granice a regionalizm w Afryce Subsaharyjskiej: afrykańska i europejska percepcja. In: Żukowski A (ed) Przestrzeń i granice we współczesnej Afryce, vol 10. Forum Politologiczne series, Olsztyn, p 207
10. Mannan M (2008) Islamic capital market. In: Anwar H (ed) Islamic finance: a guide for international business and investment. GMB Publishing, London, p 106
11. Akkizidis I, Khandelwal SK (2008) Financial risk management for Islamic banking and finance. Palgrave Macmillan, New York, pp 42–79
12. Brugnoni A (2008) Sharia governance at work: from asset-based to asset back Sukuk. Shirkah 7:21

Chapter 6
Example of Investments in the Formula of Public-Private Partnership Using the Heterodox Perspective

Referring to the previous chapters, this chapter presents a practical model of the deliberations into the adequacy of the proposed heterodox approach in public finance for the implementation of PPP projects. It points to the process of risk management in PPP projects, taking into account the management objectives of various partners, i.e. public and private, conventional and Islamic. The subject of the analysis is a model of a healthcare institution specialising in the provision of highly specialised medical services in the field of cardiac surgery and rehabilitation. The entity is located in one of the countries of sub-Saharan Africa—Botswana. The specific location is only intended to underline the specificities of emerging countries, especially in sub-Saharan Africa, which may become new areas of interest to investors and require the development of public finance management functions and rules. The sources of information used to create the model are the results of research carried out, among others at the Rhodes University in South Africa, within the framework of the research project "Public-private partnership as a solution for the development of the health care system in East Cape Province, SA" and at the Glasgow University (Scotland) within the framework of the scientific project "Public-private partnership projects in healthcare sector: Theoretical and practical implications for EU countries". At the same time, the knowledge of the medical sector, especially in the area of cardiac surgery, is the result of 1.5-year scientific cooperation with a company operating in this sector in Poland. As part of the funding of scientific and implementation research by the City of Wrocław, a research project entitled "Development of DCChS Medinet sp. z o.o. and Public-Private Partnership" was carried out within the framework of the Mozart Programme, and a project of internationalisation of this company has been developed.

An example of an investment project is the establishment of a *special purpose vehicle* (SPV) in Botswana. The shares are distributed as follows: Polish private investor, Islamic private investor, Ministry of Health & Wellness of Botswana, any public entity from Poland. The total value of the shares is USD 7 million, including:

H. Kociemska, *Public-Private Partnership for Sub-Saharan Africa*,
Advances in African Economic, Social and Political Development,
https://doi.org/10.1007/978-3-030-14753-2_6

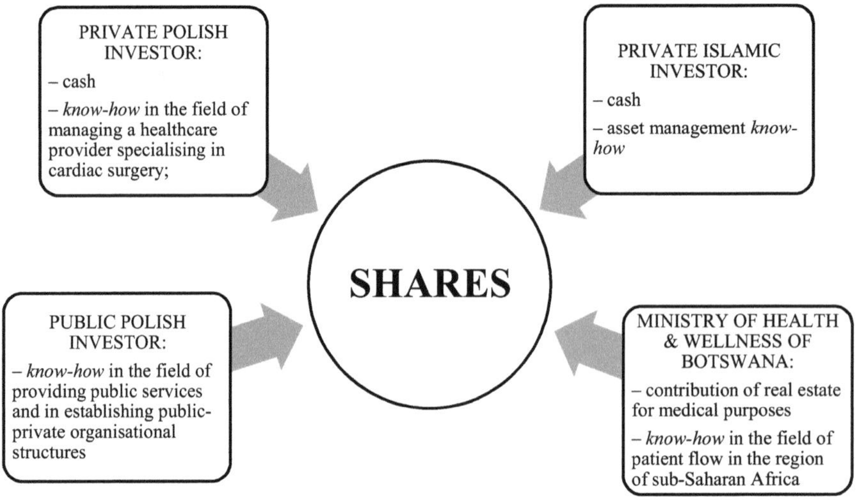

Fig. 6.1 Distribution of shares in the planned SPV. *Source* Own compilation

- a Polish private investor contributes financial resources in cash and *know-how* in the field of managing a healthcare provider specialising in cardiac surgery;
- an Islamic private investor brings in cash and *know-how* in the field of asset management;
- the Ministry of Health & Wellness of Botswana brings in real estate for medical purposes and *know-how* in the field of patient flow in the region of sub-Saharan Africa;
- a public investor from Poland contributes *know-how* in the field of provision of public services and in the establishment of public-private organisational structures (Fig. 6.1).

The purpose of establishing the "Heart Disease Treatment Centre for the People of Sub-Saharan Africa" company (hereinafter referred to as SPV) is to run a cardiac surgery hospital with a cardiac rehabilitation ward for adults and children—in the future, as well as a cardiology clinic. The contract term for a public-private partnership company (SPV) is 20 years.

Before the decision on the planned investment was made, a market analysis was carried out, including an analysis of demographic and epidemiological trends, as well as the existing potential of the medical services market in Botswana. The following characteristics of the market in which the project is planned were identified: population of Botswana, demographic trend, existing potential of other healthcare providers operating in the field in question, epidemiological trend, including in particular the incidence of heart diseases or cardiovascular diseases, mortality rate with the indication of the main causes of death and their possible links with cardiac surgery treatment (Table 6.1).

Table 6.1 Demographic and epidemiological data: Botswana

Market characteristics	Description	Trend	Comparison with Poland
Population of Botswana	2,007,000	Since 1990, there has been an increase in the population of Botswana every year	The population of Poland is much higher (38.53 million)
Life expectancy	In 2015, average life expectancy was 65.7 years. The average life expectancy for women is 68.1 years, while for men it is 63.3 years	...only 4% of the population is aged 65 and over, 63.4% is aged between 15 and 65	In 2015, average life expectancy was 77.5 years. On average, women lived around 81.3 years and men 73.6 years
The most common cause of death	HIV/AIDS—44.93%, stroke—5.79%, coronary heart disease—4.86%	Since 1990, the most common cause of death in Botswana has been HIV/AIDS	Stroke—19.47%, lung cancer—7.06%
Morbidity of heart and cardiovascular diseases	Mortality caused by heart and cardiovascular diseases: coronary heart disease—4.75%, hypertension—3.16%, myocarditis—1.75%	Mortality due to all heart and cardiovascular diseases increased compared to 2011: coronary heart disease—4.86%, hypertension—0.97%, myocarditis—0.72%	Mortality caused by heart and cardiovascular diseases: coronary heart disease—26.92%, hypertension—2.8%, myocarditis—1.81%
Number of cardiac surgery wards	1 within the cardiology ward		37
Number of cardiac surgeons	0		240
Number of cardiovascular wards	2		283

Source Own compilation based on the data from: www.worldlifeexpectancy.com/botswana-life-expectancy; www.worldlifeexpectancy.com/poland-life-expectancy; www.worldlifeexpectancy.com/country-health-profile/poland; www.worldlifeexpectancy.com/country-health-profile/botswana; www.worldlifeexpectancy.com/country-health-profile/poland; www2.mz.gov.pl/wwwfiles/ma_struktura/docs/raportzkardiochir_201210221550.pdf; www2.mz.gov.pl/wwwfiles/ma_struktura/docs/raportzkardiochir_201210221550.pdf; www.rynekzdrowia.pl/Serwis-Kardiologia/Specjalisci-za-dwa-lata-dogonimy-UE-w-liczbie-kardiologow,141697,1014.html

These figures show that there is a negative trend in Botswana concerning the high mortality rate of working-age people due to infectious diseases such as HIV. Thus, the life expectancy of the inhabitants is more than ten years shorter than in European countries. In the face of changing epidemiological trends and lifestyle, cardiovascular diseases are becoming an increasingly serious medical problem. Lack of medical infrastructure and limited access to diagnostic tests may cause that the indications as to the level of incidence are not reliable, although it is the case that the number of cases is on an upward trend. It should be noted that official data make it possible to estimate the market potential on the basis of the registered population, but the population register system is still not fully effective—for example according to UNICEF, more than 25% of children are not registered.[1] Thus, the incidence of heart disease should be related to similar communities characterised by lack of everyday access to medical facilities, lack of prevention, poor eating habits resulting in the consumption of large amounts of fats and sugars, low consumption of fish and rice, immunological characteristics of Black people. South Africa is therefore the closest country which can be used as a basis for comparison, with estimated 210 people dying of heart diseases in a population of nearly 55 million[2] every day.[3]

The public form is dominant with regard to the ownership structure of the healthcare providers in Botswana. The Ministry of Health & Wellness is the founding body for 98% of the entities. According to the government data, there are 101 inpatient clinics, 171 outpatient clinics and over 800 mobile medical centres.[4] These values seem to be sufficient and adequate for the needs of 2.3 million people. However, both the infrastructure standards of these entities, as well as access to medical staff, are far from being in line with European conditions. Certainly, the newly built Medical University in Gaborone is a healthcare provider that meets all standards in terms of medical and educational facilities in the field of medicine.[5] In addition, there are two private healthcare providers, also considered adequate in terms of the needs and standards of developing societies, namely: Bokamoso Private Hospital and Gaborone Private Hospital.[6] When taking into account the access to healthcare providers for general population, it is worth noting that the population is dispersed over an area of over 581,000 km^2,[7] which makes it much more difficult to provide effective medical assistance in one highly specialised treatment centre. From the institutional point of view, the Botswana Ministry of Health & Wellness is organised to the highest standards. It was divided into seven departments responsible for particular substantive areas. The entire scope of responsibilities includes key activities in the following

[1] www.unicef.org/botswana/stories_17968.html.

[2] www.data.worldbank.org/indicator/SP.POP.TOTL?locations=ZA.

[3] South Africa Heart Association, www.saheart.org/cms/content/54-why-heart-disease-is-on-the-rise-in-south%C2%A0africa.

[4] www.gov.bw/en/Ministries--Authorities/Ministries/MinistryofHealth-MOH/About-MOH/About-MOH/.

[5] www.ub.bw/home/ac/1/fac/23/Faculty-of-Medicine/.

[6] Own data collected during the visit.

[7] www.tradingeconomics.com/botswana/surface-area-sq-km-wb-data.html.

areas: HIV/AIDS prevention, prevention of mother-to-child infections, retrovirus control programme, reduction of waiting times for doctor visits, monitoring the incidence of HIV/AIDS, coordination of the medical and management staff, increasing access to medicines and medical equipment, maintenance of medical infrastructure.[8] A particularly interesting objective of the Botswana Ministry of Health & Wellness is, from the point of view of foreign investors, the creation of the so-called Health-Hub (medical cluster), the mission of which will be to create a regional healthcare quality centre, stimulating the involvement of various partners. Among the specific functions of this cluster are:

- ensuring efficiency in the provision of services and offering high-quality services;
- improvement of service provision through strategic partnerships (PPP) and outsourcing of selected services;
- establishing clinical and research centres of excellence that can serve both the region and customers outside the country;
- promoting "medical tourism" to meet local, regional and international healthcare needs;
- identifying ways in which the provision of high-quality health services can contribute to economic diversification and job creation;
- identifying clinical and research centres of excellence in Botswana that can serve the South African Development Community (SADC) and foreign investors;
- stimulating targeted initiatives that have a direct impact on the efficiency and quality of public health care in Botswana.

Due to the aforementioned medical area, the aim of the medical cluster is connected with the seven most important medical areas, which are to be the subject of cooperation within the framework of the agreements being established. These are, apart from modern treatment of cardiovascular diseases, centre of excellence in oncological therapy, high-quality orthopaedic services, organ transplants, neurological treatment, development of the pharmaceutical, diagnostic and laboratory industries.[9]

To sum up the market assumptions, the population of Botswana's inhabitants indicates that it is possible to perform 2000 cardiac surgery procedures and carry out the same number of rehabilitation processes. The average figure for developed countries indicates that on average, 1000 cardiac surgeries are performed per million inhabitants.[10] However, taking into account the shorter lifespan of Botswana's inhabitants and the high incidence of HIV/AIDS, it should be pointed out that the optimum number of interventions is estimated at 700 surgeries per year. Additionally, it has been assumed that this number will include patients not only from Botswana, but also from other countries in sub-Saharan Africa, where there is also a lack of medical

[8]www.moh.gov.bw/ourpriorities.html.

[9]www.gov.bw/en/Ministries--Authorities/Ministries/MinistryofHealth-MOH/The-Masters-Office112/.

[10]Direct interview with a recognised cardiac surgeon who carries out medical procedures around the world and runs cardiac surgery clinics in 2 countries.

facilities in the field of cardiovascular surgery. Taking into account the inhabitants of Zambia, Angola, Namibia and Zimbabwe, the planned number of surgeries seems realistic, especially as access to such procedures is also very difficult in these countries. The number of treatments carried out so far in Botswana is only a little over 20 per year.[11] Most patients start their treatment abroad, mainly in South Africa or the USA, but this is true for the most affluent people. Data on access to public health services indicate that the majority of the population (95% of the total population, 89% of the rural population) lives within 8 km of a healthcare facility.[12] However, access to healthcare facilities does not always translate into the use of these services to the extent that is both expected and possible. The proposed scope of services is disproportionate to the therapeutic needs. The lack of medical technology and qualified medical staff is a serious problem in fulfilling the public function in this area. These facts are confirmed by results of research carried out in 2006–2008, which indicate that over 70% of hospitals are run inefficiently. The reason for this is the strong centralisation of the management and organisation of hospitals, as well as the lack of qualified staff.[13]

The current situation regarding the potential of the medical services market is connected with the practical dimension of the implementation of the state functions and the principles of public finance management in Botswana. The Ministry of Health & Wellness of Botswana is responsible for the entire healthcare policy of the country. The tasks that directly concern the model project, i.e. the healthcare provider, have been identified. Therefore, the basic public functions in terms of health care in Botswana include providing healthcare services via public healthcare providers, as well as access to rehabilitation and prevention programmes against infectious diseases.[14]

Key data on public finances are presented in Table 6.2 (2015 data).

The data in Table 6.3 point to Botswana's stable budget situation, with its public debt-to-GDP ratio slightly above 22%. At the same time, there is a slight increase in government revenue and a significant increase in fiscal expenditure in 2015 compared to 2014. The loss of the budget surplus is mainly due to much lower-than-expected government revenue from two main sources. These are revenues from the sale of natural resources, mainly diamonds (40% of revenue) and the functioning of the Southern African Customs Union (SACU).[15] However, the country remains at a low level of social development, with a poverty rate of 19%, mainly affecting the rural population. The rate of permanent unemployment also remains high at about 17.8%; additionally, a large income inequality of the inhabitants is observed. Therefore, continuous spending on education—at the level of 9% of the country's GDP—focusing

[11] Information from the interviews carried out at BITC Botswana.

[12] www.aho.afro.who.int/profiles_information/index.php/Botswana:The_Health_System.

[13] www.ncbi.nlm.nih.gov/pmc/articles/PMC4181967/.

[14] www.moh.gov.pl11.2016. www.aho.afro.who.int/profiles_information/index.php/Botswana:Analytical_summary_-_Health_system_outcomes.

[15] www.worldbank.org/en/country/botswana/overview.

Table 6.2 Botswana's key public finance area figures in 2015

Description	2015	2014	Highest in the years 2004–2015	Lowest in the years 2004–2015	Unit
Public debt as a share of GDP	22.7	22.8	25.9	5.98	%
State budget as a share of GDP	0.2	5.6	11.2	−10.7	% GDP
State budget expenditure	1644.12	1448.55	1644.12	355.11	mln USD
Public debt	2115.06	2061.10	2115.06	222.23	mln USD
Military expenditure	436.50	378.80	436.50	188.30	mln USD
State budget revenue	994.05	832.08	1476.24	810.01	mln USD
Fiscal expenditure	1389.14	1098.54	1403.07	701.65	mln USD

Source Own compilation based on the data from: www.tradingeconomics.com/botswana/government-budget and www.waluty.pl/

Table 6.3 Level of healthcare expenditure: Botswana, South Africa, Poland

	2012		2013		2014	
	Per capita expenditure (USD)	Total public expenditure (% of GDP)	Per capita expenditure (USD)	Total public expenditure (% of GDP)	Per capita expenditure (USD)	Total public expenditure (% of GDP)
Botswana	427.50	4.00	396.60	3.50	385.30	3.20
Poland	869.70	4.60	881.80	4.50	910.30	4.50
South Africa	661.40	4.30	601.40	4.20	570.20	4.2

Source own compilation based on data from: www.databank.worldbank.org/data/reports.aspx?source=2&series=SH.XPD.PCAP&country=, www.databank.worldbank.org/data/reports.aspx?source=2&series=SH.XPD.PUBL.ZS&country=

on providing universal free education is one of the highest in the world.[16] Data on healthcare expenditure are presented in Table 6.3.

Spending per capita is at a slightly lower level of GDP than in Poland or in South Africa, which shares a border with Botswana. In value, however, these expenditures per capita are almost three times lower than in Poland and about 60% lower than in South Africa.

[16]Ibid.

Summarising the analysis of market, demographic, epidemiological and economic conditions in the context of the implementation of this investment project, the following problems should be pointed out:

- strong centralisation of public decisions;
- lack of sufficient medical infrastructure;
- insufficient medical and lower medical staff;
- a large spatial distribution of the population;
- high incidence of HIV/AIDS;
- the increasing incidence of cardiovascular diseases;
- the mediocre reliability of epidemiological data;
- a moderately positive trend in the state budget results;
- high potential for the development of the state in the conditions of reduction of bureaucracy and constant transfer of knowledge and experience of investors from the outside.

6.1 Assumptions Concerning an Exemplary Public-Private Partnership Project

The planned investment project encompasses opening a cardiac surgery ward for adults with 30 beds, child cardiac surgery ward with 10 beds and a 10-bed intensive care unit in an existing hospital building belonging to the Ministry of Health & Wellness. The hospital will have two operating rooms, equipped with the highest quality equipment, where state-of-the-art technologies will be used. The equipment and possible renovation will be a part of the investment project. The investment is planned for 2 years and will comprise equipping the already completed building with medical equipment and starting up the hospital. The cost of hospital equipment is USD 4,000,000. These costs will be covered with external financing in the amount of 30% of the investment value (USD 1,200,000). The external financing will be provided for a period of 5 years. The annual fee for providing financing was established at the level of 4.5%. The remaining part of the investment value will be executed from the investors' equity. The structure of the shares is as follows:

- *know-how* (1,000,000 USD) and cash (500,000 USD) from a Polish private investor—25% of the capital in the SPV—USD 1,500,000;
- *know-how* (USD 500,000) and real estate contribution (USD 1,000,000) from the local Ministry of Health & Wellness—25%—USD 1,500,000;
- *know-how* from the Polish public entity, USD 500,000—8%;
- cash from an Islamic investor—USD 3,500,000—42%.

A 20-year forecast period and an annual number of patients have been assumed, taking into account an 80% occupancy rate—700 patients per year. The hospital will receive income from medical activities (cardiac surgery interventions and cardiology clinic). A price of USD 8000 for cardiac surgery and USD 50 for a visit to the clinic were assumed. An annual number of patients admitted to the cardiology clinic were estimated at a level of 700 patients, and the same number is assumed to use cardiac surgery procedures. Revenues from medical activities will ultimately amount to: cardiac surgery—USD 5,600,000 annually, cardiology clinic—USD 35,000 annually. In the initial years of the hospital's operation, revenues will be lower in accordance with the following scheme: in the first year of its operation, the hospital will achieve 20% of its planned annual revenues, in the second and third year—33% of its planned revenues, in the fourth year—50%, in the fifth year—60%, in the sixth year—70%, and only in the seventh year—the hospital will achieve 100% of its planned revenues. This estimate is based on an expert assessment of the length of time taken to achieve optimum performance in highly specialised hospitals, also taking into account the potential of the local market. The hospital's operating costs depend mainly on the number of medical procedures performed. The forecasts assume costs in terms of "percentage of medical revenues" thanks to industry knowledge and verification of the accounts of similar medicines operators worldwide, namely:

- remunerations with surcharges—27.78% of revenues in a given year;
- costs of materials—27.40%;
- other operating expenses—2.5%;
- costs of external services—20%.

The forecast costs of external services include costs of salaries (with surcharges) due to medical contracts concluded in the form of civil law contracts. The investors do not bear the cost of the lease because they own the property, which was contributed to the company by the Ministry of Health & Wellness of Botswana. The model assumes the depreciation rate of hospital equipment for 7 years at 14%, which translates into USD 560,000 per year. The building's depreciation rate is 2.5% per annum, which translates into USD 25,000. The profit and loss account, balance sheet and cash flow statement for the year are presented below. Investors need USD 6,000,000 in equity at the beginning of the investment, to cover their capital expenditures and expenses in the first years of the project:

- USD 3,000,0000 for capital expenditures and liquidity in cash;
- USD 1,000,000 as a contribution of real estate to the company;
- the remaining USD 2,000,000 is the investors' valued *know-how*.

Lack of liquidity is caused by incurring external financing costs during the construction of the investment and the operation of the facility in the first years at a lower level of target revenues. At the beginning of the hospital's operations, the net profit is negative due to external financing costs and depreciation write-offs. It is only after four years that the investment will be profitable. Under the above assumptions, the cash flows will be positive throughout the entire forecast period. Due to the foreign nature of the investment and its location in the conditions of the medical cluster, there is no income tax; instead, a fixed percentage of the contribution above the value of *Niṣāb* in the amount of 10% (in accordance with the assumptions of the proposed

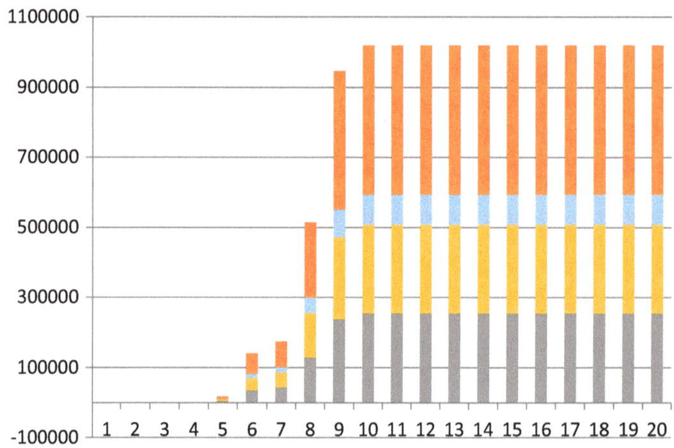

Fig. 6.2 Forecast of dividend distribution to each shareholder in subsequent years. *Source* Own compilation. *Legend* Orange—cash input from Islamic investors; Blue—public partner input know-how; Yellow—local Ministry of Health; Grey—private partner input of know-how and cash

heterodox approach to public finances) was applied. The company also intends to pay dividends in the amount of the total net profit achieved in the previous year. A simulation of the value of dividend payments for each shareholder is presented in Fig. 6.2.

The target value of dividend paid to shareholders, for example, the Polish public investor, is over USD 81,000. This is an amount that could be used in Poland to finance medical services for uninsured persons, such as cardiac surgery, which would mean the possibility of carrying out about 15 highly specialist cardiac surgery procedures (free flow of dividend funds to the country of origin is assumed). That dividend, in accordance with the assumptions of the heterodox PPP approach, it could be partially transferred to the investor's country of origin (in this case, it concerns a public or private investor from Poland), but it is partially assumed that a specific amount of money above the value of *Niṣāb* will be allocated to the needy. These people could be, in the case of this project, those who, for various reasons, do not have access to the public health service, for example, because they are not insured. Admission of such persons and the provision of medical services to them involve, for the healthcare provider, a cost which is not covered by financial transfers from the payer. In this case, the cover for the treatment subject would be the levies above the *Niṣāb* limit. It does not expose the operator to losses, and at the same time, it ensures the fulfilment of the function of social responsibility, which is the essence of the discussed heterodox approach to PPP. Every year, the number of people not covered by insurance who receive medical services at the expense of the state budget generates a cost; only in Łódź Voivodeship, the total cost amounted to PLN 22 million. Moreover, from the point of view of the implementation of public policy and the fulfilment of public functions, the value of an annual contribution above the value of *Niṣāb*, transferred to the local community, is important. These amounts constitute 10% of the net financial result and exceed USD 100,000 per year. This has a significant impact on the availability of medical services, e.g. for uninsured persons in Botswana. In the example, a fixed level of the levy was established due to the constant level of profit since the 9th year of the entity's operation. According to the proposed heterodox approach to public finances, this constitutes a permanent share in the financial result of the project, allocated to the local community.

NPV, IRR and period of return were used to assess the profitability of the investment. The investment is financed with existing equity and borrowed capital. The cost of equity is 5%, and the weighted average cost of WACC capital is 4.77% per annum. The assumed forecast period for the investment is 20 years. *Net present value* (NPV) is the most popular indicator used for investment project assessment. The main advantage of this method is that it can be used to analyse all types of investments. Since it takes inflation into account, it allows us to calculate quite accurately what the value of a future investment is today. NPV is the sum of all discounted (converted from future value to present value) cash flows that a given project will generate during its lifetime. The discount rate used in the calculation is set at such a level as to reflect the time value of money, the cost of capital and the risk related to the realisation of a given investment. An investment project only makes sense if the NPV is greater than zero. This means that the cost of capital (equity and debt) is covered and an additional bonus is obtained, thanks to which the company value increases. The analysis assumes an annual discount rate of 4.77%. The NPV indicator for FCFF is USD 5397,434 and USD 4,563,206 for FCFE. It is bigger than zero, so the investment is profitable. The *internal rate of return* (IRR) is another method of assessing the effectiveness of a project. Like NPV, it takes inflation and risk into account. IRR is a measure of the return on investment. It shows the rate of return from a given project, or in layman's terms, how much is the entity going to gain from the investment. On the other hand, it is also a maximum rate of investment loan, which will allow to finance the project without loss for the owners. The IRR value is determined by the interest rate at which the NPV referred to above is zero. An investment project is profitable if the IRR is higher than the cost of capital (the assumed discount rate). This means that the cost of capital was covered, and an additional bonus was received. The analysis assumes an annual discount rate of 4.77% and an IRR of 14.38% for FCFF and 12% for FCFE. Therefore, the actual return on investment exceeds the expectations of investors—the project is profitable. The investment will pay for itself after 9 years under the given assumptions. From the point of view of an Islamic investor, the above profitability indicators do not carry any economic importance and do not constitute a basis for making an investment decision. As mentioned earlier, Islam prohibits the use of interest rates and interest, which are understood as an unjustified profit. Instead, the concept of a rate of return based on the profitability of the project in question is used. The rate of return cannot be equated with the return on investment defined as the ratio of the return on investment to the market price of instruments. In market practice, in determining the rate of return, reference is sometimes made to the level of the commonly accepted rate, for example LIBOR, which is referred to as the so-called markup.[17] However, this carries a risk of non-compliance with the investment project structure with the *Shari'ah* law. One of the basic Islamic instruments used in the model investment is *murabahah*—the sale of medical equipment and necessary products at a price in which the aforementioned bonus for the seller is already included, and both parties to the contract are aware of it. The price is paid on deferred dates; in this case, the full amount will be paid within five years. Other features of this type of transactions are:

- simple formula, clear to all partners;
- similarity to a conventional trade credit instrument;
- relatively short-term nature;
- lack of possibility to manipulate the price.

A possible solution for the discussed project is also the construct of *sukuk*, described earlier in Sect. 5.4. From an Islamic accounting point of view, attention should be paid to the focus of Islamic investors on the balance sheet showing socio-economic behaviour, especially:

- showing all executed business transactions, which are prohibited by *the Quran*;
- indicating the obligations under the *zakat* and the grounds for their calculation;
- defining activities in the area of social responsibility, including the aspect of charity, shaping desirable relations with employees, caring for other public goods, etc.[18]

The Islamic accounting system has been codified in Bahrain by *The Accounting and Auditing Organization for Islamic Financial Institutions—AAOIFI*. Thanks to the activities of this organisation, 25 accounting standards, a code of ethics for accountants and auditors as well as other documents were established.[19] However, the key in this case is the transparency of the documents being prepared, since the recipients are not only investors or owners, as is the case with conventional finance, but also the society or general community to a large extent, as required by the principles of *the Quran*, in accordance with corporate social responsibility, which is a key element of the *Islamic Moral Economy*. The sensitivity analysis of the revenue level showed that assuming cost and revenue variability, only a drop-in revenue by 32.3% that will cause a lack of financial liquidity. This means that the number of treatments performed, and the number of patients served by the clinic would have to fall to 473 patients before investors are forced to make capital contributions. On the other hand, assuming constant costs in the forecasts (costs at the level of 700 patients), the sensitivity analysis showed that a decrease in revenues by more than 7.2% will already cause a lack of financial liquidity. This means that the number of patients served by a hospital can fall to a maximum of 650 for the investment to continue to pay off and for investors not to have to make capital contributions. The financial projections are presented in Appendix 3.

---

[17] Piotrowski [1].

[18] Cf. Hameed [2].

[19] www.aaofi.com, data from the website accessed on 11th of November 2016.

6.2 Risk Management in Public-Private Partnerships on the Basis of the Proposed Heterodox Approach

In accordance with the proposed heterodox approach, the PPP adopted the principle of risk management of a PPP project based on the following assumptions:

- The risk is not transferred to the shareholders outside the scope of their responsibility resulting from the articles of association of the established special purpose vehicle. In this way, the principle of realisation of the investment in the *ring-fenced* formula is fulfilled.
- The majority of the risk areas are identified, and instruments are used for hedging against risks in the form of appropriate contractual provisions, which emphasises the nature and importance of the contract in accordance with the pillars of the *Islamic Moral Economy* are sought.
- No insurance is used.
- The criterion of qualifying liabilities of public shareholders to the total public liabilities of these public entities is based only on the principle of necessity, or lack thereof, of consolidation of financial statements of the public entity with the financial statements of the entities in which they hold shares.[20]
- The requirement to classify PPP liabilities as public liabilities based on the adopted risk-sharing methodology, where the majority of risk areas are assumed by a special purpose vehicle rather than individual partners of the company independently, does not apply.

The first step in the risk analysis was to identify risk areas. Appendix 1 presents a list of the selected ones, together with their symbols. Subsequently, each of the identified risk areas was assigned a value of its potential impact on the course of the investment project. The impact of the negative consequences of the project resulting in a change in the average annual costs of the project between 1 and 5% was considered to be minor. Major consequences are characterised by the increase of the current costs of the project by 5–10%. Critically negative consequences will mean the realisation of risk that will result in an increase in current costs by 10–20% annually (which would cause the loss of liquidity of the company). On the other hand, if the predicted consequences of the implementation of the identified risk area would result in an increase in costs exceeding 20%, then such consequences were determined as extreme. In view of the methodology thus adopted, a minimum value for each of the identified areas has been determined. Then, each risk area was assigned a probability value based on the expert method. The distribution of all risk areas, taking into account their potential value, is presented in Fig. 6.3.

---

[20] In Polish conditions, the need to consolidate the financial statements of public entities with the financial statements of companies in which they hold shares is strictly defined by the provisions concerning the obligation to submit consolidated JST financial statements to the Regional Chamber of Auditors [www.bip.lodz.rio.gov.pl/?cid=29].
However, in the example discussed there will be no need for preparing such a report due to the fact that the Polish public entity holds only 8% of the share in SPV covered by the contribution of intangible assets, in this case *know-how*.

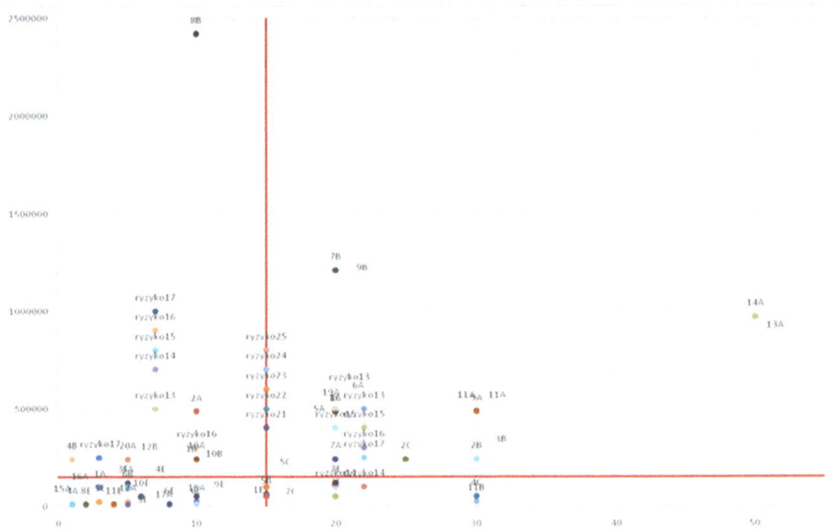

Fig. 6.3 Risk distribution. The Y-axis is the risk value; the X-axis is the probability of occurrence. *Source* Own compilation

Table 6.4 Coefficients for risk mapping

20	15	10	5	Probability: almost certain	5
16	12	8	4	Probability: very likely	4
12	9	6	3	Probability: possible	3
8	6	4	2	Probability: rare	2
4	3	2	1	Probability: unlikely	1
Extreme	Critical	Major	Minor	Coefficient for the risk map	
4	3	2	1		
Negative consequences					

Source Own compilation

The vertical straight line represents the median of probability, while the horizontal straight line represents the maximum value of the realisation of risk that investors are able to finance, set at USD 100,000. The risk areas presented in such a way provide managers with an overview of the risk distribution, taking into account the probability and potential value of the damage.

Subsequently, for identical risk areas, a risk map was prepared, the methodology of which takes into account the frequency of management of each of the identified risk areas, and a coefficient for the risk map, determined in accordance with the matrix presented in Table 6.4.

An example of a risk analysis for a part of a selected group of risk areas is presented in Appendix 2.

Table 6.5 Selected list of risk factors

Risk	Probability	Cost	Coefficient of negative consequences	Coefficient of probability of occurrence	Product of coefficients
1A	3	45,023	1	4	4
2A	10	225,113	2	4	8
3A	5	225,113	2	2	4
4A	1	45,023	1	1	1
5A	20	450,227	3	3	9
6A	20	450,227	3	3	9
7A	20	225,113	1	3	3
8A	20	450,227	3	3	9
9A	30	225,113	2	4	8
10A	10	225,113	2	3	6
11A	30	225,113	2	4	8
12A	5	45,023	1	2	2
13A	50	225,113	2	5	10
14A	50	225,113	2	5	10
15A	1	45,023	1	1	1
16A	1	45,023	1	1	1
17A	5	45,023	1	2	2
18A	10	45,023	1	2	2
19A	20	450,227	3	3	9
20A	5	450,227	3	2	6

Source Own compilation

An example of a matrix of negative consequence and probability coefficients is presented in Table 6.5.

This resulted in a risk map indicating the distribution of individual areas by the frequency of control of the risk area and its coefficient (based on the degree of consequences and probabilities) (Fig. 6.4).

In practice, the application of the risk management methodology presented above boils down to retaining most of the risk areas in the special purpose vehicle and

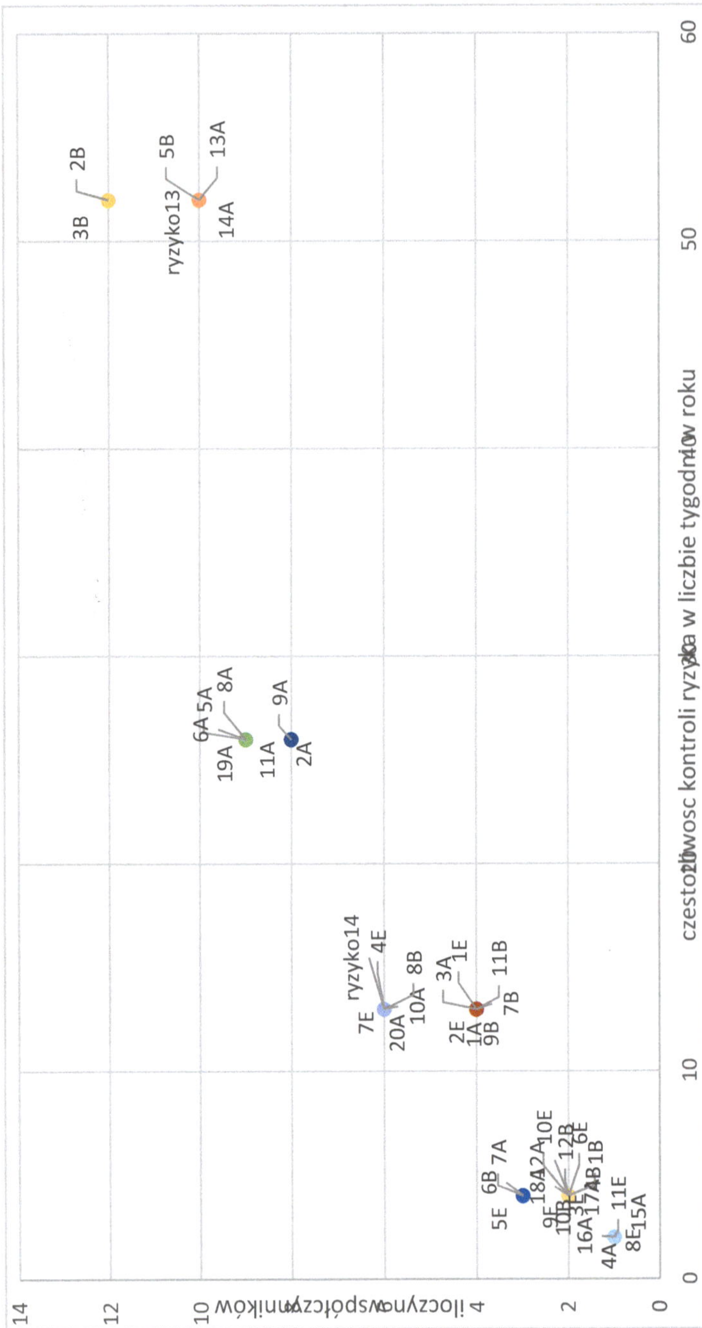

Fig. 6.4 Risk map. *Source* Own compilation

managing them effectively. Skilful division of these risk areas into groups with the highest, average and lowest frequency of controls guarantees constant monitoring of risk factors in an orderly manner. In the example described, the frequency of risk monitoring is determined in weeks from once a week to once a year.

6.3 Advantages and Disadvantages of the Investment in the Proposed Formula According to the Heterodox Approach

Taking into account the management objectives of a private conventional investor, the following set of advantages and disadvantages can be identified from its point of view.

Advantages of the heterodox approach in a specific PPP entity model:

- access to new markets;
- stable levels of profit sources;
- access to knowledge of the use of Islamic financial instruments and the exercise of public functions.

Disadvantages of the heterodox approach in a specific PPP entity model:

- difficult transfer of profits, the possible need for reinvestment in the country of original investment;
- renouncement of a part of profits in favour of a stable level of revenues in the long term;
- the need to verify the instruments used in the Islamic *Shari'ah board*, which lengthens the process of organising the investment project;
- transferring part of the profit to the local community by financing a contribution above the *Niṣāb* value determined by the partners.

An important role in the described model cooperation in the PPP formula, based on the heterodox approach, is played by a conventional public investor. Theoretically, it could be any public entity interested in performing public functions and obtaining additional sources of financing. Certain advantages and disadvantages can be attributed to its presence in the modelled investment formula.

Advantages from the point of view of a public conventional investor:

- obtaining an additional, stable, long-term source of public revenue, derived from the annual dividend in the public-private special purpose vehicle;
- a contribution in the form of a valuation of intangible assets only, such as *know-how* regarding the field of performing public medical services;
- internationalisation of the public entity, an aspect of promoting the region as innovative and open to various forms of investments;
- execution of investments *off-balance*, i.e. without impact on the level of indebtedness of the public entity and without loss of the asset components.

Disadvantages from the point of view of a conventional public investor:

- possibility of not receiving a dividend in case a reinvestment of profit is necessary. Such a situation does not mean, however, that the public function is not carried out, as it is always carried out before a decision is made on profit distribution as a compulsory contribution to the local community in the amount of 10% of the net financial result. Therefore, holding a stake in a special purpose vehicle is always connected with pursuing a public objective and is not only linked to a positive financial result;
- negligible influence on the management, given the minority stake;
- taking on risks based on the principle of solidarity and partner risk management in the special purpose vehicle by transferring the risk to insurers;
- the need to accept cultural, linguistic and religious differences in the place where the investment is carried out;
- the possibility of an outflow of part of the medical and nursing staff to work abroad as part of the investment in question, in a situation where the number of medical staff in the country of origin of the conventional public investor is limited.

The key partner in the model project is the private Islamic investor. External financing represents only 30% of the value of the investment, and thus, the rest is financed by partners, with the leading role of an Islamic investor, whose capital value in this exemplary project is USD 3.5 million. Thus, we need to point out advantages and disadvantages of undertaking the investment in Botswana from the point of view of an Islamic investor.

The advantages are as follows:

- access to new markets, with the possibility of shaping political and economic conditions consistent with the *Islamic Moral Economy*;
- stable, long-term source of profit;
- access to knowledge and experience of partners in the field of public finance and management of health care providers;
- promoting the principles of *the Islamic Moral Economy;*
- risk management based on the pillars of the proposed heterodox approach and the *risk follows responsibilities* principle, where the distribution of risk indicates to a large extent its acceptance by the SPV (due to the fact that the SPV also retains the project risk) and the possible partial transfer of risk, but only on the basis of contracts, for example with sub-contractors, when the scope of responsibility in a specific area is also transferred;
- building trust and prestige thanks to the implementation of the investment with an Islamic partner;
- understanding of cooperation with a public partner, resulting from extensive experience of cooperation with a public partner in Islamic countries, where public authorities often have a majority stake in investment projects;
- introduction of the principle of paying 10% of the value of profit to the local community in order to fulfil the social function of prosperity, which is part of the *Islamic Moral Economy*;

- the possibility of promoting Islamic economic principles in new areas which are characterised by assets in the form of natural resources; the proposed heterodox approach would ensure their effective and safe use by retaining a part of the profit from their exploitation in the country of origin.

Among the disadvantages of the proposed project from the point of view of the interest of an Islamic investor, the following need to be pointed out:

- the need to implement the principles of the proposed heterodox approach to PPPs, as well as Islamic instruments, from scratch;
- a small base of Islamic financial institutions in the new area;
- difficulties in transferring funds outside Botswana;
- extended return on investment period;
- cultural and linguistic diversity of partners in the company and clients/patients, influencing the smoothness of cooperation, document management or shaping organisational and management principles in conditions different from the full principles of Islam.

The key to the success of an investment project is the local public partner. In the case of this model project, it is the Ministry of Health & Wellness of Botswana. It provides funding for medical services on the same contractual basis as for any other healthcare provider in Botswana. However, the essence of the cooperation is a long-term contract for financing a predetermined number of procedures, in accordance with financial forecasts. Independent approval from the Ministry of Health & Wellness would only be required for SPV to provide medical services to a patient from outside Botswana, where funding from the patient's country of origin would have to be transferred to the Ministry of Health & Wellness of Botswana. Thus, the contract value for the special purpose vehicle would be determined in advance in the following years, and the financing of the performed services could be carried out in cooperation with other budgets of the Health Ministries in the countries of sub-Saharan Africa. The distribution of a 10% share of the profit to be used to finance benefits to uninsured persons would be subject to the distribution of the ratio between the countries in which they participated in the financing of the special purpose vehicle's core contract.

From the point of view of the Ministry of Health & Wellness of Botswana, the advantages of the model are as follows:

- implementation of public finance tasks by ensuring unlimited access to medical services of appropriate quality for eligible residents;
- implementation of social policy by financing 10% of the target company's profits with regard to the treatment of cardiovascular diseases for uninsured or excluded persons;
- access to knowledge and experience of the foreign public partner in the field of providing public services and managing public-private infrastructure in the long term;
- securing the interest of the state through fair management of its resources, accumulation of assets and minimisation of the necessary debt financing within the special purpose vehicle;

- implementation of the *off-balance* investment project without impacting on the level of state budget commitments;
- achieving a stable level of profit in the long term, derived from the dividend of the special purpose vehicle.

The most important disadvantages from the point of view of the public entity from Botswana are as follows:

- making the fate of the investment project dependent on the majority shareholders in the special purpose vehicle;
- the transfer of assets to the special purpose vehicle, hence the conversion of the budget item in the form of tangible assets into a % stake in the special purpose vehicle;
- reducing part of the budget revenue by granting tax exemptions to companies operating in the medical cluster;
- the need to implement new principles of the heterodox approach to PPP, which is connected with the period of implementation, learning, controlling, etc.

It is important for the completeness of the research process to highlight the advantages and disadvantages of the project from the point of view of the population in Botswana. Among the most important advantages, the following may be indicated:

- access to highly specialised medical services in the field of cardiac surgery and rehabilitation;
- obtaining access to these benefits by a specified number of uninsured persons;
- promotion of the region as friendly to investors from different legal and economic systems, which can serve as a good example for other investors, and thus contribute to the professional, economic and educational activation of local communities;
- transparency of the rules governing the performance of public functions;

Drawbacks include:

- problems with communication and understanding of cultural and linguistic differences between patients and hospital staff;
- fear of losing national identity.

References

1. Piotrowski D (2015) Ryzyko finansowe inwestycji w sukuk. Annales Universitatis Marie Curie Skolodwska, Lublin, Polonia, vol XLIX, 4, p 473
2. Hameed S (2000) The need for Islamic accounting; perceptions of its objectives and characteristics by Malaysian Muslim accountants and accounting academic, Ph.D. thesis, University of Dundee, Chapter 6, p 260

Chapter 7
Conclusion: Heterodox Approach to Public-Private Partnership

The emergence of public finance crises in conventional economies urges us to reflect on the causes of imperfections in public fund management. Governments' previous initiatives to stabilise finances and to improve social well-being, using existing science achievements in finance and the experience of the economic society, have failed and have not brought the expected results. Reducing public spending and increasing fiscal burdens are met with social resistance. In addition, progressing stagnation in the implementation of both public and private investments reflects the uncertainty of current market conditions and the impasse in the performance of state functions. Within the confines of the European Union arc its pillars, such as the monetary alliance, regional and social policy, which, despite the progressing globalisation and internationalisation of individual economies, are inadequate to the current domestic problems of the individual countries. The unification of public policy, including the level of public debt, does not contribute to the improvement of the situation. The unfavourable demographic trends in Europe and the migration of the population both deepen the crisis of social policy. Meanwhile, Islamic countries have seen another type of challenge facing public finance managers, who have found it necessary to find greater opportunities for budgetary income diversification and the disappearance of the Islamic system's isolation from the conventional financial system. The large Islamic capital and assets facilitate their expansion into external markets and the widespread use of assets and financial structures based on them to make the necessary investments. Opening up to new markets will contribute to the acquisition of knowledge, which is often a barrier to the development of Islamic countries. It seems necessary to popularise the principles of the Islamic Moral Economy as honest, transparent canons of performing state functions, economic development and ensuring social well-being in a globalising world. The sub-Saharan African region is a key area that is dependent on both conventional and Islamic financial systems. The countries of this area represent high economic and social potential, but they require real, deliberate interventions to introduce public policy, transparent public

H. Kociemska, *Public-Private Partnership for Sub-Saharan Africa*, Advances in African Economic, Social and Political Development, https://doi.org/10.1007/978-3-030-14753-2_7

finances and profitable economic bases for private investors. The necessity of protecting these markets against "new colonialists", depriving the continent of valuable assets, is increasingly clear.

Therefore, to undertake multidisciplinary research related to the search for new public finance rules appears to be particularly relevant and useful. The presented scientific analysis confirmed the hypotheses:

- Convergence exists, understood as convergence in selected areas of conventional public finance and of Islamic Moral Economy, for the development of emerging and developing economies wishing to implement PPP investments.
- Promoting public-private partnerships in emerging countries can help stabilise their economies.
- It is possible to manage risks of public-private projects on the bases of applying both conventional financing and Islamic finance.
- Applying the proposed heterodox approach to PPP can help increase conventional investors involvement in Islamic finance countries, also on new markets, where both can cooperate.
- Heterodox approach to PPP can be a solution to the public finance crisis in different economic circumstances, especially those that convene convergence of the principles and philosophy of managing conventional and Islamic investors.

This monograph is a manifestation of the search for a theoretical model that explains the ever-changing reality. It gives the foundation for shaping new theoretical solutions in the area of public finance in emerging, developing countries, particularly in sub-Saharan Africa region. It is a kind of provocation that encourages the revision of the perception of the often-disjointed systems of conventional public finances and Islamic finance. As a consequence, it allowed the creation of a new concept called heterodox approach to public-private partnership, theoretical solution, attractive and adequate to the needs of the market, in times of uncertainty and crisis of public worldwide. The conducted discourse is a contribution to the further discussion on the development of public finance theories and the inclusion of various developments, including the Islamic Moral Economy. Thus, the heterodox approach in PPP directs to obtain the convergence between selected goals: conventional private investors—maximising profits, Islamic investors—maximising social well-being and profits, as well as public entities goals—provision of public services with specified quality and accessibility. At the same time, the proposed platform for the interpenetration of both financial systems and the principles of financial management (public or private) guarantees equal opportunities for cooperation between those parties from different socio-economic and religious orders. Each partner waives some of their rights, invests what is their key, material or financial capital and seeks to achieve stable, predetermined shared profits over the long term, with particular emphasis on the positive impact of cooperation on the society. The proposal for a heterodox approach to PPP may prove to be an appropriate solution for many globalising economies, not just emerging or developing countries but mainly those looking for new financial management pillars and shifting away from cumulative external financing for greater use of their own economic or social attributes and assets. Due to the inadequacy of the current theoretical models, which do not fully explain the reality and do not permit the possibility of permeating selected conventional and Islamic finances, new, more reliable solutions are sought. The heterodox approach to PPP presents a solution that is beneficial for many types of partners, including: public and multicultural societies, conventional investors and Islamic countries, as well as from sub-Saharan Africa region. It contributes to the aforementioned continuous development of the financial discipline and the shaping of the new trend in the subdisciplines of public finance.

Bibliography

1. 2015 Statistics Regarding Religion Growth in Sub-Saharan Africa, The Future of World Religions Population Growth Projections 2010–2050. PEW Research Center. www.nairaland.com. Accessed on 1 Sept 2016
2. AAOIFI Standards 2008
3. Ab Aziz MR (2013) Islamic banking and finance in Malaysia. System, Issues and Challenges, University Sains Islam Malaysia, pp 147–173
4. Adamek J (2014) Mikrofinanse islamskie: założenia, produkty, praktyka. CeDeWu, Warsaw
5. AFFI Brochure (2016) Arab financing facility for infrastructure: developing infrastructure for growth and regional integration in Arab countries. Africa Studies Center, University of Pennsylvania. www.africa.upenn.edu/Home_Page/mcgee.html
6. African Health Observatory. World Health Organization. Botswana: analytical summary—health system outcomes. www.aho.afro.who.int/profiles_information/index.php/Botswana:Analytical_summary_-_Health_system_outcomes
7. African Health Observatory. World Health Organization. Botswana: health system. www.aho.afro.who.int/profiles_information/index.php/Botswana:The_Health_System
8. Aging in the UAE and Services Available for the Elderly: Structured Interviews with Experts in Field, Policy Brief, no 34, Dubai School of Government, Feb 2013
9. A Guide to the Statistical Treatment of PPPs, Sept 2016 EPEC and EBI
10. Akkizidis I, Khandelwal SK (2008) Financial risk management for Islamic banking and finance. Palgrave Macmillan, New York
11. Al Bitar B (2015) Risk management under Sharia Law: products, techniques and competitiveness. Anchor Academic Publishing, Hamburg
12. Al Qardawi Y (1986) Fiqh Al. Zakah (Volume I) A comparative study of Zakah, regulations and philosophy in the light of Qur'an and Sunnah. Scientific Publishing Centre, King Abdulaziz University, Jeddah, Saudi Arabia, pp 5–82. http://islamfuture.les.wordpress.com/2010/07/qh-az-zakat-a-comparative-study-volume-i.pdf. Accessed on 1 Sept 2015
13. Alexander AJ (2011) Shifting title and risk: Islamic project finance with western partners. Mich J Int Law 32(3):571–621
14. Arrow JK (1979) Eseje o teorii ryzyka. PWN, Warsaw
15. Arrow JK (1951) Social choice and individual values. Wiley, New York
16. Assessing Investment Policies of Member Countries of the GULF Cooperation Council, MENA OECD Investment Programme, presented 5 Apr 2011, Abu Dhabi. http://www.oecd.org/mena/competitiveness/Preliminary%20assessment%20GCC%20invt%20policies.pdf

H. Kociemska, *Public-Private Partnership for Sub-Saharan Africa*,
Advances in African Economic, Social and Political Development,
https://doi.org/10.1007/978-3-030-14753-2

17. Association for Heterodox Economics. www.hetecon.net
18. Asutay M, Yilmaz I (2015) Constituting Islamic social welfare function: an exploration in Islamic finance. http://pubdocs.worldbank.org/en/777314466550917l/pdf/P2-Isa-Yilmaz.pdf
19. Asutay M, Yilmaz I (2009) Attracting investors to African public-private partnerships: a project preparation guide. The International Bank for Reconstruction and Development/The World Bank
20. Badawi M, How does the UAE government generate revenue without any income tax? Quora. Last updated 9 May 2018. www.quora.com/How-does-the-UAE-government-generate-revenue-without-any-income-tax
21. Bailey SJ (1999) Local government economics. MacMillan Press Ltd., London
22. Becker GS (1983) A theory of competition among pressure groups for political influence. Q J Econ 98(3):371–400
23. Beidleman CR (1990) On allocating risk: the essence of project finance. Sloan Manag Rev 1:48–51
24. Bernstein PL (1996) Against the gods. Wiley, Hoboken, NJ
25. Bloomberg LP, Snapshot for China monthly foreign exchange reserves CNGFOREX, accessed 24 Apr 2015. https://www.bloomberg.com/quote/CNGFOREX%3AIND
26. Boardman AE (2012) The political economy of public private partnerships and analysis of their social value. Ann Public Coop Econ 83(2):117–141
27. Boć J, Błaś A, Jeżewski J (2013) Nauka administracji. Publisher Kolonia Limited, Wroclaw
28. Bochenek M (2012) Ryzyko i niepewność w naukach ekonomicznych: rozważania semantyczne. Ekonomia [Economics] 4(21):43–64
29. Boudot Y (2014) Director African Department AFD: challenges and issues of financing infrastructures—case studies of public-private partnerships (PPP)
30. BP Statistical Review 2011
31. Bremer J (2013) Zakat and economic justice: emerging international models and their relevance for Egypt, Takaful. In: 3rd annual conference on Arab philanthropy and civic engagement, Tunis, Tunesia, June 4–6
32. Bremmer I (2012) Every nation for itself: winner and losers in a G-zero world. Penguin-Portfolio, New York
33. Broadman HG (2008) China and India go to Africa. Foreign Affairs 87:85–109
34. Brugnoni A (2008) Sharia governance at work: from asset-based to asset back Sukuk. Shirkah 7
35. Buchanan JM, Tullock G (2004) The calculus of consent: the logical foundation of constitutional democracy. University of Michigan Press, Ann Arbor, MI
36. Buchanan JM (1997) Finanse publiczne w warunkach demokracji. PWN, Warsaw
37. Buchanan JM (1968) The collected works of J.M. Buchanan, vol. 5. The Demand and Supply of Public Goods, Liberty Fund Inc. http://oll.libertyfund.org/titles/buchanan-the-collected-works-of-james-m-buchanan-vol-5-the-demand-and-supply-of-public-goods
38. Caballero RJ (2006) On the macroeconomics of asset shortages. The National Bureau of Economic Research, Working Paper no 12753, 12/2006, pp 3–4
39. Cattelan V (2014) In the name of God: managing risk in Islamic finance. Oxford Center for Islamic Studies, eabh Papers, no 14-07
40. Chazbijewicz S, Skarbek K, Turowski M (2012) Nowoczesność, Europa, Islam: Religia a dylematy obywatelstwa i wykluczenia, 1st edn. Institute for Islam Studies, Wrocław
41. Choudhury MA, Bhatti I (2017) Heterodox Islamic economics: the emergence of an ethico-economic theory. Routledge, London
42. Choudhury MA (1996) The nature of globalization and the Muslim world. Manag Finan Struct Change 22(special issue 5/6):7–30
43. Choudhury MA (1999) Global megatrends and the community. World Futures 53(3):229–252

44. CoFace for Trade. Region Bliskiego Wschodu i Afryki Północnej: postęp po arabskiej wiośnie, 02.02.2015. http://www.coface.pl/layout/set/print/AKTUALNOSCI-I-MEDIA/Biuro-prasowe/Region-Bliskiego-Wschodu-i-Afryki-Polnocnej-postep-po-Arabskiej-Wiosnie
45. Countryeconomy.com. National Debt Ethipia and Zambia. www.countryeconomy.com/national-debt/ethiopia, http://countryeconomy.com/national-debt/zambia
46. Countryeconomy.com. National Debt Germany. www.countryeconomy.com/national-debt/germany
47. Countryeconomy.com. National Debt Italy. www.countryeconomy.com/national-debt/italy
48. Countryeconomy.com. National Debt Kuwait. www.countryeconomy.com/national-debt/kuwait
49. Countryeconomy.com. National Debt Saudi Arabia. www.countryeconomy.com/national-debt/saudi-arabia
50. Countryeconomy.com. National Debt South Africa. www.countryeconomy.com/national-debt/south-africa
51. Countryeconomy.com. National Debt Spain. www.countryeconomy.com/national-debt/spain
52. Countryeconomy.com. National Debt United Arab Emirates. www.countryeconomy.com/national-debt/united-arab-emirates
53. Ćwikliński K (2013) Specyfika zadłużenia publicznego krajów Afryki Subsaharyjskiej. Nierówności Społeczne a Wzrost Gospodarczy [Social inequalities and economic growth]. Rzeszow University Publishing House, nr 30, pp 270–285
54. Dealogic Projectware database, extraction 7 Dec 2015. www.ec.europa.eu/economy_finance/events/2016/20160302-pfn/documents/03_tomasi_presentation_on_en.pdf
55. Deloitte (2016) International tax: United Arab Emirates tax highlights. https://www.resourcedata.org/dataset/rgi-deloitte-international-text-highlights-for-uae-2016/resource/e289f3e1-289d-4c13-a4bb-54b42b2a24a1
56. de Nahlik DJ (1992) Rutherford and Montgomerie Handbook of UK Corporate Finance, 2nd edn. Butterworths, London
57. de Soto JH (2010) Szkoła austriacka. Ład rynkowy, wolna wymiana I przedsiębiorczość. Fijorr Publishing, Warsaw
58. DESA Working Paper No. 148, ST/ESA/2016/DWP/148, Public-Private Partnerships and the 2030 Agenda for Sustainable Development: Fit for Purpose?, 2016, pp 8–11
59. Domagała S, Rodzaje sprawozdań badanych przez Regionalne Izby Obrachunkowe: Sprawozdawczość budżetowa [Types of reports examined by the Regional Chambers of Auditors: budget reporting], 15 July 2013. Biuletyn Informacji Publicznej. Regionalna Izba Obrachunkawa w Lodzi [Regional chamber of statistics in Lodz]. www.bip.lodz.rio.gov.pl/?cid=29
60. Dornbusch R (2001) The National Bureau of Economic Research, Cambridge, June 2001, Working Paper, no 8326, pp 1–2
61. Dubai International Financial Centre Sukuk Guidebook, Clifford Chance, pp 28–29
62. Dylewski M, Filipiak B (2010) Ryzyko w finansach i bankowości. Difin, Warsaw
63. Dziennik Ustaw [Journal of Laws]. Rzeczypospolitej Polskiej [Republic of Poland]. www.dziennikustaw.gov.pl/
64. Eatwell J (1899) Dictionary of political economy. Palgrave Macmillan, London
65. Eisenhardt KM (1989) Agency theory: an assessment and review. Acad Manag Rev 14(I):57–74
66. Ekonomia dla przyszłości. Odkrywać naturę i przyczyny zjawisk gospodarczych, congress materials PTE. http://kongres.pte.pl/kongres/upload/files/Kongres_streszczenia_internet.pdf
67. El-Gamal MA (2006) Islamic finance: law, economics and practice. Cambridge University Press, New York
68. El-Awa MD (1980) On the Political System of the Islamic State. American Trust Publications, Indiana

69. El Shazly MR (2004) Sukuk structures, profiles and risk. Columbia College. www.isfin.net
70. Elementy prawa cywilnego, ze szczególnym uwzględnieniem prawa własności, w świetle prawa islamskiego. In: Kozerskiej E, Sadowskiego P, Szymańskiego A, Problemy własności w ujęciu historyczno-prawnym, Opole 2008, pp 47–56
71. EPEC (2013) The PPP market European trends and developments, pp 2–7. www.eib.org/epec/resources/publications/epec_market_update_2014_en
72. Erdem E (2010) The functions of state in determining economic policies in Islam tradition. Erciyes Üniversitesi İktisadi ve İdari Bilimler Fakültesi Dergisi [Erciyes University Journal of the Faculty of Economics & Administrative Sciences] 35(Ocak-Temmuz):19–36
73. Estache A, Strong J (200) The Rise, the Fall, and... the emerging recovery of project finance in transport. World Bank Working Papers 2000, no 2385, pp 8–9
74. Ethica Institute of Islamic Finance (2013) Zakah Q&A Handbook
75. European Commission. Eurostat. www.ec.europa.eu/eurostat/tgm/table.do?tab=table&init=1&language=en&pcode=tsdde410&plugin=1
76. European Commission. Eurostat. File: public balance and general government debt, 2012–2015 (% of GDP) YB16 III.png. https://ec.europa.eu/eurostat/statistics-explained/index.php?title=File:Public_balance_and_general_government_debt,_2012%E280%932015_(%25_of_GDP)_YB16_III.png&oldid=321243
77. European Commission. Eurostat. Glossary: exchange rate mechanism (ERM). www.ec.europa.eu/eurostat/statistics-explained/index.php/Glossary:Exchange_rate_mechanism_(ERM)
78. European Investment Bank. The EPEC PPP Guide. Project finance. www.eib.org/epec/g2g/annex/1-project-finance/
79. European Investment Bank. EPEC—European PPP Expertise Centre, s. 18. www.eib.org/epec/resources/publications/epec_eurostat_guide_ppp
80. European Commission Directorate General Regional Policy (2003) Report: guidelines for successful public private partnerships. European Commission, Brussels
81. Ferlie E, Ashburner L, Fitzgerald L, Pettigrew A (1996) The new public management in action. Oxford University Press, Oxford
82. FFP (2015) The fund for peace. Fragile States Index. www.library.fundforpeace.org/library/fragilestatesindex-2015.pdf
83. Fijor JM (2011) Czy dobra publiczne są naprawdę publiczne. Studia Ekonomiczne [Economic Studies] 1(68):87–100
84. Filipak B (2007) Finanse samorządu terytorialnego. PWN, Warsaw
85. Filipak B (2011) Finanse samorządowe, nowe wyzwania bieżące perspektywy. Difin, Warsaw
86. Filipowicz L, Opawski K (1992) Teoria wyboru publicznego wybrane koncepcje badawcze. Ekonomista 3:378–379
87. Finnerty JD (1996) Project financing: asset based engineering. Wiley, New York
88. Frank H (1986) Project financing: ein Verfahren zur finanziellen Absicherung des Unternehmenswachstums. Service Fachverlag of the University of Economics Vienna, Vienna
89. Focus Economics. Country Indicator: South Africa—Public Debt. www.focus-economics.com/country-indicator/south-africa/public-debt
90. Future trends and market opportunities in the world's largest 750 cities: how the global urban landscape will look in 2030, Oxford Economics
91. Galor Z (2010) Socjologiczno-własnościowy sens „problemu gapowicza": stosunki lumpenwłasności w Polsce. In: Galor Z. Odmiany życia społecznego współczesnej Polski, instytucje-polityka-kultura. WSN Humanities and Journalism Publishing, Poznań
92. Global Turning Points (2012) Understanding the challenges for business in the 21st century. Cambridge University Press, Cambridge

93. Górniewicz G, Determinanty i konsekwencje bezpośrednich inwestycji zagranicznych: Definicja bezpośrednich inwestycji zagranicznych. Studia z Zakresu Prawa, Administracji i Zarządzania [Studies in the Field of Law, Administration and Management] 4(24):61–78. Uniwersytetu Kazimierza Wielkiego w Bydgoszczy [University of Casimir the Great in Bydgoszcz]. www.repozytorium.ukw.edu.pl/bitstream/handle/item/412/Grzegorz%20G%C3%B3rniewicz.pdf?sequence=1
94. Government of Poland: Ministry of Finance. Zadłużenie Skarbu Państwa. www.finanse.mf.gov.pl/zadluzenie-skarbu-panstwa/-/document_library_display/a7KU/view/4079196
95. Grimsey D, Lewis MK (2002) Accounting for public private partnership. Account Forum 26(3/4). https://doi.org/10.1111/1467-6303.00089
96. Gruszka B, Zawadzka Z (1992) Ryzyko w działalności bankowej, Zabezpieczenia systemowe. SGH, Warsaw
97. Guziejewska B, Meandry sanacyjnej roli finansów publicznych, IX Congress of Polish Economists. www.pte.pl
98. Guidelines for Successful Public Private Partnerships. European Commission, Brussels
99. Guillen MF, Ontiveros E (2012) Global turning points: understanding the challenges for business in the 21st century. Cambridge University Press, Cambridge
100. Habib A (2002) Incentive—compatible profit sharing contracts: a theoretical treatment. In: Iqbal M, Llewellyn DT (eds) Islamic banking and finance: new perspectives on profit sharing and risk. Edward Elgar Publishing, Cheltenham
101. Hallaq S (2002) Individual, society and social choice in Islamic thought. In: Habib A (ed) Theoretical foundations of Islamic economics, Book of Readings, no 3. Islamic Development Bank, Islamic Research and Training Institute, pp 101–123
102. Hall D (2014) Why public private partnership don't work. Public Services International Research Unit, University of Greenwich, Greenwich, UK
103. Hall D (2011) PPP's in the EU: a critical appraisal, pp 1–32. www.psiru.org/publicationsindex.asp
104. Hameed S (2000) The need for Islamic accounting: perceptions of its objectives and characteristics by Malaysian Muslim accountants and accounting academic. Ph.D. Thesis, University of Dundee
105. Hassan K, Lewis M (2007) Handbook of Islamic banking. Edward Elgar Original Reference, Cheltenham
106. Harries H (1989) The contract law of project financing. The Law of International Trade Finance, vol 6
107. Hausnera J (2002) Od idealnej biurokracji do zarządzania publicznego. In: Hausner J, Kukiełka M (eds) Studia z zakresu zarządzania publicznego, vol II. Akademia Ekonomiczna w Krakowie [Economic Academy Krakow], Krakow 2002, pp 64–65
108. Hausnera J (ed) (2013) Raport o partnerstwie publiczno-prywatnym w Polsce [Report on Public Private Partnership]. Centrum PPP, Warsaw. http://www.centrum-ppp.pl/templates/download/rap_PPP_ostateczna_wersja.pdf
109. Helman GB, Ratner S (1992/1993) Saving Failed States. Foreign Policy 89(Winter):3–20
110. Herbst I, Jadach Sepioło A (2012) Report: Analizy potencjału podmiotów publicznych i przedsiębiorstw do realizacji projektów PPP dla Polskiej Agencji Rozwoju Przedsiębiorczości
111. Heterodox Economics Newsletter. 1 Aug 2016. www.heterodoxnews.com/directory/intro.htm
112. HM Treasury. Guidance: Orange Book—management of risk-principles and concepts. 29 May 2013. *Gov.uk*. https://www.gov.uk/government/publications/orange-book
113. Hood Ch (1991) A public management for all seasons? Public Adm 69(Spring):3–19
114. Horodecka A (2001–2002) Instytucjonalizm i podejście instytucjonalne do polityki gospodarczej. Polityka Gospodarcza [Economic Policy] 5/6:115–143
115. Hua Jin X, Zhang G, Yang RJ (2012) Factor analysis of partners' commitment to risk management in public private partnership projects. Emerald Insight 12(3):297–316

116. Human capital development: Sustaining the growth of Islamic finance, Malaysia's Islamic Finance Marketplace, 15th Nov 2013, Malaysia International Islamic Financial Center
117. Hupe M (1995) Steuerung und Kontrolle internationaler Projektfinanzierungen. Peter Lang, Frankfurt am Main
118. India International Reserves and Foreign Currency Liquidity, 24.04.2015
119. InfraPPP Partners S.L. PPP-Projects in Bahrain. www.infrapppworld.com/pipeline-html/projects-in-bahrain
120. InfraPPP Partners S.L. PPP-Projects in Kuwait. www.infrapppworld.com/pipeline-html/projects-in-kuwait
121. InfraPPP Partners S.L. PPP-Projects in Oman. www.infrapppworld.com/pipeline-html/projects-in-oman
122. InfraPPP Partners S.L. PPP-Projects in Qatar. www.infrapppworld.com/pipeline-html/projects-in-qatar
123. InfraPPP Partners S.L. PPP-Projects in Saudi Arabia. www.infrapppworld.com/pipeline-html/projects-in-saudi-arabia
124. InfraPPP Partners S.L. PPP-Projects in United Arab Emirates. www.infrapppworld.com/pipeline-html/projects-in-united-arab-emirates
125. International Monetary Fund. www.imf.org/external/pubs/ft/fandd/2015/09/prasad.htm
126. International Reserves and Foreign Currency Liquidity, 24.04.2015
127. Islamic Markets. Sukuk Al-Mudaraba. www.islamicbanker.com/education/sukuk-al-mudaraba
128. IUGG 2015 General Assembly. Earth and Environmental Sciences for Future Generations. Prague, Czech Republic 22 June–2 July 2015. List of Developing Countries. www.iugg2015prague.com/list-of-developing-countries.htm
129. Jajuga K, Nauka o finansach: nowe wyzwania metodyczne. IX Congress of Polish Economists. www.pte.pl
130. Jajuga K (2007) Zarządzanie ryzykiem. PWN, Warsaw
131. Jastrzębska M (2015) Zarządzanie: podejście normatywne do zagadnienia pod kątem procesów decyzyjnych i ryzyka. Finanse Komunalne (Miesięcznik Regionalnych Izb Obrachunkowych) 1–2:72–78
132. Lam KC, Chow WS (1999) The significance of financial risks in BOT procurement. Build Res Inf 27(2):87–95
133. Kachniarz M (2008) Mierzenie efektywności samorządu terytorialnego. Współczesne Zarządzanie [Contemporary Management] 3:56–66
134. Kaczmarek TT (2006) Ryzyko i zarządzanie ryzykiem: Ujęcie interdyscyplinarne, 2nd edn. Difin, Warsaw
135. Karwowski J (1997) Operacje zagraniczne banków centralnych. Wroclaw University of Economics Publishing, Poznań
136. Karwowski J (2011) Sukuk: islamskie certyfikaty inwestycyjne. In: Jajuga K (ed) Finanse: nowe wyzwania teorii i praktyki. Rynki finansowe. Wroclaw University of Economics Publishing, Wroclaw, pp 233–234
137. Karwowski J (2012) Zakazy i nakazy w finansach islamskich. Studia Ekonomiczne [Economic Studies] 106:89–99
138. Karwowski J (2012) Zakazy i nakazy w finansach islamskich. In: Harasim J, Cichy J (eds) Finanse w niestabilnym otoczeniu: dylematy i wyzwania – Rynki finansowe. Katowice University of Economics Publishing, Katowice, pp 89–99
139. Kenton W, Emerging market economy. Investopedia. Last updated 6 July 2018. www.investopedia.com/terms/e/emergingmarketeconomy.asp
140. Khoutem BJ, Hichem H (2014) Profit and losses sharing paradigm in Islamic banks: constraints or solutions for liquidity management? J Islamic Econ Bank Finan 10(3):29–45
141. Kleer J (2006) Sektor publiczny w Polsce i na świecie. CeDeWu, Warsaw

142. Klimczak B (2001) Teoretyczne podstawy badania działań grup interesu na rzecz ładu rynkowego. In: Klimczak B (ed) Samorząd gospodarczy i zawodowy w procesie powstawania ładu rynkowego. University of Economics, Wroclaw, pp 11–64
143. Klimczak MK (2008) Dylematy ujęcia ryzyka w teorii ekonomii. Acta Universitatis Lodziensis: Folia Oeconomica 221:359–367
144. Kłosowicz R, Mormul J (2013) Pojęcie dysfunkcyjności państw: geneza i definicje. In: Kłosowicz R (ed) Państwa dysfunkcyjne i ich destabilizujący wpływ na stosunki międzynarodowe, series Studia nad Rozwojem [Studies on Development]. Jagiellonian University Publishing, Krakow, pp 11–36
145. Kłosowicz R (2014) Państwa dysfunkcyjne w Afryce Subsaharyjskiej. In: Kłosowicz R (ed) Państwa dysfunkcyjne i międzynarodowe wysiłki zmierzające do ich naprawy. Jagiellonian University Publishing, Krakow, pp 11–64
146. Knight FH (1921) Risk, uncertainty and profit. Hart Schaffner&Marx Houghton Miffin Co., Boston, MA. www.econlib.org/library/Knight/knRUP1.html#Pt.I,Ch.II
147. Kociemska H (2010) Public-private partnership project success circumstances. J Mod Account Auditing 6(11, Serial no. 66):53–63
148. Kociemska H (2015) Ryzyko w partnerstwie publiczno-prywatnym w teorii finansów publicznych i w praktyce. In: Patrzałek L, Kociemska H (eds) Research Work Wroclaw University of Economics, no 404, Finanse samorządu terytorialnego, University of Economics, Wrocław
149. Kollatz-Ahnen M (2011) Vice President European Investment Bank, 17. http://ec.europa.eu/economy_finance/events/2011/2011-05-17-joint_ec-epec_private_sector_forum/kollatz_en.pdf
150. Komitet Organizacji Sponsorujących Komisji Treadwaya (COSO), (Committee of Sponsoring Organizations of the Treadway Commission) (2004). http://www.coso.org/documents/coso_erm_executivesummary_polish.pdf, w opracowaniu pt.: Zarządzanie ryzykiem korporacyjnym: zintegrowana struktura ramowa ERM
151. Komunikat Komisji: Europa 2020. Strategia na rzecz inteligentnego i zrównoważonego rozwoju sprzyjającego włączeniu społecznemu, Komisja Europejska, 2010 (Communication from the Commission: Europe 2020. A strategy for smart, sustainable and inclusive growth, European Commission, 2010.)
152. Konopczak M (2014) Ocena wpływu zmian poziomu rezerw walutowych na premię za ryzyko kredytowe Polski: wykorzystanie metody roszczeń warunkowych. Bank i Kredyt 45(5):467–490
153. Konstytucja Rzeczpospolitej Polskiej z dnia 2 kwietnia 1997 Dz.U. 1997, nr 78, poz. 483
154. Kopańska A (2006) Partnerstwo publiczno-prywatne – wzory brytyjskie: Czego możemy się z nich nauczyć? Studia Regionalne i Lokalne 3(25):83–98
155. *Koran* 2009, sura II, verse 284
156. *Koran*, sura XLII, verse 38
157. Kosikowski C (2011) Naprawa finansów publicznych w Polsce. Temida Publishing House 2, Bialystok
158. Kowalczyk M (2001) Zarządzanie ryzykiem w project finance. Narodowy Bank Polski, Departament Analiz i Badań (National Polish Bank Department of Research and Analysis). Warsaw, www.nbp.pl/publikacje/materialy_i_studia/137.pdf
159. Kozerska E, Sadowski P, Szymański A (eds) (2008) Problemy własności w ujęciu historyczno-prawnym. Wydawnictwo Uniwersytetu Opolskiego (Opole University Publishing House), Opole
160. Krukowska M, Zróżnicowanie poziomu wzrostu gospodarczego w wybranych krajach Afryki Subsaharyjskiej. Kolegia Szkoły Głównej Handlowej, Warsaw, Kwartalnik Archiwum (Colleges of the Warsaw School of Economics, Warsaw, Quarterly Journal, Archive), pp 69–73
161. Kubiczek A (2014) Jak mierzyć dziś rozwój społeczno-gospodarczy krajów? Nierówności społeczne a wzrost gospodarczy 38:40–56

162. Kuhn T (2003) Droga po strukturze: Eseje filozoficzne z lat 1970–1993 i wywiad rzeka z autorem słynnej "Struktury rewolucji naukowych". transl. Stefan Amsterdamski, Wydawnictwo Sic!, Warsaw
163. Kuhn T (2001) Struktura rewolucji naukowych, transl. H. Ostrołęcka. Warsaw
164. Kulesza M (2003) Partnerstwo publiczno-prywatne: Uwagi wstępne. Finanse Komunalne (Municipal Finance), no 8, supplement
165. Kumpiałowska A (2011) Skuteczne zarządzanie ryzykiem a kontrola zarządcza w sektorze publicznym. CeDeWu, Warsaw
166. Kuran T (1995) Further reflections on the behavioral norms of Islamic economics. J Econ Behav Organ 27(1):159–163
167. Kwiatkowski S (2014) Teoria dóbr publicznych i rynkowe mechanizmy ich produkcji pod prąd głównego nurtu ekonomii, Institute Misesa
168. Lapidus IM (2002) A history of Islamic societies, 2nd edn. Cambridge University Press, Cambridge
169. Lee FS, Heterodox economics. Association for Heterodox Economics. www.hetecon.net/?page=about&side=heterodox_economics
170. Le Menestrel M (2002) Economic rationality and ethical behavior: ethical business between vanity and sacrifice. Bus Ethics Eur Rev 11(2):157–166
171. LHV Persion Gulf Fund. Gulf Cooperation Council. www.persiangulffund.com/gulf-area/gulf-cooperation-council
172. Loughlin M (2002) Foundations of public law. Oxford University Press, 27.09.2012
173. Mannan M (2008) Islamic capital market. In: Anwar H (ed) Islamic finance: a guide for international business and investment. GMB Publishing, London, pp 103–116
174. Mapping Africa's Islamic economy: A report by the economist intelligence unit. The Economist, 2015
175. Market Update, Review of the European PPP Market in 2013, European PPP Expertise Centre
176. McKinnon RI, Pill H (1996) Credible liberalizations and international capital flows: the over borrowing syndrome. In: Ito T, Krueger AO (eds) Financial deregulation and integration in East Asia, NBER-EASE vol 5. National Bureau of Economic Research, University of Chicago Press, Chicago, pp 10–15
177. McPhee I, Risk and management in the public sector. 1 Sept 2005. Australian National Audit Office. Public sector governance and risk forum. www.anao.gov.au/sites/g/files/net616/f/McPhee_risk_and_risk_management_in_the_public_sector_2005.pdf
178. Merna T, Njiru C (1998) Financing and managing infrastructure projects. Euromoney Publications, Jersey
179. Miller MH, Modigliani F (1958) The cost of capital, corporation finance and the theory of investment. Am Econ Rev 48(3):261–297
180. Ministry of Finance. Rozporządzenie Ministra Finansów z dnia 2 grudnia 2010r w sprawie wzoru oświadczenia o stanie kontroli zarządczej, 2 December 2010. Dz.U., no 238, poz. 1581
181. Ministry of Finance. Rozporządzenie Ministra Finansów z dnia 3 lutego 2010r., w sprawie sprawozdawczości budżetowej, 3 Feb 2010. Dz.U., no 20, poz. 103
182. Tabash MI, Dhankar RS (2014) The relevance of Islamic finance principles in economic growth. Int J Emerg Res Manag Technol 3(2):49–54
183. MRC Consulting, Report "Zarzadzanie ryzykiem w działalności jednostek samorządu terytorialnego: ze szczególnym uwzględnieniem ryzyka katastroficznego", Qualifact, Market Research & Analysis, Gdańsk University, May 2013. http://www.wzieu.pl/zn/794/ZN_794.pdf
184. Muñoz J, Snowden N (2012) Building a BRIC: stock market opening and investment finance in India since liberalization. World Dev J 40(6):1109–1121

185. Muñoz J (2011) Ortodox versus heterodox (Minskyan) perspectives of financial crisis: explosion in the 1990s versus implosion in the 2000s. Levy Economics Institute, Working Paper no. 695, Nov 2011
186. Musgrave RA, Musgrave PB (1980) Public finance in theory and practice. McGraw-Hill, New York
187. Musgrave RA (1959) The theory of public finance: a study in public economy. McGraw-Hill, New York
188. Nagji B, Tuff G (2012) Jak zarządzać portfelem innowacji, Harvard Business Review Polska, no 115, Sept 2012
189. National Zakat Foundation, What is Zakat All About? Mercy Mission UK. www.nzf.org.uk/Content/PDF/NZF_Zakat_Guide.pdf
190. Nazmi A, Ekonomia Muzulmanska [Muslim Economy]. PWN Encyclopedia. https://encyklopedia.pwn.pl/haslo/ekonomia-muzulmanska;3897007.html
191. Nejatullah SM (2006) Islamic banking and finance in theory and practice: a survey of state of the art. Islamic Econ Stud 13(2):1–48
192. Nejatullah SM (1992) Teaching public finance in Islamic perspective. Center for Research in Islamic Economics, Kind Abdulaziz University, Jeddah, Saudi Arabia, published Jan 2008
193. Never mind the balance sheet: the dangers posed by PPP in Central and Eastern Europe. Bankwatch Network 11.2008. http://bankwatch.org/documents/never_mind_the_balance_sheet.pdf. Accessed on 10 Sept 2016
194. Nevit PK, Fabozzi F (1995) Project financing, 6th edn. Euromoney Publications, London
195. New Decision of Eurostat on Deficit and Debt: Treatment of Public Private Partnership. Eurostat News Release, 11.02. 2004, Eurostat Press Office Philippe Bautier, Luxemburg 2004. www.europa.eu.int/comm/eurostat
196. New York Times, October 28, 2010, page B1 of the New York edition with the headline: Rapid Growth in Dubai Outstrips Its Resources
197. Nobel Prize Organization (1986) Economic sciences: laureates. www.nobelprize.org/nobel_prizes/economic-sciences/laureates/1986/
198. Noblisci.pl. Nobel Prize Winners. 1998: Amartya Sen. www.noblisci.pl/1998-amartya-sen/
199. Obaidullah M (2005) Islamic financial services. Islamic Economics Research Center, Kind Abdul Aziz University, Jeddah. http://islamiccenter.kau.edu.sa/english/publications/Obaidullah/ifs/ifs
200. OECD, Principles for public governance of public private partnerships, May 2012
201. OECD Statistics. www.stats.oecd.org/glossary/detail.asp?ID=7315
202. Olson M (1977) The logic of collective action: public goods and the theory of groups. Harvard University Press, Harvard, MA
203. Ormerod P (1997) The death of the economics. Wiley, New York
204. Ostaszewski J (2014) Zamiast wstępu. In: Ostaszewski J, Kosycarz E (eds) Rozwój nauki o finansach. Stan obecny i pożądane kierunki jej ewolucji. Department of Finance, College of management and Finance, SGH, Warsaw, pp 9–14
205. Owsiak S (1999) Finanse publiczne. PWN, Warsaw
206. Owsiak S (2001) Finanse publiczne: Teoria i praktyka, 2nd edn. PWN, Warsaw
207. Owsiak S (2005) Finanse publiczne: Teoria i praktyka. PWN, Warsaw
208. Oxford Business Group. Income breakdown: A look at the government's main revenue streams. www.oxfordbusinessgroup.com/analysis/income-breakdown-look-government's-main-revenue-streams
209. Piotrowski D (2015) Ryzyko finansowe inwestycji w sukuk. Annales Universitatis Marie Curie-Skolodwska: Sectio H Oeconomia 49(4):469–478
210. Piotrowski D (2014) Zastosowanie podstawowej zasady finansów islamskich PLS celem ograniczenia zjawiska moralnego hazardu na rynku usług finansowych. Acta Universitatis Nicolai Copernici: Ekonomia 45(1):99–113

211. Pollio G (1998) Project finance and international energy development. Energy Policy 26(9):687–697
212. Poniatowicz M (2011) Partnerstwo publiczno-prywatne w sektorze samorządowym a problematyka lokalnego długu publicznego. Optimum Studia Ekonomiczne 3(51):33–53
213. Polskie Towarzystwo Ekonomiczne [Polish Economic Society]. Ekonomia dla przyszłości
214. Odkrywać naturę i przyczyny zjawisk gospodarczych. IX Kongres Ekonomistów Polskich [9th Conference of Polish Economists]. www.kongres.pte.pl/kongres/upload/files/Kongres_streszczenia_internet.pdf
215. Popławski B, [Afryka] Failed States Index: państwa kruche czy upadłe? Kultura Liberalna. No 287, 27/2014, 9 July 2014. www.kulturaliberalna.pl/2014/07/09/afryka-panstwa-kruche-czy-upadle-failed-states-index/
216. PPP Institute. Report: "Rynek partnerstwa publiczno-prywatnego i koncesji w Polsce w 2014 r. na tle stanu obowiązującego w latach 2009–2013". http://ippp.pl/raport-nt-rynku-ppp-i-koncesji-w-polsce-w-2014-r/
217. Program ramowy UE w zakresie badań naukowych i innowacji "Horizon 2020". European Commission, 2014. www.ec.europa.eu
218. PRO INNO Europe, Inno Metricks, European Public Sector Innovation Scoreboard: Methodology Report, 2012
219. Publikacja Ministerstwa Gospodarki [Publication of the Ministry of Economy], Zawarcie umowy o PPP: PPP od pomysłu do wyboru partnera prywatnego, Dec 2014, pp 102–06. www.ppp.gov.pl/Publikacje/E_przewodnik/Documents/Raport_MG_umowa_ppp.pdf
220. Qatar Statistics Authority from 2009, accessed 2011
221. Rehman AA (2010) Gulf capital and Islamic finance: the rise of the new global players. McGraw-Hill, New York
222. Republic of Botswana. Government of Botswana. Ministry of Health (MOH). About MOH. www.gov.bw/en/Ministries–Authorities/Ministries/MinistryofHealth-MOH/About-MOH/About-MOH/
223. Republic of Botswana. Government of Botswana. Ministry of Health (MOH). http://www.gov.bw/en/Ministries–Authorities/Ministries/MinistryofHealth-MOH/
224. Republic of Botswana. Government of Botswana. Ministry of Health. Our priorities. www.moh.gov.bw/ourpriorities.html
225. Republic of Botswana. Government of Botswana. The Master's Office. www.gov.bw/en/Ministries–Authorities/Ministries/MinistryofHealth-MOH/The-Masters-Office112/
226. Ricardo D, On the principles of political economy and taxation. In: Sraffa P (ed) The works and correspondence of David Ricardo, 11 vols. Cambridge University Press, Cambridge 1951–1973, chapter 6.31. http://www.econlib.org/library/Ricardo/ricP.html
227. Rodriguez F, What the new HDI tells us about Africa. Development Research Initiative, New York University. From Aid to Euqality. www.nyudri.org/what-the-new-hdi-tells-us-about-africa/
228. Rogowska B (2016) Na obrzeżach ekonomii: Znaczenie współczesnej heterodoksji. Studia Ekonomiczne: Zeszyty Naukowe 259:108–118
229. Rotberg RJ (2003) When states fail: causes and consequences. Princeton University Press, Princeton, NJ
230. Rynard TW (1991) Insurance and risk management for state and local governments. Matthew Bender & Co., Inc., Lexis Nexis, New York
231. Ryner M (2012) Financial crisis, orthodoxy and heterodoxy in the production of knowledge about the EU. Millennium J Int Stud 40(3):647–673
232. Shazly El MR (2004) Sukuk structures, profiles and risk. Columbia College. www.isfin.net
233. Sadka E (2007) Public private partnership: a public economics perspectives. CESifo Econ Stud 53(3):466–490
234. Sadowski M (2008) Elementy prawa cywilnego, ze szczególnym uwzględnieniem prawa własności, w świetle prawa islamskiego. In: Kozerska E, Sadowski P, Szymański (eds) Problemy własności w ujęciu historyczno-prawnym. University Opole, Opole

235. Salanie B (2005) The economics of contract: a primer, 2nd edn. MIT Press, Cambridge, MA
236. Sanni AO, Hashim M (2014) Building infrastructure through public private partnership in sub-Saharan Africa: lessons from South Africa. Procedia—Soc Behav Sci, 143
237. Schumm WR, Kohler AL (2006) Social cohesion and five pillars of Islam: a comparative perspective. Am J Islamic Soc Sci 23(2):126–136
238. Sciulli N (2008) Public private partnership: an exploratory study in healthcare. Asian Rev Accoun 16(1):21–38
239. Sedjari A (2004) Public private partnership as a tool for modernising public administration. Int Rev Adm Sci 70(2):291–306
240. Seitio-Kgokgwe O, Gauld RD, Hill PC, Barnett P (2014) Assessing performance of Botswana's public hospital system: the use of the World Health Organization Health System Performance Assessment Framework. Int J Health Policy Manag 3(4):179–189. Published 2014 Sept 13. https://doi.org/10.15171/ijhpm.2014.85, www.ncbi.nlm.nih.gov/pmc/articles/PMC4181967/
241. Sen AK (1998) The concept of Developmenti. In: Chenery H, Srinivasan TN (eds) Handbook of development economics, vol 1, Handbooks in Economics. Elsevier, North-Holland, pp 9–26
242. Shendy R, Kaplan Z, Mousley P (2011) Towards better infrastructure: conditions, constraints, and opportunities in financing public-private partnerships, evidence from Cameroon, Cote d'Ivoire, Ghana, Kenya, Nigeria, and Senegal. The World Bank, Public-Private-Partnership Legal Resource Center. https://library.pppknowledgelab.org/PPIAF/documents/2987
243. Siddiqi M (2008) Teaching public finance in Islamic perspectives. Center for Research in Islamic Economics King Abdulaziz University Jeddah, Saudi Arabia
244. Śmiechowicz J (2015) PPP and using EU funds in its financing in terms of crisis and budgetary restrictions. In: Management, Knowledge and Learning: Joint International Conference, 27–29 May 2015, Bari, Italy, pp 2063–2071. www.toknowpress.net/ISBN/978-961-6914-13-0/papers/ML15-435.pdf
245. South Africa Heart Association, Why heart disease is on the rise in South Africa. 29 Sept 2016. www.saheart.org/cms/content/54-why-heart-disease-is-on-the-rise-in-south%C2%A0africa-
246. Sochacka-Krysiak H (2010) Niektóre problemy efektywności w gospodarce finansowej samorządu terytorialnego. In: Wieteska S, Wypych M (eds) W poszukiwaniu efektywności finansów publicznych. Łodz University Publishing House, pp 192–194
247. Sovereign Wealth Fund Institute. Ranking "Largest Sovereign Wealth Funds by Assets under Managements", 2017, www.swfinstitute.org
248. Statista. Kenya: National debt from 2012 to 2022 (in billion U.S. dollars). www.statista.com/statistics/531654/national-debt-of-kenya/
249. Statista. Public debt of the United States from 1990 to 2018* (in billion U.S. dollars). www.statista.com/statistics/187867/public-debt-of-the-united-states-since-1990/
250. Stiglitz JE (1999) Economics of the public sector, 3rd edn. W.W. Norton & Company, New York
251. Strauss G (2016) Six challenges facing Africa in 2016. Providence J Christianity Am Foreign Policy. www.providencemag.com/2016/01/six-challenges-facing-africa-2016/
252. Sygut M (2014) Specjaliści: za dwa lata dogonimy UE w liczbie kardiologów. Rynekzdrowia.pl. www.rynekzdrowia.pl/Serwis-Kardiologia/Specjalisci-za-dwa-lata-dogonimy-UE-w-liczbie-kardiologow,141697,1014.html
253. Szumlicz T (2016) O niedostatecznej ochronie prawnej jako ryzyku społecznym. Wiadomości Ubezpieczeniowe [Insurance News] 1:53–62
254. Tariq A, Humayon D (2007) Risk of Sukuk structures: implications for resource mobilization. Thunderbird Int Bus Rev 49(2):203–223

255. Thawani S (2015) Achieving & sustaining excellence in public service, pp 1–17. www.kwinta.be/sites/default/files/bijlage/artikel/achieving-excellence-in-govt-service-adopting-efqm.pdf
256. The Bulletin of the Commission Terminology of the American Risk Association, vol 1, no 1, March 1966
257. Thomson Reuters. Zawya. www.zawya.com
258. Tiffen A, The new neo-colonialism in Africa, 19.08.2014, www.globalpolicyjournal.com. Accessed on 10 Sept 2016
259. Tiong R (1990) BOT projects: risk and securities. Constr Manag Econ 8(3):315–328
260. Trading Economics. Botswana: Government Budget. www.tradingeconomics.com/botswana/government-budget
261. Trading Economics. Botswana: Surface area (sq. km). www.tradingeconomics.com/botswana/surface-area-sq-km-wb-data.html
262. Trading Economics. Kenya Government Debt to GDP. www.tradingeconomics.com/kenya/government-debt-to-gdp
263. Trading Economics. United States Gross Federal Debt to GDP. www.tradingeconomics.com/united-states/government-debt-to-gdp
264. Traktat o Unii Europejskiej [Treaty on the European Union], 7 Feb 1992. www.oide.sejm.gov.pl
265. UAE Ministry of Economy, The Annual Economic Report 2014, 22nd ed
266. UAE National Bureau of Statistics. Labor force figures for 2005
267. UK Government. 04.09.2016. www.gov.uk
268. UN Capital Development Fund. Unlocking Public and Private Funding for the Poor. Documents and Reports. LFI Project Workshop 21.10.2014. www.uncdf.org/sites/default/files/Documents/uncdf_lfi_project_workshop-21.10.2014daressalaam.pdf. Accessed 11 Oct 2016
269. Unicef Botswana. Mobile birth registration Inititative Addresses Challenges in the Okavango Area. www.unicef.org/botswana/stories_17968.html
270. University of Botswana. Faculties and Departments: Faculty of Medicine. https://www.ub.bw/faculties-and-departments
271. Usmani M, Qazi B (2010) Guide to Zakah Understanding & Calculation, Maktaba Ma'ariful Qur'an [Quranic Studies Publishers], Meezan Bank, Product Development & Shariah Compliance
272. Ustawa z dnia 19 grudnia 2008 r. o partnerstwie publiczno-prywatnym, Dz.U., 2015, poz. 696, 1777. [Act dated 19 December 2008 on public private partnership of 2015, 696 item 1777 as amended]
273. Ustawa z dnia 27 sierpnia 2009 r. o finansach publicznych, Dz.U. 2013, poz 885 z późn. zm., rozdział 6 "Kontrola zarządcza oraz koordynacja kontroli zarządczej w jednostkach sektora finansów publicznych" od art. 68 do art. 71, art. 5 ust. 2, art. 69. [Act dated 27 August 2009 on Public Finance of 2013 item 885 as amended]
274. Ustawa z dnia 22 czerwca 2016 r. o zmianie ustawy *Prawo zamówień publicznych* oraz niektórych innych ustaw, Dz.U. z dnia 13 lipca 2016 r., poz.1020. [Act dated 22 June 2016 on the Change of Public procurement and other act of 2016 item 1020 as amended]
275. Ustawa z dnia 9 stycznia 2009 o koncesji na roboty budowlane lub usługi, Dz.U. 2009, nr 19, poz. 101. [Act dated 9 January 2009 on concession on construction and other public services on 2009 no 19 item 101 as amended]
276. Visser H (2009) Islamic finance principles and practice. Edward Elgar, Northampton, USA
277. Walasik A (2008) Redystrybucyjna funkcja finansów publicznych w ujęciu teoretycznym. Katowice University of Economics Publishing, Katowice
278. Walker C, Smith AJ (1995) Privatized infrastructure: the build operate transfer approach. Thomas Telford Ltd., London
279. Waluty.pl. Currency calculator. www.waluty.pl/

280. Wasilewski B, Teoria wyboru publicznego a proces podejmowania decyzji w Radzie Unii Europejskiej. 27.01.2010. PolitykaGlobalna.pl. www.politykaglobalna.pl/2010/01/teoria-wyboru-publicznego-a-proces-podejmowania-decyzji-w-radzie-unii-europejskiej/2/
281. Whitaker B (2014) Arabs without god: atheism and freedom of belief in the Middle East. CreateSpace Independent Publishing Platform
282. Wikipedia. Geographic map of Sub-Saharan Africa [Public Domain]. https://commons.wikimedia.org/wiki/File:Sub-Saharan-Africa.png
283. Wikipedia. Demographics of the European Union. www.en.wikipedia.org/wiki/Demographics_of_the_European_Union
284. Wikipedia. www.wikipedia.org/wiki/Kraje_rozwijaj%C4%85ce_si%C4%99.pl
285. Wiliamson OE (1998) Ekonomiczne instytucje kapitalizmu. PWN, Warsaw
286. Wiliamson OE (2000) The new institutional economics: taking stock, looking ahead. J Econ Lit 38(3):595–613
287. Wilkin J (2012) Teoria wyboru publicznego: Główne nurty i zastosowania. Scholar, Warsaw
288. Willett A (1951) Economic theory of risk and insurance (1901). The Committee of the Theory of Risk, S.S. Huebner Foundation for Insurance Education, University of Pennsylvania
289. Williams CA Jr, Smith ML, Young PC (2002) Zarządzanie ryzykiem a ubezpieczenia. PWN, Warsaw
290. Woody W, Pourian H (1992) Risk assessment and options in project finance. Project Manag J 23(4):21–28
291. Woodward D (1992) Risk management of BOOT projects. Project 3:10–11
292. World Bank. Data bank. www.databank.worldbank.org/data/reports.aspx?source=2&series=SH.XPD.PCAP&country
293. World Bank. Data Bank. www.databank.worldbank.org/data/reports.aspx?source=2&series=SH.XPD.PUBL.ZS&country=
294. World Bank. Data bank: South Africa. www.data.worldbank.org/indicator/SP.POP.TOTL?locations=ZA
295. World Bank. Guidelines Procurement under IBRD Loans and IDA Credits. May 2004, revised 1 Oct 2006 & 1 May 2010. www.siteresources.worldbank.org/INTPROCUREMENT/Resources/ProcGuid-10-06-RevMay10-ev2.pdf
296. World Bank. Public-Private-Partnership Legal Resource Center: About public-private-partnerships. https://ppp.worldbank.org/public-private-partnership/about-public-private-partnerships
297. World Bank. Public-Private-Partnership Legal Resource Center: guidance note. Procurement arrangements applicable to Public-Private Partnerships (PPP) contracts financed under World Bank projects. Sept 2010. https://ppp.worldbank.org/public-private-partnership/sites/ppp.worldbank.org/files/ppp_testdumb/documents/GuidanceNote_PPP_September2010.pdf
298. World Bank. Public-Private-Partnership Legal Resource Center: Procurement Laws. www.ppp.worldbank.org/public-private-partnership/legislation-regulation/laws/procurement
299. World Bank. PPP in Infrastructure Resource Center. www.ppp.worldbank.org, 2015
300. World Bank. The World Bank in Botswana: overview. www.worldbank.org/en/country/botswana/overview
301. World Bank. World trade indicators country classification by region and income (July 2009–July 2010). www.worldbank.org (25.09.2010)
302. World Health Rankings: Live Longer Live Better. Botswana: Life Expectancy. www.worldlifeexpectancy.com/botswana-life-expectancy
303. World Health Rankings: Live Longer Live Better. Health Profile: Botswana. www.worldlifeexpectancy.com/country-health-profile/botswana
304. World Health Rankings: Live Longer Live Better. Health Profile: Poland. www.worldlifeexpectancy.com/country-health-profile/poland

305. World Health Rankings: Live Longer Live Better. Poland: Life Expectancy. www.worldlifeexpectancy.com/poland-life-expectancy
306. Wspólnoty Europejskie. Report: "Przezwyciężanie niestabilności w Afryce: Nowe europejskie podejście" [Overcoming instability in Africa: A new European approach]. European Report on Cooperation 2009, Robert Schuman's Center for Advanced Studies at the European University Institute San Domenico di Fiesole
307. Yescombe ER (2007) Project finance, wybrane elementy finansowania strukturalnego. Wolters Kluwer Business, Krakow
308. Yescombe ER (2007) Public private partnerships: principles of policy and finance, 1st edn. Elsevier-Butterworth-Heinemann, Oxford
309. Yousri A-R, The role of taxation, expenditure and debt in an Islamic economy. University of Alexandria, Egypt
310. Zajączkowski K (2010) Przestrzeń i granice a regionalizm w Afryce Subsaharyjskiej: afrykańska i europejska percepcja. Forum Politologiczne, vol 10, INP UWM Olsztyn, pp 189–224
311. Zalewski D (2016) Rynek PPP w Polsce: siedem lat za nami, Forum PPP: Magazyn Inwestycji Publicznych [Public Investment Magazine] 1(31):3–21
312. Zembala M, National consultant in the field of cardiosurgery. 14 Sept 2002. www.2.mz.gov.pl/wwwfiles/ma_struktura/docs/raportzkardiochir_201210221550.pdf

MIX
Papier aus verantwortungsvollen Quellen
Paper from responsible sources
FSC® C105338

If you have any concerns about our products,
you can contact us on
ProductSafety@springernature.com

In case Publisher is established outside the EU,
the EU authorized representative is:
Springer Nature Customer Service Center GmbH
Europaplatz 3, 69115 Heidelberg, Germany

Printed by Libri Plureos GmbH
in Hamburg, Germany